Online Learning Analytics

Data Analytics Applications

Series Editor
Jay Liebowitz

Online Learning Analytics

Edited by
Jay Liebowitz

CRC Press
Taylor & Francis Group
Boca Raton London New York

CRC Press is an imprint of the
Taylor & Francis Group, an **informa** business
AN AUERBACH BOOK

First Edition published 2022
by CRC Press
6000 Broken Sound Parkway NW, Suite 300, Boca Raton, FL 33487-2742

and by CRC Press
2 Park Square, Milton Park, Abingdon, Oxon, OX14 4RN

ISBN: 978-1-032-20097-2 (hbk)
ISBN: 978-1-032-04777-5 (pbk)
ISBN: 978-1-003-19462-0 (ebk)

DOI: 10.1201/9781003194620

Dedication

To all those students, educators, and
practitioners entering the "new normal."

Contents

Chapter 12   213
Face Detection with Applications in Education
Juan Carlos Bonilla-Robles, José Alberto Hernández Aguilar, and
Guillermo Santamaría-Bonfil

Index   229

List of Figures

List of Tables

Foreword

Pete Smith

University of Texas at Arlington

In 2017, I asked in a book chapter title: Has learning analytics had its Moneyball moment? The world of education was and is awash with data about and from our learners. And researchers in the emerging field of learning analytics were beginning to make significant breakthroughs in our understanding of the classroom, the learning process, and curricula writ large. As educators and scholars we were poised, as were the Oakland As in the well-known book and film, to transform and deepen understanding of "our sport."

Add to that momentum the "Great Onlining" of 2020, when so many of our institutions of higher education in particular moved quickly to online teaching and learning in the face of a pandemic. This rapidly increased our available data related to instruction and learning. If anything, institutions were faced with not only "big data," but also "even bigger data" to use for both learning as well as institutional analytics.

But what has been clearly emerging in the past several years, in both the research and practitioner literatures, is a palpable sense of professional unease in the learning analytics area. Beyond research, educational practitioners at all levels focused on the data and analytics of our profession, with a nagging voice asking us all for ROI, often in a business sense, proof of the impact of our work. Can we clearly and cleanly link improved student retention or graduation rates to interventions based on our ever-accumulating data? And did the costs in tools, technology, and talent justify further focus and investment of human and financial resources?

There were and are, in fact, early ROI successes in learning analytics. Institutions in the U.S. and around the world are applying systems to monitor and model student performance and success, providing a window into student engagement that we honestly have lacked at the institutional level. The educational data market has seen the emergence of a range of these applied tools specifically designed for supporting students and measuring impact in our big data world.

Academic administrators at my institution make use of data and modeled outcomes from our *Civitas* machine learning models to better understand the learners in their colleges and departments. AI models today reveal clear indicators of student success and engagement, as well as potential pathways for intervention when a learner struggles. Faculty and staff across my campus use these modeled data to better communicate with and support learners at my institution. It is having a demonstrable impact. This is the "real world" of learning analytics—learning analytics "on the ground."

However, beyond the pristine cases of student progression and graduation rates, ROI remains a challenging concept in the teaching and learning space. Truth be told, there are very few clean business cases for analytics investment even in the worlds of business and industry. In the higher ed setting, our growth in analytics-trained personnel takes place alongside the general development of a campus culture of data usage, training of faculty and staff in learning analytics, and personnel growth in areas such as advising, coaching, and scaffolding students on their educational journeys. Can I as an administrator pinpoint the clear and identified fiscal impact of one particular new data analytics tool, or a single new staff position specialized in learning data and their analysis? Too often the answer to that question is "yes . . . but," and that does leave that same sense of unease.

Without using a sports metaphor, Neil Selwyn (2019) asked a similar question, perhaps slightly more bluntly: "What's the problem with learning analytics?" That author raised concerns about the "profit-driven machinations" of the "data economy," and cited in particular a "blind faith in data," techno-solutionism and the issues of fairness and equity in the socio-economic and political contexts of learners." To restate Selwyn's concerns: Are we putting blind faith in the data and the emerging technologies we have at our disposal as educators? And are the algorithms that drive student retention modeling also algorithms of economic and societal misrepresentation?

The challenges of data-solutionism in our field are concrete. In my role as an analytics leader, I often open presentations to faculty colleagues with the question: Where is the data in your teaching? That query frequently leads to spirited discussion, and I do more often than not come away from such encounters with a stronger sense of the very human nature of teaching and learning. Indeed, Selwyn (2019) notes the larger tension between "'dataphiles' who consider that everything is quantifiable, calculable, and potentially party to statistical control" and "'data sceptics' who feel that education is an area where this logic is not appropriate"—the larger concept that education simply cannot be viewed through what Beer (2018) has called the "data gaze."

And there is no shortage of techno-solutionism in the rapid rise of artificial intelligence. Wajcman (2019) cautions against the belief, perhaps idealistic, that individuals and social systems are essentially programmable machines, and argues that a technology-centered approach clearly underestimates the complexity of our educational settings. To this, the technological idealists will point out that in fact our AI models today are ever-increasing in complexity and the subtlety of the insight they provide. And today we are demanding of the algorithms not only increased efficiency but also results that can not only be acted upon but also better understood. Large scale responses to machine intelligence such as the European Union's AI regulation plan will bring these debates center-stage for several years to come.

Indeed, as analytics professionals, educational researchers, and applied data scientists, we all are faced daily with questions of fairness and equity: do the data we collect equitably portray the broadest range and depth of our diverse learners, and offer avenues for student success that are sensitive to our multicultural and multidimensional student body? Obviously, there is work to be done in our now-global context for teaching and learning.

Despite these critical concerns and a palpable sense of disillusion or transition in the larger field, it is important to note that learning analytics remain, for many of us, the most visible and oftentimes the only large-scale implementation of big data and machine learning to have a "real world" impact on teaching and learning on our campuses today. In many ways, learning analytics remains a key player on the educational field, "the show" to continue the baseball metaphor, where on a daily basis AI models of our learners are built and used to guide student learning and success. Our students in "Generation AI" increasingly expect intelligent tools and services to support and guide them.

No other instance of machine learning on my campus impacts students and their success daily. Critics may argue that this data and modeling work is reductivist, or theoretically less "user respectful" than it could be—fair points, and obvious topics for future research and scholarship. Yet across the educational research literature, writers implicitly posit through their research methods, in almost every issue of every scholarly journal, that machine learning can help us to better understand our learners and their learning processes, in all of their complex social contexts.

Today, we can and do use AI to teach, coach, and scaffold students in ways that are more complex and more user-respectful than just a few years ago.. Each semester now, at hundreds of higher education institutions such as my own, hundreds of thousands of college and university students benefit from increased scaffolding and focused communication with faculty and staff based on retention and engagement models. "Mega-models" which munge the modeling and outcome data from multiple institutions are providing deeper and more nuanced understandings of our higher education game plan. We do, daily and year-round, impact the broadest range of learners, their study, and their success, in higher education as well as in secondary settings.

However, it remains true that the field faces very real philosophical and operational challenges, perhaps symbolized by that nagging, amorphous feeling of unease. Yet I would argue that it is specifically at this point that new research themes and emerging scholarly voices will energize us. The present time is the juncture for us to expand our thinking, to "complexify" our frameworks, our audiences, and our toolsets to address expanding understandings of teaching and learning and the broadest set of learners in the socio-cultural and political settings in our multicultural and global age.

The authors in this volume do just that, addressing areas of concern such as those outlined by Selwyn, but also serving as voices to energize the field of learning analytics again. Their range of topics is both broad and one which recognizes the humanness and depth of the educational act. Their work includes learning analytics applications, trends, and future research, ethics and privacy in learning analytics, social impacts, settings from both K-12 and higher education. They write about technologies such as gamification and augmented reality, and the fair and just application of AI and machine learning, in addition to considering the future of online learning itself.

The writers here, I can say, do not fall prey to the threats of data- or techno-solutionism. Their ideas and case studies are "socially sympathetic" learning analytic designs, which respect the needs and rights of learners. These applications of learning analytics clearly engage the emerging topic of algorithmic bias, as well as broader frameworks of fairness, equity, and social justice in data science generally.

The work in this volume asks us all to confront our field's philosophical unease, and then leads us further to reflect on and engage with the power of learning analytics and modeled data in new, complex, and nuanced ways. Through these insights and real-world applications, learning analytics will continue to live up to its potential on the field: to deepen and make more complex our understanding of the very human act of teaching and learning every day. With this collection, we further the vital academic thread of learning analytics and deepen our insight into and appreciation of the educational process for the years ahead on a global scale.

References

Beer, D. (2018). *The Data Gaze: Capitalism, Power and Perception.* Sage.

Selwyn, N. (2019). What's the problem with learning analytics? *Journal of Learning Analytics, 6*(3), 11–19.

Wajcman, J. (2019). The digital architecture of time management. *Science, Technology, & Human Values, 44*(2), 315–337.

Preface

Due to the COVID-19 pandemic and after effects, we have begun to enter the "new normal" of education. Instead of online learning being an "added feature" of K–12 schools and universities worldwide, it will be incorporated as an essential feature in one's education.

There are many questions and concerns from parents, students, teachers, professors, administrators, staff, accrediting bodies, and others regarding the quality of virtual learning and its impact on student learning outcomes. These are reasonable reservations to consider, but I feel the answer lies in the field of "learning analytics," particularly in the online environments of today and tomorrow.

We have witnessed innovations over the recent years in adding more "intelligence" to the virtual learning experience, and certainly more will be coming in the near future. In today's data-driven environment, we must develop the right assessments and metrics through learning analytics in order to ensure that the effectiveness and efficacy of the student learning process are optimized.

This book is conceived on trying to answer the questions of those who may be skeptical about online learning. Through better understanding and applying learning analytics, we can assess how successful learning and student/faculty engagement, as examples, can contribute towards producing the educational outcomes needed to advance student learning for future generations.

Much research is still needed in many areas of learning analytics. For example, the ethical aspects of learning analytics systems and cultural diversity of studies on ethics in technology-enhanced learning require additional work (Pargman & McGrath, 2021). A Spring 2020 New York University/LEARN study of 298 university students from 50 different schools across the United States found that online learning during the COVID-19 times could be improved by more active student/faculty engagement, having more compassion and better organization of the material. A McKinsey teacher survey in March 2021 found that there is a significant learning loss in remote learning around the world (Chen et al., 2021).

However, as explained through the chapters in this book, learning analytics has proven to be successful in many areas, such as the impact of using learning analytics in asynchronous online discussions in higher education (Martinez et al., 2020). In addition, according to the 2020 L&D Global Sentiment Survey, with about 2,300 respondents from 86 countries, the majority said that learning analytics will take the center stage in global learning and development trends going forward (Robinson, 2021).

I also feel that learning analytics are paramount and will become even more important in our post-COVID era. To substantiate this claim, I am so thankful for having such a distinguished group of contributing authors worldwide (from 10 countries) to add their keen insights on online learning analytics. I am also greatly appreciative to Peter Smith for including his knowledgeable perspectives in the Foreword on learning analytics for online environments in the future.

This book would never have been possible without John Wyzalek's continuing support, along with his Taylor & Francis colleagues, Theron Shreve and Susan Culligan of DerryField Publishing Services. Certainly, my students and colleagues over the past 40 years have pushed me to "get ahead of the game" (as my 99-year-old mother-in-law's father would always tell her). And finally, my family gets the greatest accolades for having to put up with me for all these years.

Enjoy the book!

Jay Liebowitz, DSc
Washington, DC

References

Chen, L. K., Dorn, E., Sarakatsannis, J., and Wiesinger, A. (2021). *Teacher Survey: Learning Loss is Global—and Significant.* McKinsey & Co.

Martinez, J. P. C., Catasus, M. G., and Fontanillas, T. R. (2020). Impact of using learning analytics in asynchronous online discussions in higher education. *International Journal of Educational Technology in Higher Education,* 17.

Pargman, T. C., and McGrath, C. (2021). Mapping the ethics of learning analytics in higher education: A systematic literature review of empirical research. *Journal of Learning Analytics.* https://doi.org/10.18608/jla.2021.1

Robinson, S. (2021, March 1). Learning Analytics Trends Driving Education in 2021, https://donaldhtaylor.co.uk/insight/the-ld-global-sentiment-survey-2020-first-thoughts/

Contributing Authors

José Alberto Hernández Aguilar has a PhD in Engineering and Applied Sciences from the Autonomous University of the State of Morelos (UAEMor). In 2018 he made a postdoctoral sabbatical at the National Institute of Electricity and Clean Energies. Since 2010 he has been a full-time research professor at the Faculty of Accounting, Administration and Informatics (FCAeI) of the UAEMor. His scientific interests include data science, big data analytics, and computer security.

Juan Carlos Bonilla-Robles has a degree in Computer Science, originally from the Autonomous University of the State of Morelos (UAEMor). He has worked in the private sector as a software developer and analyst. He is currently a student of the master's degree in Optimization and Applied Computing at the UAEMor. His main lines of research and interest include digital image processing, machine learning techniques, and data science.

John Fritz is Associate Vice President for Instructional Technology in the UMBC Division of Information Technology. He is responsible for UMBC's focused efforts in teaching, learning, and technology and has been an active thought leader in the emerging field of learning analytics. Prior to his professional IT career, John served as a public information officer, editor, writer, and webmaster for 10 years at three University System of Maryland (USM) schools. John is a frequent presenter and author for numerous higher ed IT events and publications and has served on the EDUCAUSE Learning Initiative (ELI) advisory board.

Samuel Greiff is head of research group, principal investigator, and Full Professor of Educational Assessment and Psychology at University of Luxembourg. He joined the institution in 2012. He holds a PhD in cognitive and experimental psychology from the University of Heidelberg, Germany. His research focuses on educational psychology, psychological assessment, personality psychology, cognitive psychology, and psychological methodology. He has been awarded several national and international research funds by diverse funding organizations such as the German Ministry of Education and Research and the European Union, was fellow in the Luxembourg research programme of excellency, and has published articles in national and international scientific journals and books (>150 contributions in peer-reviewed journals, many of them leading in their field). Samuel has been working for several years on the assessment of transversal skills such as problem solving and collaboration and their role in the classroom, at work, and in private life. He also takes a strong interest in the use of log file data and learning analytics for summative and formative assessment purposes. He and his team are dedicated to increasing the understanding, measurement, and application of cognitive and non-cognitive skills that shape our lives.

Åke Grönlund is Professor in Informatics, Örebro University School of Business, Department of Informatics, Örebro, Sweden. Åke's research concerns the use of digital technologies in various human activities. The common denominator involved in all projects is to understand how people arrange their work, their organizations, and other activities pertaining to private life, such as socializing on the web, and how technology can be used to make improvements. In particular, focus is on the fields of education and e-government.

Mariann Hawken is the Acting Director of Instructional Technology at UMBC and has more than 21 years of experience in educational technology. As a member of the Blackboard Community Leadership Circle, Hawken coordinates professional development for faculty who are preparing to teach online; supports online and hybrid course development; and spearheads the campus transition to Ultra. She maintains several Blackboard applications on campus, including Learn and Collaborate. Mariann is a certified Peer Reviewer and Facilitator for the Applying the Quality Matters Rubric.

Kristen Herrick serves as a Learning Scientist within Educational Testing Service's Personalized Learning and Assessment Laboratory. In this role, she facilitates the application of learning design principles, learning models, and learning sciences insights to the development of digital learning capabilities and solutions. Since 2012, Kristen has worked in various assessment, learning improvement, and learning science-based roles in higher education and industry settings. Her previous research focused on incorporation of implementation fidelity into student learning outcomes assessment practices, assessing and improving students' ethical reasoning skills, and connecting assessment practices with teaching and pedagogy to demonstrably improve student learning. Her current research interests include self-regulated learning and strengths-based pedagogies. Kristen holds a master's degree in Psychology and a PhD in Assessment and Measurement from James Madison University.

Dirk Ifenthaler is the Chair and Professor for Learning, Design and Technology at University of Mannheim, Germany and UNESCO Deputy Chair of Data Science in Higher Education Learning and Teaching at Curtin University in Australia. Dirk Ifenthaler's research focuses on the intersection of cognitive psychology, educational technology, learning science, data analytics, and computer science. His research outcomes include numerous co-authored books, book series, book chapters, journal articles, and international conference papers, as well as successful grant funding in Australia, Germany, and USA. He is the Editor-in-Chief of the Springer journal *Technology, Knowledge and Learning*.

Mohammad Khalil is a senior researcher in learning analytics at the Centre for the Science of Learning & Technology (SLATE) at the faculty of psychology, University of Bergen, Norway. Mohammad has a master's degree in Information Security and Digital Criminology and a PhD from Graz University of Technology in Learning Analytics in Massive Open Online Courses (MOOCs). He has published over 50 articles on learning analytics in high-standard and well-recognized journals and academic conferences, focusing on understanding and improving student behavior and engagement in digital learning platforms using data sciences. His current research focuses on learning analytics in Open and Distance Learning (ODL), self-regulated learning, mobile, visualizations, and gamification, as well as inclusiveness, privacy, and ethics.

Justian Knobbout obtained the MSc degree in Supply Chain Management from the Erasmus University Rotterdam in 2013. He will obtain the PhD degree in Learning Analytics at the Open University, the Netherlands in 2021. Justian's research interests include learning analytics and educational data mining. Next to researcher, he is lecturer at the Institution of Design & Engineering at HU University of Applied Sciences Utrecht.

Moria Levy, PhD, serves as CEO and owner of ROM Knowledgeware, a leading KM solutions firm in Israel (40 employees). She has 35 years of experience, among them over 20 years in Knowledge Management. She is chairman of the global expert committee of ISO (TC260/WG6) and led the team of worldwide experts in writing the global Knowledge Management ISO standard (30401). Moria initiated Knowledge Management studies, taught in high schools in Israel, as part of an official program of the Ministry of Education of Israel, for digital knowledge and information. This is the first program of its kind in the world. She has published several books on the discipline of KM. She is the author of the books *A Holistic Approach to Lessons Learned: How Organizations Can Benefit from Their Own Knowledge* (CRC Press) and *21st Century Management*; she is also the editor of the books *Knowledge Development and innovation: KM articles: 2019, Knowledge Sharing: KM articles 2017, Knowledge Management in Israel: KM articles 2015,* and *Knowledge Management in Israel: KM articles 2012.* Moria serves as the deputy chair of KMGN (KM Global Network) and leads the KMGN Taskforce: Bringing the KM future. She is the known to be the most active researcher of KM in Israel. Her research "WEB2.0 Implications on Knowledge Management" has been cited over 600 times and was recognized as a KM "classic research" and indexed Thomson Reuters "Journal Impact Factor" as to her achievements. Moria is the chairman of the Israeli Knowledge Management Forum, which unites all KM parties in Israel.

Kara McWilliams is Associate Vice President of the ETS AI Research Laboratories, responsible for the development of innovative AI-powered capabilities across three laboratories—The Natural Language Processing Lab, the Personalized Learning and Assessment Lab, and the Language Learning, Teaching, and Assessment Lab. Her vision in the labs is the development of solutions that are research based, user obsessed, and technology enabled. Most of Kara's work has focused on how to understand user needs from the perspective of their values, beliefs, and experiences and merge the research on how people learn most effectively with the application of innovative technology. She has conducted extensive work on the efficacy of educational technology, ethical use of AI, and communicating both to users in meaningful ways. Kara holds a master's degree in Curriculum & Instruction and a PhD in Educational Research, Measurement and Evaluation from Boston College.

Chris Millet has 20 years of experience in the fields of educational technology and online learning. He is currently the Director of Penn State World Campus Learning Design. In this role, he oversees the design and development of online courses for a portfolio of over 45 academic programs and 500 courses. He provides leadership at the university on policies and organizational processes related to online learning and educational technology. He also teaches at Penn State's College of Education. Chris co-lead the creation of the IMS Caliper learning analytics standard. His current work focuses on online learner retention, learning analytics, virtual reality and immersive learning, and organizational effectiveness. He holds a master's degree in instructional systems from Penn State and is currently pursuing a PhD in Learning, Design, and Technology at Penn State.

Pablo Munguia is the Associate Director, Student Learning Support Service at Flinders University. His research areas have been ecology and evolution of marine organisms, and learning analytics. Within the learning analytics field, Pablo has focused on student behaviour, metric design, scaling solutions for learning analytics, and tactical approaches to deploy student-driven insights to academics. Pablo has published extensively in these fields and received funding from different agencies. He is currently Editor in Chief of the *Journal of Marine Biology and Ecology* and Editor of *Oecologia,* having served on several other boards.

Ronit Nehemia serves as the head supervisor of the Technological Data Analysis discipline for high school students at the Israeli Ministry of Education. She has a master's degree from Bar Ilan University in Israel in Data Science. She served as a national supervision supervisor and is responsible for the 21st Century Education System Adaptation Program at the Ministry of Education.

Andreas Oranje is Vice President of Assessment and Learning Technology Development for Educational Testing Service (ETS)'s Research & Development (R&D) division, responsible for developing and maintaining testing programs with an emphasis on optimizing structure and processes to increase efficiency and innovation. A key member of the R&D leadership team, he is also responsible for leading and optimizing the assessment and learning development portfolio and provides strategic, tactical, and financial oversight. Andreas joined ETS in 2001 as an associate research scientist. During his tenure at ETS, Oranje has held a variety of roles, including Psychometric Manager and Psychometric Director; NAEP Project Director for Design, Analysis, and Reporting; and Principal Research Director. His most recent position was General Manager, Research, where he directed, managed and set strategy for several of ETS's core innovation areas, including Natural Language Processing and Speech, Artificial Intelligence, Cognitive Sciences, Virtual Performance Assessments, and Accessibility Technology. He holds a master's degree and PhD in quantitative psychology from the University of Amsterdam. He served on the editorial board of the *Journal of Educational Measurement* and was program chair for AERA Division D. He has presented at numerous conferences and has written extensively on large-scale assessment methodology, game-based assessment, and artificial intelligence in education.

Joanna Paliszkiewicz works as the Director of the Management Institute at the Warsaw University of Life Sciences in Warsaw, Poland. She is an adjunct professor at the University of Vaasa in Finland. She is well recognized in Poland

and abroad for her expertise in management issues: knowledge management and trust management. She has published over 210 papers and manuscripts and is the author/co-author/editor of 13 books. She has been a part of many scholarship endeavors in the United States, Ireland, Slovakia, Taiwan, the United Kingdom, and Hungary. She has actively participated in presenting research results at various international conferences. Currently, she serves as the Deputy Editor-in-Chief of the *Management and Production Engineering Review.* She is an associate editor for the *Journal of Computer Information Systems, Expert Systems with Applications,* and *Intelligent Systems with Applications.* She is the Vice President of the Polish Association for Production Engineering. She also serves as chair of the International Cooperation in European Business Club. She serves as the Vice President of the International Association for Computer Information Systems in the United States. She is a board member of the Intellectual Capital Accreditation Association. She has successfully supervised many PhD students, leading them to completion of their degrees. She has also served as an external reviewer for several PhD students in Poland, India, and Finland. She is actively involved in participating in the scientific committees of many international conferences. She was named the 2013 Computer Educator of the Year by IACIS.

Paul Prinsloo is a Research Professor in Open and Distance Learning (ODL) in the Department of Business Management, in the College of Economic and Management Sciences, University of South Africa (Unisa). Since 2015, he is also a Visiting Professor at the Carl von Ossietzky University of Oldenburg, Germany, a Fellow of the European Distance and E-Learning Network (EDEN), and serves on several editorial boards. Paul is an internationally recognized speaker, scholar, and researcher and has published numerous articles in the fields of teaching and learning, student success in distance education contexts, learning analytics, and curriculum development. His current research focuses on the collection, analysis, and use of student data in learning analytics, graduate supervision, and digital identity.

Bart Pursel is the Director of Innovation within Teaching and Learning with Technology (TLT) at Penn State. In this role, Bart ensures the University is positioned to effectively incorporate various technologies into the teaching and learning ecosystem. By utilizing expertise in instructional design, research, learning spaces, and emerging technology, he works with faculty to align TLT's programs, platforms, and services to the needs of the Penn State community. Coming from a diverse background of instructional design, teaching, and research, his interests reside at the intersection of technology and pedagogy. Bart's current projects focus on areas such as AI in education, learning spaces, and immersive experiences. He is also an Affiliate Associate Research Professor in the College of Information Sciences and Technology, where he teaches large, general education courses. Bart received his PhD from Penn State in Workforce Education and Development, his MS from Bloomsburg University in Instructional Technology, and BA from Bloomsburg University in Mass Communications.

Jessica Resig is a Senior Instructional Designer with Penn State World Campus and is the lead designer for the World Campus business portfolio. She joined Penn State in 2013 and has collaborated with faculty and program directors to design, develop, and offer a variety of online, hybrid, and executive-style programs. Jessica teaches courses in instructional technology and maintains an active research portfolio. She holds a master's degree in instructional technology from Duquesne University and a PhD in Instructional Design and Technology from Old Dominion University.

Bart Rienties is Professor of Learning Analytics and programme lead of the learning analytics and learning design research programme at the Institute of Educational Technology at the Open University UK. He leads a group of academics who provide university-wide learning analytics and learning design solutions and conduct evidence-based research of how students and professionals learn. As an educational psychologist, he conducts multi-disciplinary research on work-based and collaborative learning environments and focuses on the role of social interaction in learning, which is published in leading academic journals and books.

K. Rebecca "Becca" Marsh Runyon serves as Managing Sr. Learning Scientist within Educational Testing Service's Personalized Learning & Assessment Laboratory. She has worked primarily in higher education technology digital strategy development and product design as a learning researcher, scientist/designer, and assessment specialist. She's passionate about innovative, integrated learning and formative assessment solutions; learning analytics; and the holistic insights and actionable interventions these afford learners. She is committed to advancing quality and equity in education and is grateful to contribute to work at ETS, given its mission and ability to deliver on this promise. Becca holds a master's degree in Cognitive Science and PhD in Assessment and Measurement from James Madison University.

Guillermo Santamaría-Bonfil has a bachelor's degree in Computer Systems and a PhD in Computer Sciences from the Monterrey Institute of Technology and Higher Education (ITESM). He has two postdoctoral years of experience at the Applied Mathematics and Systems Research Institute from the National Autonomous University of Mexico (IIMAS-UNAM) with Dr. Carlos Gershenson, working with complex systems and data science. He is an enthusiastic data scientist with experience in applied machine learning and over six years of time series forecasting insight in the fields of finance, renewable energies, and learning analytics. He has experience as a data scientist in risk modelling for the banking sector and learning analytics for the power systems sector. He has published seven articles in high-impact journals such as *Renewable Energy and Computers & Education.* He is member of the Applied Computational Intelligence Network (RedICA), the Mexican Academy of Computation (AMEXCOMP), the International Institute of Forecasters (IIF), to mention a few.

Sharon Slade worked for 20 years as a senior lecturer at the Open University (UK), where she led projects which fed into teaching and learning across the university. She led the team which developed policy for the ethical use of learning analytics and acted as an active member of several international teams developing ethical codes of practice for uses of student data. Ongoing interests relate to ethical issues in learning analytics. Sharon currently works for an environmental charity, The Earth Trust, in the UK.

Sarah J. Shin is Associate Provost for Academic Affairs at UMBC, where she is also Professor of Education and the 2017–2020 Presidential Research Professor. A member of the Provost's Office senior leadership, Shin coordinates academic program reviews and new program development and leads a number of campus-wide initiatives aimed at improving student success. Shin brings extensive experience in leadership and shared governance, including her two-term service as president of Faculty Senate and as an American Council on Education (ACE) Fellow (2017–2018).

Edyta Skarzyńska earned her master's degree in 2020 at the Faculty of Economics at the Warsaw University of Life Sciences. The area of her master's thesis was knowledge management. Currently, she is a first-year PhD student at the Doctoral School of the Warsaw University of Life Sciences. Her area of research is intellectual capital. Her scientific achievements include a publication in the field of knowledge management.

Pete Smith is Chief Analytics Officer and Professor of Modern Languages at the University of Texas at Arlington, where he also holds the AP Endowed Chair in Online Learning and Innovation. He is the founding administrator of University Analytics at UTA, which engages data scientists toward achieving the strategic academic and business goals of the university. His teaching and scholarship focus on big data in education, natural language processing and natural language understanding, as well as machine translation. Additionally, he oversees UTA's Localization and Translation program, offered to students of seven critical languages as an introduction to the language services industry.

Esther van der Stappen obtained her MSc degree in Computer Science from the University of Groningen in 2003 and her PhD in Computer Science at Utrecht University in 2008. Until 2020, she was an Associate Professor at HU University of Applied Sciences Utrecht, leading a research group on digital innovation in education. Currently, she is a Professor of Applied Sciences, leading the research group Digital Education at Avans University of Applied Sciences. Her research interests include learning analytics, technology-enhanced learning, and blended and hybrid learning.

Olga Viberg is Associate Professor in Media Technology with specialization in Technology-Enhanced Learning, Department of Media Technology and Interaction Design, KTH Royal Institute of Technology, Stockholm, Sweden. She received her PhD in Informatics from Örebro University (Sweden). Her fields of expertise include technology-enhanced learning, self-regulated learning, learning analytics, mobile learning, learning design, and design science research in education. Her work has been published in many high-ranked, referred journals and conferences. She is an active member of the Society for Learning Analytics Research and the European Association of Technology-Enhanced Learning.

Deborah West is Pro Vice Chancellor (Learning and Teaching Innovation) and oversees the Centre for Innovation in Learning and Teaching at Flinders University. Her research has encompassed both her discipline (social work) and learning and teaching, with a particular focus on the use of technology in higher education learning and teaching. Since 2012, this research has focused on the use of learning analytics to support and improve pedagogical approaches, teaching practice, and learning in the online space. She has published extensively, providing insights into the application of learning analytics from the perspective of students, teaching academics, and institutions as well as ethical considerations for responsible use of data to support these purposes.

About the Editor

Dr. Jay Liebowitz is a Visiting Professor in the Stillman School of Business and the MS-Business Analytics Capstone & Co-Program Director (External Relations) at Seton Hall University. He previously served as the Distinguished Chair of Applied Business and Finance at Harrisburg University of Science and Technology. Before HU, he was the Orkand Endowed Chair of Management and Technology in the Graduate School at the University of Maryland University College (UMUC). He served as a Professor in the Carey Business School at Johns Hopkins University. He was ranked one of the top 10 knowledge management researchers/practitioners out of 11,000 worldwide, and was ranked #2 in KM Strategy worldwide, according to the January 2010 *Journal of Knowledge Management*. At Johns Hopkins University, he was the founding Program Director for the Graduate Certificate in Competitive Intelligence and the Capstone Director of the MS-Information and Telecommunications Systems for Business Program, where he engaged over 30 organizations in industry, government, and not-for-profits in capstone projects.

Prior to joining Hopkins, Dr. Liebowitz was the first Knowledge Management Officer at NASA Goddard Space Flight Center. Before NASA, Dr. Liebowitz was the Robert W. Deutsch Distinguished Professor of Information Systems at the University of Maryland-Baltimore County, Professor of Management Science at George Washington University, and Chair of Artificial Intelligence at the U.S. Army War College.

Dr. Liebowitz is the Founding Editor-in-Chief of *Expert Systems With Applications: An International Journal* (published by Elsevier; ranked as a top-tier journal; Thomson Impact Factor from June 2021 is 6.45). He is a Fulbright Scholar, IEEE-USA Federal Communications Commission Executive Fellow, and Computer Educator of the Year (International Association for Computer Information Systems). He has published over 45 books and myriad journal articles on knowledge management, analytics, financial literacy, intelligent systems, and IT management.

Dr. Liebowitz served as the Editor-in-Chief of *Procedia-CS* (Elsevier). He is also the Series Book Editor of the *Data Analytics Applications* book series (Taylor & Francis), as well as the Series Book Editor of the new *Digital Transformation: Accelerating Organizational Intelligence* book series (World Scientific Publishing).

In October 2011, the International Association for Computer Information Systems named the "Jay Liebowitz Outstanding Student Research Award" for the best student research paper at the IACIS Annual Conference. Dr. Liebowitz was the Fulbright Visiting Research Chair in Business at Queen's University for the Summer 2017 and a Fulbright Specialist at Dalarna University in Sweden in May 2019. He is in the Top 2% of the top scientists in the world, according to a 2019 Stanford Study. His recent books are *Data Analytics and AI* (Taylor & Francis, 2021), *The Business of Pandemics: The COVID-19 Story* (Taylor & Francis, 2021), and *A Research Agenda for Knowledge Management and Analytics* (Elgar Publishers, 2021). He has lectured and consulted worldwide.

Chapter 1

Leveraging Learning Analytics for Assessment and Feedback

Dirk Ifenthaler[1] and Samuel Greiff[2]

Abstract

This chapter critically reflects the current state of research in learning analytics and educational assessment. Given the omnipresence of technology-enhanced assessment approaches, vast amounts of data are produced in such systems, which open further opportunities for advancing assessment and feedback systems as well as pedagogical assessment practice. A yet-to-be-solved limitation of learning analytics frameworks is the lack of a stronger focus on dynamic or real-time assessment and feedback, as well as the improvement of learning environments. Therefore, a benefits matrix for analytics-enhanced assessment is suggested, which provides examples on how to harness data and analytics for educational assessment. Further, a framework for implementing analytics-enhanced assessment is suggested. The chapter concludes with a critical reflection on current challenges for making use of analytics data for educational assessments. Clearly,

---

[1] University of Mannheim and Curtin University
[2] University of Luxembourg

stakeholders in the educational arena need to address ethics and privacy issues linked to analytics-enhanced assessments.

Keywords: Assessment, feedback, learning analytics, analytics-enhanced assessment

Introduction

A recent search in scientific databases identified an increase of research publications focusing on assessment from the 1950s to the 2020s by over 380%. Despite an intense debate over the past seven decades, the distinction between formative and summative assessment has not resulted in a precise definition, and the distinction between the two remains blurry (Newton, 2007). To the contrary, other terms have been introduced, such as learning-oriented assessment (Carless, 2007), emphasizing the development of learning elements of assessment; sustainable assessment (Boud, 2000), proposing the support of student learning beyond the formal learning setting; or stealth assessment (Shute et al., 2016), denoting assessments that take place in the background without the user noticing it.

More recently, technology-enhanced assessments enriched standard or paper-based assessment approaches, some of which hold much promise for supporting learning (Webb et al., 2013; Webb & Ifenthaler, 2018b). While much effort in institutional and national systems is focused on harnessing the power of technology-enhanced approaches in order to reduce costs and increase efficiency (Bennett, 2015), a range of different technology-enhanced assessment scenarios have been the focus of educational research and development—however, often at small scale (Stödberg, 2012).

For example, technology-enhanced assessments may involve a pedagogical agent for providing feedback during a learning process (Johnson & Lester, 2016). Other scenarios of technology-enhanced assessments include analyses of a learner's decisions and interactions during game-based learning (Bellotti et al., 2013; Ifenthaler et al., 2012; Kim & Ifenthaler, 2019), scaffolding for dynamic task selection including related feedback (Corbalan et al., 2009), remote asynchronous expert feedback on collaborative problem-solving tasks (Rissanen et al., 2008), or semantic rich and personalized feedback as well as adaptive prompts for reflection through data-driven assessments (Ifenthaler, 2012).

Accordingly, it is expected that technology-enhanced assessment systems meet a number of specific requirements, such as (a) adaptability to different subject domains, (b) flexibility for experimental as well as learning and teaching settings, (c) management of huge amounts of data, (d) rapid analysis of complex and unstructured data, (e) immediate feedback for learners and educators, as well as (f) generation of automated reports of results for educational decision making (Ifenthaler et al., 2010).

With the increased availability of vast and highly varied amounts of data from learners, teachers, learning environments, and administrative systems within educational settings, further opportunities arise for advancing pedagogical assessment practice (Ifenthaler et al., 2018). Analytics-enhanced assessment harnesses formative as well as summative data from learners and their contexts (e.g., learning environments) in order to facilitate learning processes in near real time and help decision makers to improve learning environments. Hence, analytics-enhanced assessment may provide multiple benefits for students, schools, and involved stakeholders. However, as noted by Ellis (2013), analytics currently fail to make full use of educational data for assessment.

This chapter critically reflects the current state of research in educational assessment and identifies ways to harness data and analytics for assessment. Further, a benefits matrix for analytics-enhanced assessment is suggested, followed by a framework for implementing assessment analytics.

Current State of Educational Assessment

Tracing the history of educational assessment practice is challenging, as there are a number of diverse concepts referring to the idea of assessment. Educational assessment is a systematic method of gathering information or artefacts about a learner and learning processes to draw inferences of the persons' dispositions (Baker et al., 2016). Scriven (1967) is often referred to as the original source of the distinction between formative and summative assessment. However, formative and summative assessment are considered to be overlapping concepts, and the function depends on how the inferences are used (Black & Wiliam, 2018).

Newton (2007) notes that the distinction between formative and summative assessment hindered the development of sound assessment practices on a broader level. In this regard, Taras (2005) states that every assessment starts with the summative function of judgment, and by using this information for providing feedback for improvement, the function becomes formative. Bloom et al. (1971) were concerned with the long-lasting idea of assessment separating learners based on a summative perspective of knowledge and behavior—the assessment of learning. In addition, Bloom et al. (1971) supported the idea of developing the individual learner and supporting the learner and teacher towards mastery of a phenomenon—the assessment for learning.

Following this discourse, Sadler (1989) developed a theory of formative assessment and effective feedback. Formative assessment helps students to understand their current state of learning and guides them in taking action to achieve their learning goals. A similar line of argumentation can be found in Black (1998), in which three main types of assessment are defined: (a) formative assessment to aid learning; (b) summative assessment for review, transfer, and certification; (c) summative assessment for accountability to the public. Pellegrino et al. (2001) extend these definitions with three main purposes of assessment: (a) assessment to assist learning (formative assessment); (b) assessment of individual student achievement (summative assessment); and (c) assessment to evaluate programs (evaluative assessment).

To facilitate learning through assessment, Carless (2007) emphasizes that assessment tasks should be learning tasks that are related to the defined learning outcomes and distributed across the learning and course period. Furthermore, to foster learners' responsibility for learning (Bennett, 2011; Wanner & Palmer, 2018) and self-regulation (Panadero et al., 2017), self-assessments are suitable means. In general, self-assessments include students' judgment and decision making about their work and comprise three steps: definition of the expectations, evaluating the work against the expectations, and revising the work (Andrade, 2010). Consequently, as Sadler (1989) argues, self-monitoring and external feedback are related to formative assessment, with the aim to evolve from using external feedback to self-monitoring to independently identify gaps for improvement. Hence, self-assessments enable learners to develop independence of relying on external feedback (Andrade, 2010).

However, self-assessment demands but also fosters evaluative judgment of learners (Panadero et al., 2019; Tai et al., 2018). Thus, self-assessments might be particularly challenging for learners with lower levels of domain or procedural knowledge (Sitzmann et al., 2010). Hence, the feedback generated internally by the learners could be complemented and further enhanced with external feedback (Butler & Winne, 1995). Such external feedback may help learners to adjust their self-monitoring (Sitzmann et al., 2010). Among others, the feedback provided should clearly define expectations (i.e., criteria, standards, goals), be timely, sufficiently frequent and detailed, be on aspects that are malleable through the students, be on how to close the gap, in a way learners can react upon it (Gibbs & Simpson, 2005; Nicol & Macfarlane-Dick, 2006). Furthermore, assessment and feedback processes shall actively include the learner as an agent in the process (Boud & Molloy, 2013). However, offering formative assessments and individual feedback are limited in many ways throughout higher education due to resource constraints (Broadbent et al., 2017; Gibbs & Simpson, 2005).

Assessment as learning is a concept that reflects a renewed focus on the nature of the integration of assessment and learning (Webb & Ifenthaler, 2018a). Key aspects of assessment as learning include the centrality of understanding the learning gap and the role of assessment in helping students and teachers explore and regulate this gap (Dann, 2014). Thus, feedback and the way students regulate their response to feedback is critical for assessment as learning, just as it is for assessment for learning (Perrenoud, 1998). Other active research areas focus on peer assessment (Lin et al., 2016; Wanner & Palmer, 2018). Especially the opportunities of technology-enhanced peer interaction and the perceived potential for peer feedback to contribute to learning experiences in digital learning environments, such as massive open online courses (MOOCs), have been of recent research interest (Adachi et al., 2018; Labarthe et al., 2016; van der Kleij & Adie, 2018).

Webb and Ifenthaler (2018a) present an overview of the range of different opportunities for technology to support assessment with a view to providing a vision for assessment design to move forward with designers, educators, and learners working together to design assessments. Their contribution includes a review of key theoretical issues related to assessment and examines new and potential approaches to assessment that are facilitated by technology as well as the challenges that these new opportunities create.

The current state of research on educational assessment may be summarized with a closer look at an iterative implementation cycle (see Figure 1.1 on next page). The individual steps of the iterative implementation cycle of educational assessment include a co-design process in which learning designers, psychometricians, educators, and learners collaborate. The initial step clarifies learning intentions and defines criteria for learning success. As a result, learning tasks are designed. These tasks help to elicit evidence of individual learning processes. Evidence of learning is further used to provide feedback whenever needed in order to support ongoing learning processes. Learners are empowered as the owners of their learning processes and may be supported by peer learners as additional sources for learning and feedback. The final step of the iterative implementation cycle of educational assessment includes critical reflections on learning processes and learning outcomes as well as the previous steps of the cycle.

Clearly, each step may be supported or further enabled through technological systems—for instance, through innovative assessment formats that are administered through educational technology. Given the omnipresence of technology-enhanced assessment approaches, vast amount of data are produced in such systems, which, in turn, open further opportunities for advancing assessment and feedback systems.

Harnessing Data and Analytics for Assessment

Interest in collecting and mining large sets of educational data on student background and performance has grown over the past years and is generally referred to as learning analytics (Baker & Siemens, 2015). In recent years, the incorporation of learning analytics into educational practices and research has further developed. However, while new applications and approaches have brought forth new insights, there is still a shortage of research addressing the effectiveness and consequences of these endeavors (Vieira et al., 2018). Learning analytics, which refers to the use of static and dynamic data from learners and their contexts for

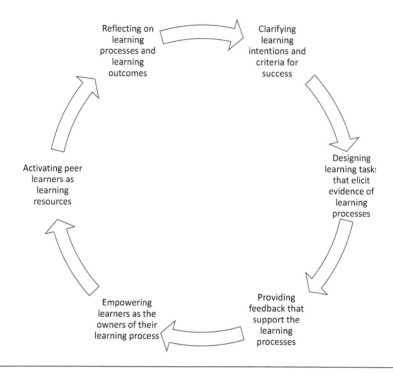

Figure 1.1   Iterative Implementation Cycle of Educational Assessment

(1) the understanding of learning and the discovery of traces of learning and (2) the support of learning processes and educational decision making (Ifenthaler, 2015), offer a range of opportunities for formative and summative assessment. Hence, the primary goal of learning analytics is to better meet students' needs by offering individual learning paths, adaptive assessments and recommendations, or adaptive and just-in-time feedback (Gašević et al., 2015; McLoughlin & Lee, 2010), ideally, tailored to learners' motivational states, individual characteristics, and learning goals (Schumacher & Ifenthaler, 2018). Research suggests that meaningful analysis of data requires sound theoretical grounding and modelling as well as verification of validity, gained, for instance, in complex evidence-based design processes (Marzouk et al., 2016; Shute et al., 2018).

Current learning analytics approaches focus on indicators based on the behavior in the digital learning environment, such as time spent online, access to various types of resources, or reading and writing posts, to relate them to learning performance (Mah, 2016; Martin & Whitmer, 2016). Only a few approaches are enriched with learner characteristics, such as demographic data or results of assessments—for instance, to predict study success (Costa et al., 2017; Vieira et al., 2018; Yau & Ifenthaler, 2020). Vieira et al. (2018) found that research studies on learning analytics analyze usage of resources in particular, with only a few approaches having a processual perspective by trying to understand learning paths or learners' actual learning progress in the tasks at hand. Therefore, learning analytics may yield only limited insight into students' actual learning, because the indicators collected are not pedagogically valid. For instance, specific indicators, such as 'time on task', might have different meanings, depending on the learning contexts and the specific domain they are embedded into (Goldhammer et al., 2014).

Learning analytics could be utilized for educational assessment, which has far-reaching consequences for modelling and analyzing available data, as well as the development of criteria to evaluate its impact (Ifenthaler et al., in press). From an assessment perspective, learning analytics for formative assessment focusses on the generation and interpretation of evidence about learner performance by teachers, learners, and/or technology to make assisted decisions about the next steps in learning and instruction (Ifenthaler et al., 2018; Spector et al., 2016). In this context, real- or near-time data are extremely valuable because of their benefits in ongoing learning interactions. Learning analytics for summative assessments are utilized to make judgements that are typically based on standards or benchmarks (Black & Wiliam, 1998). In a recent Delphi study on global trends in the educational arena, which are related to learning analytics (Ifenthaler et al., in press), the international experts agreed on the importance of developing analytics-enhanced assessments.

Accordingly, analytics-driven assessment harnesses formative and summative data from stakeholders and learning environments in order to facilitate learning processes in real time and help decision makers to improve learning environments. Distinct features of analytics-driven assessments may include, but are not limited to, the following (Ellis, 2013; Ifenthaler & Widanapathirana, 2014a):

- Semantic-rich feedback for written assignments in near real-time using natural language processing (Bektik, 2019; Gottipati et al., 2018; Whitelock & Bektik, 2018)
- Progress reports toward curricular required competences or learning outcomes, including intra-individual and inter-individual comparisons (Lockyer et al., 2013)
- Peer assessments focusing on specific learning outcomes or general study skills (e.g., learning strategies, time management) (Gašević et al., 2019; Gašević et al., 2017)
- Defining individual goals and desired achievements for subjects, modules, or classes and tracking learning-dependent progress toward them (Schumacher & Ifenthaler, 2018)
- Reflective prompts highlighting persistence of strengths and weaknesses of specific learning events and assessment results (e.g., reoccurring errors, misconceptions, learning habits) (Schumacher & Ifenthaler, 2021)

Benefits of Analytics-Enhanced Assessment

Multiple benefits from learning analytics for educational purposes can be associated with four levels of stakeholders: mega-level (governance), macro-level (organization), meso-level (curriculum, learning design, teacher/tutor), and micro-level (learner). Ifenthaler (2015) introduced a learning analytics benefits matrix that exemplifies potentials of learning analytics for the different stakeholder levels, including three analytics perspectives: (1) summative, (2) real-time, and (3) predictive. For example, the mega-level facilitates cross-institutional analytics by incorporating data from all levels of the learning analytics framework. Such rich datasets enable the identification and validation of patterns within and across institutions and therefore provide valuable insights for informing educational policy making.

The macro-level enables institution-wide analytics for better understanding learner cohorts to optimize associated processes and allocate critical resources for reducing dropout and increasing retention as well as success rates. The meso-level supports the curriculum and learning design as well as providing detailed insights about learning processes for educators. The micro-level analytics supports the learner through recommendations and help functions implemented in the learning environments.

While the learning analytics benefits matrix includes many practical examples (Ifenthaler, 2015), a specific focus on assessment is lacking. Table 1.1 exemplifies benefits of analytics-enabled assessment for stakeholders and analytics perspectives.

Table 1.1 Benefits Matrix of Analytics-Enhanced Assessments

	Perspective		
Stakeholder	Summative	Formative/Real-time	Predictive/Prescriptive
Governance	• Compare assessment standards across institutions	• Analyze assessments and performance	• Model impact of assessment regulations
Institution	• Evaluate assessment practices and regulations	• Adjust assessment practices and regulations	• Forecast performance
Learning design	• Increase quality of task design	• Adjust task design • Modify task difficulty	• Predict outcomes of task design changes
Educator	• Compare task design and related feedback	• Understand assessment progress and use of feedback	• Identify assessment and feedback issues
Learner	• Visualize successful tasks • Compare assessment outcomes	• Dynamic task recommendation • Adaptive feedback	• Optimize task difficulty • Predict task mastery

Despite the rich reflection of research on the benefits of learning analytics, the implementation of organization-wide analytics systems is scarce (Buckingham Shum & McKay, 2018). A common explanation is the lack of a learning analytics framework (Chatti & Muslim, 2019; Chatti et al., 2020; Dyckhoff et al., 2012) as well as limited staff and technology being available for learning analytics projects (Ifenthaler, 2017; Ifenthaler & Yau, 2019). However, the demand toward analytics-enhanced assessments require a further development of existing frameworks for learning analytics.

Analytics-Enhanced Assessment Framework

One important strand within learning analytics research is the development of frameworks for the implementation of systems into existing legacy systems or newly-to-be-designed infrastructure (Klasen & Ifenthaler, 2019). Such frameworks are also regarded as a key component of change processes when implementing learning analytics into organizational structures and procedures (Ifenthaler, 2020; Leitner et al., 2019). Learning analytics frameworks have been proposed, including surface-level approaches combining stakeholders, objectives, data, instruments, and internal and external constraints (Greller & Drachsler, 2012).

Chatti and Muslim (2019) proposed the PERLA (Personalization and Learning Analytics) framework that focusses on effective analytics-enhanced personalized learning. It guides researchers and developers through a systematic perspective in the design process and suggests the development of indicators to support personalized learning.

Blackmon and Moore (2020) suggest a framework to support interdisciplinary approaches among stakeholders. The major components of the framework focus on data—specifically, on awareness, access, and resources. The LAVA (Learning Analytics and Visual Analytics) framework includes four dimensions of learning analytics (Chatti et al., 2020): What?, Why?, Who?, How? An important assumption of the LAVA framework is the active involvement of human stakeholders in the learning analytics process. Still, elaborated, and more importantly, empirically validated learning analytics frameworks are scarce (Ifenthaler & Widanapathirana, 2014a). Another limitation of learning analytics frameworks is the missing link of learner characteristics (e.g., prior learning), learning behavior (e.g., access of materials), and curricular requirements (e.g., competences, sequencing of learning).

Ifenthaler and Widanapathirana (2014a) addressed most of these limitations by introducing a holistic learning analytics framework. Their PASS (Personalized Adaptive Study Success) framework includes a holistic perspective on learning analytics and combines data sources directly linked to individual stakeholders, their interaction with the online learning environment, as well as curricular requirements.

Additionally, data from outside of the educational system are integrated (e.g., reading a textbook from a public library). The processing and analysis of the combined data is carried out in a multilayer data warehouse and returned to the stakeholders—e.g., institution, teacher, learner—in a meaningful way. Each of these stakeholders has unique needs for understanding and interpreting data that is most relevant for the decisions that need to be made (e.g., by a student for re-working, by a teacher for assisting in providing guidance and advice to the learner, by an institutional leader for aggregating results to make programmatic and curriculum decisions). However, a yet-to-be-solved limitation of learning analytics is the lack of a stronger focus on dynamic or real-time assessment and feedback as well the improvement of learning environments. While the above-mentioned holistic learning analytics framework includes allusions to assessment data (e.g., prior academic performance, self-tests) and accompanying feedback (e.g., metacognitive prompts, personalized scaffolds) (Ifenthaler & Widanapathirana, 2014a), distinct assessment analytics or analytics-enhanced formative and evaluative assessment features are not integrated.

Following the core components of the above-mentioned PASS learning analytics framework (Ifenthaler & Widanapathirana, 2014b), Figure 1.2 shows a holistic learning analytics framework with a specific emphasis on analytics-enhanced assessment.

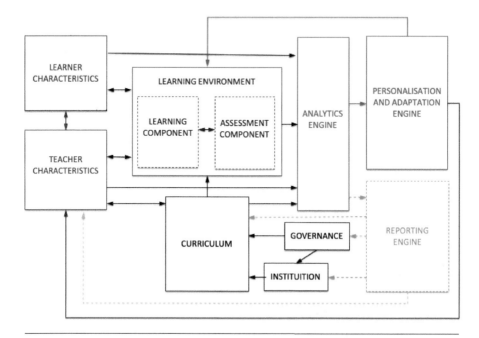

Figure 1.2 Analytics-Enhanced Assessment Framework (adapted from Ifenthaler, 2015)

While governance and institutions define formal components of the curriculum (e.g., competences), including assessment regulations, the learning environment includes components for learning (e.g., videos, reading materials) as well as aligned assessment tasks (e.g. single/multiple-choice quizzes, essays, case or project tasks). Both learners and educators demonstrate specific personal characteristics (e.g., learning/teaching strategies) and dispositions (e.g., interests, beliefs), which may influence their interaction with the learning environment. Data from the afore-mentioned framework entities (e.g., trace-data, self-report data, historic data) are collected and analyzed using algorithms within the analytics engine (e.g., support vector machines, natural language processing). Based on the analytics results, the personalization and adaption engine produces features to be pushed through auto-mated procedures into the learning environment (e.g., dashboard, visualization) or through specific features for educators, which facilitate pedagogical action and decision making (e.g., highlighting clusters of students at risk, high-performing students). Additionally, reporting features may be included which help to further improve the design of the learning environment and advance the curriculum as well as assessments and feedback.

Conclusion

The complexity of designing technology- and analytic-enhanced assessment and feedback systems has been discussed widely over the past few years (Sadler, 2010; Shute, 2008; Webb & Ifenthaler, 2018a). The current challenge is to make valid use of analytics data—from learners, teachers, and learning environments—for assessments and feedback. In addition to embracing opportunities provided by analytics-enhanced assessment, educational decision makers need to address ethics and privacy issues linked to analytics-enhanced assessments. They need to define who has access to which assessment data, where and how long the assess-ment data will be stored, and which procedures and algorithms to implement for further use of the available assessment data (Ifenthaler & Tracey, 2016). While ethics and privacy are gaining increasing attention, and first attempts of frame-works for ethics and privacy in learning analytics are established (Drachsler & Greller, 2016; Ferguson et al., 2016), most research toward privacy issues in learning analytics refers to guidelines from other disciplines, such as Internet security or medical environments. Due to the contextual characteristics of pri-vacy, an adoption from other contexts to questions of learning analytics, and more specifically analytics-enhanced assessments and feedback, seems not to be recommendable (Nissenbaum, 2004).

In conclusion, analytics-enhanced assessments may reveal personal information and insights into an individual learning history; however, they are not accredited and far from being unbiased, comprehensive, and fully valid at this point in time. Much remains to be done to mitigate these shortcomings in a way that learners will truly benefit from learning analytics.

References

Adachi, C., Tai, J. H.-M., and Dawson, P. (2018). Academics' perceptions of the benefits and challenges of self and peer assessment in higher education. *Assessment & Evaluation in Higher Education, 43*(2), 294–306. https://doi.org/10.1080/02602938.2017.1339775

Andrade, H. J. (2010). Students as the definitive source of formative assessment: Academic self-assessment and the self-regulation of learning. In: H. J. Andrade & G. J. Cizek (Eds.), *Handbook of Formative Assessment,* 90–105. Routledge.

Baker, E. L., Chung, G. K. W. K., and Cai, L. (2016). Assessment, gaze, refraction, and blur: The course of achievement testing in the past 100 years. *Review of Research in Education, 40,* 94–142. https://doi.org/10.3102/0091732X16679806

Baker, R. S. J. d., and Siemens, G. (2015). Educational data mining and learning analytics. In: R. K. Sawyer (Ed.), *The Cambridge Handbook of the Learning Sciences* (2 ed.), 253–272.

Bektik, D. (2019). Issues and challenges for implementing writing analytics at higher education. In: D. Ifenthaler, J. Y.-K. Yau, and D.-K. Mah (Eds.), *Utilizing Learning Analytics to Support Study Success,* 143–155. Springer.

Bellotti, F., Kapralos, B., Lee, K., Moreno-Ger, P., and Berta, R. (2013). Assessment in and of serious games: An overview. *Advances in Human-Computer Interaction, 136864.* https://doi.org/10.1155/2013/136864

Bennett, R. E. (2011). Formative assessment: A critical review. *Assessment in Education: Principles, Policy & Practice, 18*(1), 5–25. https://doi.org/10.1080/0969594X.2010.513678

Bennett, R. E. (2015). The changing nature of educational assessment. *Review of Research in Education, 39*(1), 370–407. https://doi.org/10.3102/0091732x14554179

Black, P., and Wiliam, D. (1998). Assessment and classroom learning. *Assessment in Education: Principles, Policy & Practice, 5*(1), 7–74. https://doi.org/10.1080/0969595980050102

Black, P. J. (1998). *Testing: Friend or Foe? The Theory and Practice of Assessment and Testing.* Falmer Press.

Black, P. J., and Wiliam, D. (2018). Classroom assessment and pedagogy. *Assessment in Education: Principles, Policy & Practice, 25*(6), 551–575. https://doi.org/10.1080/0969594X.2018.1441807

Blackmon, S. J., and Moore, R. L. (2020). A framework to support interdisciplinary engagement with learning analytics. In: D. Ifenthaler and D. C. Gibson (Eds.), *Adoption of Data Analytics in Higher Education Learning and Teaching,* 39–52. Springer.

Bloom, B. S., Hastings, J. T., and Madaus, G. F. (1971). *Handbook of Formative and Summative Evaluation of Student Learning.* McGraw-Hill.

Boud, D. (2000). Sustainable assessment: Rethinking assessment for the learning society. *Studies in Continuing Education, 22*(2), 151–167. https://doi.org/10.1080/713695728

Boud, D., and Molloy, E. (2013). Rethinking models of feedback for learning: The challenge of design. *Assessment & Evaluation in Higher Education, 38*(6), 698–712. https://doi.org/10.1080/02602938.2012.691462

Broadbent, J., Panadero, E., and Boud, D. (2017). Implementing summative assessment with a formative flavour: A case study in a large class. *Assessment & Evaluation in Higher Education, 43*(2), 307–322. https://doi.org/10.1080/02602938.2017.1343455

Buckingham Shum, S., and McKay, T. A. (2018). Architecting for learning analytics. Innovating for sustainable impact. *EDUCAUSE Review, 53*(2), 25–37.

Butler, N., and Winne, P. H. (1995). Feedback and self-regulated learning: A theoretical synthesis. *Review of Educational Research, 65*(3), 245–281.

Carless, D. (2007). Learning-oriented assessment: Conceptual bases and practical implications. *Innovations in Education and Teaching International, 44*(1), 57–66.

Chatti, M. A., and Muslim, A. (2019). The PERLA framework: Blending personalization and learning analytics. *The International Review of Research in Open and Distributed Learning, 20*(1). https://doi.org/10.19173/irrodl.v20i1.3936

Chatti, M. A., Muslim, A., Guliani, M., and Guesmi, M. (2020). The LAVA model: Learning analytics meets visual analytics. In: D. Ifenthaler and D. C. Gibson (Eds.), *Adoption of Data Analytics in Higher Education Learning and Teaching*, 70–93. Springer.

Corbalan, G., Kester, L., and van Merriënboer, J. J. G. (2009). Dynamic task selection: Effects of feedback and learner control on efficiency and motivation. *Learning and Instruction, 19*(6), 455–465. https://doi.org/10.1016/j.learninstruc.2008.07.002

Costa, E. B., Fonseca, B., Santana, M. A., de Araújo, F., and Rego, J. (2017). Evaluating the effectiveness of educational data mining techniques for early prediction of students' academic failure in introductory programming courses. *Computers in Human Behavior, 73*, 247–256. https://doi.org/10.1016/j.chb.2017.01.047

Dann, R. (2014). Assessment as learning: Blurring the boundaries of assessment and learning for theory, policy and practice. *Assessment in Education: Principles, Policy & Practice, 21*(2), 149–166. https://doi.org/10.1080/0969594x.2014.898128

Drachsler, H., and Greller, W. (2016). Privacy and analytics—it's a DELICATE issue. A checklist for trusted learning analytics. *Sixth International Conference on Learning Analytics & Knowledge,* Edinburgh, UK.

Dyckhoff, A. L., Zielke, D., Bültmann, M., Chatti, M. A., and Schroeder, U. (2012). Design and implementation of a learning analytics toolkit for teachers. *Educational Technology & Society, 15*(3), 58–76.

Ellis, C. (2013). Broadening the scope and increasing usefulness of learning analytics: The case for assessment analytics. *British Journal of Educational Technology, 44*(4), 662–664. https://doi.org/10.1111/bjet.12028

Ferguson, R., Hoel, T., Scheffel, M., and Drachsler, H. (2016). Guest editorial: Ethics and privacy in learning analytics. *Journal of Learning Analytics, 3*(1), 5–15.

Gašević, D., Dawson, S., and Siemens, G. (2015). Let's not forget: Learning analytics are about learning. *TechTrends, 59*(1), 64–71. https://doi.org/10.1007/s11528-014 -0822-x

Gašević, D., Joksimović, S., Eagan, B. R., and Shaffer, D. W. (2019). SENS: Network analytics to combine social and cognitive perspectives of collaborative learning. *Computers in Human Behavior, 92*, 562–577. https://doi.org/10.1016/j.chb.2018.07.003

Gašević, D., Jovanović, J., Pardo, A., and Dawson, S. (2017). Detecting learning strategies with analytics: Links with self-reported measures and academic performance. *Journal of Learning Analytics, 4*(2), 113–128. https://doi.org/jla.2017.42.10

Gibbs, G., and Simpson, C. (2005). Conditions under which assessment supports students' learning. *Learning and Teaching in Higher Education, 1*, 3–31.

Goldhammer, F., Naumann, J., Stelter, A., Toth, K., Rölke, H., and Klieme, E. (2014). The time on task effect in reading and problem solving is moderated by task difficulty and skill. Insights from a computer-based large-scale assessment. *Journal of Educational Psychology, 106*, 608–626.

Gottipati, S., Shankararaman, V., and Lin, J. R. (2018). Text analytics approach to extract course improvement suggestions from students' feedback. *Research and Practice in Technology Enhanced Learning, 16*(6). https://doi.org/10.1186/s41039-018-0073-0

Greller, W., and Drachsler, H. (2012). Translating learning into numbers: A generic framework for learning analytics. *Educational Technology & Society, 15*(3), 42–57.

Ifenthaler, D. (2015). Learning analytics. In: J. M. Spector (Ed.). *The SAGE Encyclopedia of Educational Technology* (Vol. 2), 447–451. Sage.

Ifenthaler, D. (2017). Are higher education institutions prepared for learning analytics? *TechTrends, 61*(4), 366–371. https://doi.org/10.1007/s11528-016-0154-0

Ifenthaler, D. (2020). Change management for learning analytics. In: N. Pinkwart and S. Liu (Eds.), *Artificial Intelligence Supported Educational Technologies*, 261–272. Springer.

Ifenthaler, D., Eseryel, D., and Ge, X. (2012). Assessment for game-based learning. In: D. Ifenthaler, D. Eseryel, and X. Ge (Eds.), *Assessment in Game-Based Learning. Foundations, Innovations, and Perspectives*, 3–10. Springer.

Ifenthaler, D., Gibson, D. C., Prasse, D., Shimada, A., and Yamada, M. (in press). Putting learning back into learning analytics: Actions for policy makers, researchers, and practitioners. *Educational Technology Research and Development*. https://doi.org/10.1007 /s11423-020-09909-8

Ifenthaler, D., Greiff, S., and Gibson, D. C. (2018). Making use of data for assessments: Harnessing analytics and data science. In: J. Voogt, G. Knezek, R. Christensen, and K.-W. Lai (Eds.), *International Handbook of IT in Primary and Secondary Education* (2 ed.), 649–663. Springer.

Ifenthaler, D., Pirnay-Dummer, P., and Seel, N. M. (Eds.), (2010). *Computer-Based Diagnostics and Systematic Analysis of Knowledge*. Springer.

Ifenthaler, D., and Tracey, M. W. (2016). Exploring the relationship of ethics and privacy in learning analytics and design: Implications for the field of educational technology. *Educational Technology Research and Development, 64*(5), 877–880. https://doi.org/10.1007/s11423-016-9480-3

Ifenthaler, D., and Widanapathirana, C. (2014a). Development and validation of a learning analytics framework: Two case studies using support vector machines. *Technology, Knowledge and Learning, 19*(1–2), 221–240. https://doi.org/10.1007/s10758-014-9226-4

Ifenthaler, D., and Widanapathirana, C. (2014b). Development and validation of a learning analytics framework: Two case studies using support vector machines. *Technology, Knowledge and Learning, 19*(1–2), 221–240. https://doi.org/10.1007/s10758-014-9226-4

Ifenthaler, D., and Yau, J. (2019). Higher education stakeholders' views on learning analytics policy recommendations for supporting study success. *International Journal of Learning Analytics and Artificial Intelligence for Education, 1*(1), 28–42. https://doi.org/10.3991/ijai.v1i1.10978

Johnson, W. L., and Lester, J. C. (2016). Face-to-face interaction with pedagogical agents, twenty years later. *International Journal of Artificial Intelligence in Education, 26*(1), 25–36. https://doi.org/10.1007/s40593-015-0065-9

Kim, Y. J., and Ifenthaler, D. (2019). Game-based assessment: The past ten years and moving forward. In: D. Ifenthaler and Y. J. Kim (Eds.), *Game-Based Assessment Revisted*, 3–12. Springer.

Klasen, D., and Ifenthaler, D. (2019). Implementing learning analytics into existing higher education legacy systems. In: D. Ifenthaler, J. Y.-K. Yau, and D.-K. Mah (Eds.), *Utilizing Learning Analytics to Support Study Success, 61*–72. Springer.

Labarthe, H., Bouchet, F., Bachelet, R., and Yacef, K. (2016). Does a peer recommender foster students' engagement in MOOCs? *International Conference on Educational Data Mining.*

Leitner, P., Ebner, M., and Ebner, M. (2019). Learning analytics challenges to overcome in higher education institutions. In: D. Ifenthaler, J. Y.-K. Yau, and D.-K. Mah (Eds.), *Utilizing Learning Analytics to Support Study Success, 91*–104. Springer.

Lin, J. W., Lai, Y. C., Lai, Y. C., and Chang, L. C. (2016). Fostering self-regulated learning in a blended environment using group awareness and peer assistance as external scaffolds. *Journal of Computer Assisted Learning, 32*(1), 77–93.

Lockyer, L., Heathcote, E., and Dawson, S. (2013). Informing pedagogical action: Aligning learning analytics with learning design. *American Behavioral Scientist, 57*(10), 1439–1459. https://doi.org/10.1177/0002764213479367

Mah, D.-K. (2016). Learning analytics and digital badges: Potential impact on student retention in higher education. *Technology, Knowledge and Learning, 21*(3), 285–305. https://doi.org/10.1007/s10758-016-9286-8

Martin, F., and Whitmer, J. C. (2016). Applying learning analytics to investigate timed release in online learning. *Technology, Knowledge and Learning, 21*(1), 59–74. https://doi.org/10.1007/s10758-015-9261-9

Marzouk, Z., Rakovic, M., Liaqat, A., Vytasek, J., Samadi, D., Stewart-Alonso, J., Ram, I., Woloshen, S., Winne, P. H., and Nesbit, J. C. (2016). What if learning analytics were based on learning science? *Australasian Journal of Educational Technology, 32*(6), 1–18. https://doi.org/10.14742/ajet.3058

McLoughlin, C., and Lee, M. J. W. (2010). Personalized and self regulated learning in the Web 2.0 era: International exemplars of innovative pedagogy using social software. *Australasian Journal of Educational Technology, 26*(1), 28–43.

Newton, P. E. (2007). Clarifying the purposes of educational assessment. *Assessment in Education: Principles, Policy & Practice, 14*(2), 149–170. https://doi.org/10.1080/09695940701478321

Nicol, D. J., and Macfarlane-Dick, D. (2006). Formative assessment and self-regulated learning: A model and seven principles of good feedback practice. *Studies in Higher Education, 31*(2), 199–218. https://doi.org/10.1080/03075070600572090

Nissenbaum, H. (2004). Privacy as contextual integrity. *Washington Law Review, 79*(1), 119–157.

Panadero, E., Broadbent, J., Boud, D., and Lodge, J. M. (2019). Using formative assessment to influence self- and co-regulated learning: The role of evaluative judgement. *European Journal of Psychology and Education, 34*(3), 535–557. https://doi.org/10.1007/s10212-018-0407-8

Panadero, E., Jonsson, A., and Botella, J. (2017). Effects of self-assessment on self-regulated learning and self-efficacy: Four meta-analyses. *Educational Research Review, 22*(74–98). https://doi.org/10.1016/j.edurev.2017.08.004

Pellegrino, J. W., Chudowsky, N., and Glaser, R. (Eds.), (2001). *Knowing What Students Know: The Science and Design of Educational Assessment.* National Academy Press.

Perrenoud, P. (1998). From formative assessment to a controlled regulation of learning processes. Towards a wider conceptual field. *Assessment in Education: Principles, Policy & Practice, 5*(1), 85–102. https://doi.org/10.1080/0969595980050105

Rissanen, M. J., Kume, N., Kuroda, Y., Kuroda, T., Yoshimura, K., and Yoshihara, H. (2008). Asynchronous teaching of psychomotor skills through VR annotations: Evaluation in digital rectal examination. *Studies in Health Technology and Informatics, 132*, 411–416.

Sadler, D. R. (1989). Formative assessment and the design of instructional systems. *Instructional Science, 18*, 119–144.

Sadler, D. R. (2010). Beyond feedback: Developing student capability in complex appraisal. *Assessment & Evaluation in Higher Education, 35*(5), 535–550.

Schumacher, C., and Ifenthaler, D. (2018). The importance of students' motivational dispositions for designing learning analytics. *Journal of Computing in Higher Education, 30*(3), 599–619. https://doi.org/10.1007/s12528-018-9188-y

Schumacher, C., and Ifenthaler, D. (2021). Investigating prompts for supporting students' self-regulation—A remaining challenge for learning analytics approaches? *The Internet and Higher Education, 49*, 100791. https://doi.org/10.1016/j.iheduc.2020.100791

Scriven, M. (1967). *The Methodology of Evaluation.* American Educational Research Association.

Shute, V. J. (2008). Focus on formative feedback. *Review of Educational Research, 78*(1), 153–189.

Shute, V. J., Rahimi, S., and Emihovich, B. (2018). Assessment for learning in immersive environments. In: D. Lui, C. Dede, R. Huang, and J. Richards (Eds.), *Virtual, Augmented, and Mixed Realities in Education,* 71–89. Springer.

Shute, V. J., Wang, L., Greiff, S., Zhao, W., and Moore, G. (2016). Measuring problem solving skills via stealth assessment in an engaging video game. *Computers in Human Behavior, 63,* 106–117. https://doi.org/10.1016/j.chb.2016.05.047

Sitzmann, T., Ely, K., Brown, K. G., and Bauer, K. N. (2010). Self-assessment of knowledge: A cognitive learning or affective measure? *Academy of Management Learning & Education, 9*(2), 169–191. https://doi.org/10.5465/amle.9.2.zqr169

Spector, J. M., Ifenthaler, D., Sampson, D. G., Yang, L., Mukama, E., Warusavitarana, A., Lokuge Dona, K., Eichhorn, K., Fluck, A., Huang, R., Bridges, S., Lu, J., Ren, Y., Gui, X., Deneen, C. C., San Diego, J., and Gibson, D. C. (2016). Technology enhanced formative assessment for 21st century learning. *Educational Technology & Society, 19*(3), 58–71.

Stödberg, U. (2012). A research review of e-assessment. *Assessment & Evaluation in Higher Education, 37*(5), 591–604. https://doi.org/10.1080/02602938.2011.557496

Tai, J. H.-M., Ajjawi, R., Boud, D., Dawson, P., and Panadero, E. (2018). Developing evaluative judgement: Enabling students to make decisions about the quality of work. *Higher Education, 76*(3), 467–481. https://doi.org/10.1007/s10734-017-0220-3

Taras, M. (2005). Assessment—summative and formative—some theoretical reflections. *British Journal of Educational Studies, 53*(4), 466–478.

van der Kleij, F., and Adie, L. (2018). Formative assessment and feedback using information technology. In: J. Voogt, G. Knezek, R. Christensen, and K.-W. Lai (Eds.), *International Handbook of IT in Primary and Secondary Education* (2 ed.), 601–615. Springer.

Vieira, C., Parsons, P., and Byrd, V. (2018). Visual learning analytics of educational data: A systematic literature review and research agenda. *Computers & Education, 122,* 119–135. https://doi.org/10.1016/j.compedu.2018.03.018

Wanner, T., and Palmer, E. (2018). Formative self- and peer assessment for improved student learning: The crucial factors of design, teacher participation and feedback. *Assessment and Evaluation in Higher Education, 43*(7), 1032–1047. https://doi.org/10.1080/02602938.2018.1427698

Webb, M. E., Gibson, D. C., and Forkosh-Baruch, A. (2013). Challenges for information technology supporting educational assessment. *Journal of Computer Assisted Learning, 29*(5), 451–462. https://doi.org/10.1111/jcal.12033

Webb, M., and Ifenthaler, D. (2018a). Assessment as, for and of 21st century learning using information technology: An overview. In: J. Voogt, G. Knezek, R. Christensen, and K.-W. Lai (Eds.), *International Handbook of IT in Primary and Secondary Education* (2 ed.), 1–20. Springer.

Webb, M., and Ifenthaler, D. (2018b). Section introduction: Using information technology for assessment: Issues and opportunities. In: J. Voogt, G. Knezek, R. Christensen, and K.-W. Lai (Eds.), *International Handbook of IT in Primary and Secondary Education* (2 ed.), 577–580. Springer.

Whitelock, D., and Bektik, D. (2018). Progress and challenges for automated scoring and feedback systems for large-scale assessments. In: J. Voogt, G. Knezek, R. Christensen, and K.-W. Lai (Eds.), *International Handbook of IT in Primary and Secondary Education* (2 ed.), 617–634. Springer.

Yau, J., and Ifenthaler, D. (2020). Reflections on different learning analytics indicators for supporting study success. *International Journal of Learning Analytics and Artificial Intelligence for Education, 2*(2), 4–23. https://doi.org/10.3991/ijai.v2i2.15639

Chapter 2

Desperately Seeking the Impact of Learning Analytics in Education at Scale

Marrying Data Analysis with Teaching and Learning

Olga Viberg[1] and Åke Grönlund[2]

Abstract

Learning analytics (LA) is argued to be able to improve learning outcomes, learner support, and teaching. However, despite an increasingly expanding amount of student (digital) data accessible from various online education and learning platforms and the growing interest in LA worldwide, as well as considerable research efforts already made, there is still little empirical evidence of impact on practice that shows the effectiveness of LA in education settings. Based on a selection of

[1] KTH Royal Institute of Technology, Department of Media Technology and Interaction Design, Sweden

[2] Örebro University, Örebro University School of Business, Sweden

theoretical and empirical research, this chapter provides a critical discussion about the possibilities of collecting and using student data, as well as barriers and challenges to overcome in providing data-informed support to educators' everyday teaching practices. We argue that in order to increase the impact of data-driven decision making aimed at students' improved learning in education at scale, we need to better understand educators' needs, their teaching practices, the context in which these practices occur, and how to support them in developing relevant knowledge, strategies and skills to facilitate the data-informed process of digitalization of education.

Keywords: Human-centered learning analytics, digitalization of education, teacher support, data, sense-making, impact, scalability, responsible learning analytics

Introduction

Learning analytics (LA)—"the measurement, collection, analysis and reporting of data about learners and their contexts, for purposes of understanding and optimizing learning and the environments in which it occurs" (Long & Siemens, 2011, p. 34)—has the potential to impact student learning at scale (Knight, Gibson, & Shibani, 2020) by offering critical insights into the processes of online and face-to-face learning, as well as supporting learning activities via analytics tools (Ochoa, Knight, & Wise, 2020). However, the potential is far from realized due to several interrelated issues, including "lack of uptake and adoption, generalizability, and the relevance of some of our [researchers'] work to actual practice and the power dynamics of data-informed approaches" (Ochoa et al., 2020, p. 2). Moreover, scholars highlight that to be able to improve the quality of teaching and learning at scale, we also need to consider stakeholders' data literacy—i.e., the ability to understand, find, collect, interpret, visualize, and support arguments using quantitative and qualitative data (Deahl, 2014)—and leadership (Schildkamp, 2019; Henderson & Corry, 2020).

There is still very little existing empirical evidence of LA research having improved learning, learner support, and teaching at scale. Viberg et al. (2018), for example, in their systematic literature review of LA, found that only nine percent of 252 reviewed studies, conducted in higher education, showed that LA improved students' learning outcomes. Also, despite the increasing availability of student data in K–12 settings worldwide—accelerated by the forced move to online education during the pandemics—the majority of LA analyses have hitherto been conducted in the context of higher education, often at a small scale within a context of one course, or in the setting of massive online open courses (MOOCs; e.g., Yu, 2021).

There are many reasons behind the slow adoption of LA and data-driven decision-making processes in educational settings, especially in K–12 education, including challenges related to data interoperability (Dodero et al., 2017; Samuelsen, Chen, & Wasson, 2019), ethics and privacy concerns (Beerwinkle, 2021; Livingstone, 2020; Viberg, Andersson et al., 2021), development of stakeholders' data literacy (Ifenthaler et al., 2020), as well as feedback literacy skills (Jivet, 2021) and a general lack of participatory approaches that take into account the needs and preferences of the students and teachers—even less actually engage them directly—in the LA design process (Buckingham Shum, Ferguson, & Martinez-Maldonado, 2019; Jivet, 2021). We should not forget that LA is about *supporting* learning, not just reporting it (Gasevic, Dawson, & Simiens, 2015). Yet, the majority of LA analyses have so far been driven by the availability of learner data, often in the context of MOOCs (massive open online courses), rather than by the specific needs of teachers and students.

In this chapter, we argue that in order to make LA attractive to educational professionals and students there is a need to further develop a *human-centered learning analytics* approach. This approach posits that the design process of effective LA must extend beyond sound technical and pedagogical principles; it needs to carefully consider a range of contextual and human factors, including *why* and *how* they will be used (Buckingham Shum et al., 2020), as well as by *whom* and in what *context*. Moreover, it must be designed for the benefit of the users rather than imposed upon them by designers or researchers. In particular, we focus our discussion on the need to understand, engage, and support *teachers*—the key stakeholders who guide and facilitate learning activities in everyday education practices and who are responsible for the design and real-time management of students' learning processes (van Leeuwen et al., 2017)—as *enablers* and *co-designers* of LA. This is important, because if LA is to be able to help them through the provision of improved teacher support, we need to (1) carefully analyse teachers' needs before implementing LA, (2) understand what data are needed and to meet those needs, (3) investigate what type of LA support mechanisms they would like to be assisted by, and (4) understand how teachers would like such LA tools (e.g., teacher-facing learning dashboards) to be designed and used. Also, there is a need to understand what knowledge and skills (e.g., data and feedback literacy) they may need to develop so as to be able to enable everyday LA practices and use the designed tools effectively. These steps need to be taken in order to move towards the ultimate goal of achieving the intended changes in students' learning behaviors that would lead to improved learning outcomes.

Critical Aspects of LA in a Human-Centered Perspective

In this section, we review the literature organized by aspects that are critical in a human-centered, responsible perspective of LA. The aspects include:

- **Focus on teachers' needs and goals.** This should be the starting point for LA development, as this is where tools are to be applied. Unless teachers can make sense of data and take action on it, it is not meaningful.
- **Teachers' data literacy skills.** Data presentation and analysis can reveal new patterns, inspire teaching, and support learning in new ways.
- **Data.** Data sources and data analysis need to become more diverse and develop beyond summative analysis of performance towards formative guidance. In doing so, students and learning contexts also must be represented.

Focus on Teachers' Needs and Goals

In order to take advantage of the affordances of LA to assist teachers and make a difference in their everyday teaching practice, we need to enable them to conduct meaningful—i.e., such that can make a positive difference—LA activities in their everyday practices. There is also an aspect of responsibility involved; protection of students' privacy is seen as both a moral and a legal obligation. To achieve this, there is a need to increase our understanding of what problems they encounter in their daily teaching practice and how LA can provide assistance in addressing those problems.

One of the key issues in this regard relates to the fact that data use is mainly used for *accountability* purposes (i.e., data collection and use focuses on achievement and not learning) (Mandinach & Schildkamp, 2021). For example, test results are most often used summatively to measure performance, but in order to improve learning, it is more productive to use them formatively to guide teaching in a way that continuously improves conditions for student learning. Understanding *why* students have not learned something is then more interesting than the performance measure itself but also more challenging to derive from data. In daily practice, teachers regularly assess students' work formatively—both through informal, everyday observations and through continuous assessment of different individual and collaborative learning activities—in order to help them focus their thinking or improve their work processes. In formal systems, to the contrary, test results are registered for the purpose of evaluation and comparison—often of both students and teachers.

While measuring student performance is necessary, it may take up too much attention, to the detriment of learning. If there "is too much accountability pressure, this often leads to misuse of data, and even to abuse" (Mandinach & Schildkamp, 2021, p. 4). It may also lead to mistrust among teachers towards LA systems, as they can be seen as tools for control rather than for assistance.

To provide assistance that would improve students' learning by offering adequate teacher-support mechanisms, some LA researchers argue for the need of a "subversive" LA that aims to grapple with the ramifications of LA research efforts and critically engage with the ways in which power, race, gender, and class influence and are influenced by LA work (Wise, Sarmiento, & Boothe, 2021). This becomes especially critical in the context of the recent turn to online learning worldwide, which has contributed to the considerably increased *quantity* and also *kinds* of data being generated about students and by students at different levels of education. This, in turn, requires LA researchers and practitioners to address questions about bias, equity, surveillance, ownership (of data), control, and agency in LA use (Wise et al., 2021).

When developing LA tools, designers need to take a critical view by integrating ways to look at the shortcomings of data in their thinking and by incorporating stakeholder privacy protection mechanisms in the tools (Klein, 2021). Such experiences and knowledge can be adapted from relevant efforts in other research areas. This includes *human–computer interaction,* which focuses on the user- and human-centered design processes aiming to effectively meet user/stakeholder needs; and *information systems research,* in which LA scholars can draw on the affordances of relevant theoretical contributions, which may help underpin the conceptual groundings of LA technological artifacts.

For example, when developing LA tools—aiming to assist teachers in their work—an *ensemble view* of technology (Orlikowski & Iacono, 2001) can be adapted. This perspective focuses on the transformational nature of technology: Technology brings changes not only in terms of *how* we do things but also in terms of *what is doable and desirable* in teaching and learning practice—that is, in teachers' perceptions. This view undertakes the idea of sociotechnical construction, suggesting that new data-driven—in the context of this chapter—teaching practices and methods are co-constructed in a sociotechnical system rather than purely engineered by developers.

Technology develops during use and based on how it is used. This implies that there is a need to pay attention to the contexts of teaching and learning and to student behavior, preferences, and individual characteristics. These are complex phenomena, which are difficult to derive from data. Teachers regularly interpret both students and situations, but they do that based not just on structured data but also on understanding, which comes from their teaching experience, informal observations, and familiarity with students and learning situations. A teacher knows what a student *is,* the computer knows only (partially) what s/he says and does.

Data existing in digital format are typically quite simple, while teachers' interpretations are based on both quantitative and qualitative data. While LA data typically informs about student scores on a test, teachers can understand *why* a student scored well or poorly. Of course, LA systems could add more data. Student behavior data could be expanded to include, for example, interaction tracing by combining data originated from different online learning platforms, and also qualitative data, for example, about students' level of motivation. But more data alone does not create understanding. There also needs to be a way to interpret data and what they tell us about student learning—that is, to translate awareness into action. Artificial intelligence (AI) can help in understanding student development in, for example, mathematics and literacy, but the reasons for this development or lack thereof cannot be understood.

A major threshold in AI development today is precisely that—it can create texts that look like human-written text, but as long as it lacks the understanding of what the text *means,* there is a limit to its further development (Hao, 2020). In learning, teachers interacting with students are the only ones who can develop understanding and, hence, understand how to use data and automated analysis of data for improved learning.

Hence, a coherent understanding requires careful analysis of learning contexts and actors so as to be able to address critical questions about (algorithmic) bias, equity, surveillance, ownership (of data), control, and agency in LA design and use (Wise et al., 2021). Contextual understanding may also require taking into account qualitative data, yet largely unexplored by the LA community—for example, cultural differences (e.g., in terms of power distance) that may influence the adoption and the effectiveness of LA interventions (see, e.g., Davis et al., 2017; Kizilcec & Cohen, 2017).

To sum up, it is critical that data use or LA activities start with a certain improvement goal and not a sole emphasis on accountability or on the available data. Taking the teacher's perspective, in today's society such goals should focus not only on the improvement of students' subject knowledge, but also on development of their critical 21st-century skills, including collaborative and self-regulated learning skills that are directly associated with academic performance, especially in online learning settings (e.g., Viberg, Khalil, & Baars, 2020). Moreover, such goals may be directed towards the development and improvements of students' data-, feedback-, and digital-literacy skills that are crucial for their successful navigation and study success in online learning settings (see, e.g., Ifenthaler et al., 2020; Jivet, 2021).

Teachers' Data Literacy Skills

While understanding teachers, students, and learning processes is important for LA tools designers, the increased use of data also puts demands on teachers' data-literacy skills (Henderson & Corry, 2020). They need to be able to interpret data from those tools and combine it with their pedagogical knowledge so as to make it actionable in educational practices (Gummer & Mandinach, 2015). Data literacy skills include the ability to understand what data are needed to address a specific problem, collect these data, make sense of (student) data representations and feedback provided through LA tools, and, based on this sense making, provide improved student assistance. Research shows that educators frequently struggle with the use of data, including setting up clear goals for improvement, collecting data, and making sense of them (Mandinach & Schildkamp, 2021). In general, scholars argue that educators must have some level of data literacy, which refers to "the ability to transform information into actionable knowledge and practices by collecting, analyzing, and interpreting all types if data (assessment, school climate, behavioral, snapshot, longitudinal, moment-to-moment, etc.) to help determine instructional steps. It combines an understanding of data with standards, disciplinary knowledge and practices, curricular knowledge, pedagogical content knowledge, and an understanding of how [students] learn" (Mandinach & Gummer, 2016, p. 14).

Data

Data-based decision making has emerged and evolved in education for almost two decades. Understanding how to make use of data in educational settings and for educational purposes is "a complex and interpretative process, in which goals have to be set, data have to be identified, collected, analyzed, and interpreted, and used to improve teaching and learning" (Mandinach & Schildkamp, 2021, p. 1). It is critical to acknowledge that this process does not start with data but with goals to be achieved.

To address teachers' needs, there is also a necessity to understand what student data has to be considered, collected, and analysed. As highlighted by Kitchin (2021), "data-driven endeavours are not simply technical systems, but are socio-technical. That is, they are as much a result of human values, desires and social relations as they are scientific principles and technologies" (p. 5).

In the educational context, it is not always clear what data are and how to best make sense of them—that is, to translate understanding into action. This can be explained by several reasons. One of them relates to the fact that at many occasions, we need to integrate different types of data in order to achieve the intended improvement goals. In an education setting, a diversity of educational tools are frequently used in parallel. One digital system may be used for practicing and taking exams, another for supporting students' collaborative learning activities. There may also be a variety of learning management systems (LMS) employed for the purpose of delivering an educational module or a course, often including information and instructions, sharing of study materials, and collecting student assignments. More advanced LMS also provide student activity/interaction data, which can be useful for understanding reasons behind performance. There are also systems that collect various types of student demographic data, which needs to be carefully accounted for to be able to provide *equitable* and *fair* adaptive learning solutions, based on LA measurements (Baker & Hawn, 2021). Equity and fairness are becoming increasingly important goals in education (Mandinach & Schildkamp, 2021) and in the design of LA systems (e.g., Holstein & Doroudi, 2019; Hakami & Hernandez-Leo,

2020; Wise et al., 2021). An equitable approach adopts an asset-based view which builds upon student strengths, interests, and backgrounds (Datnow & Park, 2018).

In sum, many LA researchers argue that in order to improve conditions for learning and to improve teaching and learner support, "the true potential to offer meaningful insights comes from combining data from across different data sources" (Bakharia et al., 2016, p. 378; Mandinach & Gummer, 2016).

The *integration* of data plays a critical role for scalability of LA (Samuelsen et al., 2019). But how do we understand scale of impact in LA? Scholars argue that there are two key tensions in implementing LA for impact (Knight et al., 2020). The first tension refers to population versus learning gain scale. That is, there is a conflict between the ambition to reach as large populations of students as possible and the ambition to make a decisive impact on learning. The second tension relates to the issues of generalizability and adoption, suggesting that hitherto LA researchers have focused on big classes with more general models, "rather than on supporting educators to develop their own analytical tools, and to adopt tools over multiple sites" (p. 4).

Scholars, furthermore, posit that to integrate data from different sources in LA, it is vital to consider the context of the data. In what settings and for what purpose were data generated? By which technological devices were they collected? Integration of data is beneficial for interoperability—semantic, technical, legal, as well as organizational—and may be used to personalise learning and enable better querying and reporting of data (Samuelsen, Chen, & Wasson, 2021).

During the past decade, a change from a heavy focus on accountability towards more emphasis on *continuous improvement of education* has occurred. The focus is on the process of data use within a particular sociocultural context. Educators need to "tap diverse data sources [e.g., demographics, attendance, motivation, and home circumstances] to contextualise student performance and behavior" (Mandinach & Schildkamp, 2021, p. 2) and to reduce 'unfair' algorithmic educational solutions (Baker & Hawn, 2021). Researchers suggest that in order to address representational and measurement bias—that is, to increase fairness, we [researchers] need—and we need to help teachers to understand how to—collect "better data—data that includes sufficient proportions of all groups of interests, and where key variables are not themselves biased. This step is recognized as essential among learning analytics practionaries" (Baker & Hawn, 2021, p. 14). As stressed by Holstein et al. (2019), one key step for enhancing *fairness* in the algorithms' use in education would be for researchers to find ways to support practitioners, including teachers, in "collecting and curating" higher-quality data sets.

Such data sources can contribute to offering better explanations and contexts to help educators to better understand and interpret what data mean.

While it is important to interpret data in view of teaching and learning goals, 'big data' analysis also offers a new channel to understanding. As stressed by

Schildkamp (2019), one of the characteristics of big data is that various kinds of data can be linked to one another and that it is possible to look for patterns in these data sets "without having pre-defined hypotheses. In this way, patterns may be discovered that have never been thought of before, which can lead to new possible applications, purposes and goals of data use" (p. 261), as well the relevant theoretical developments. Such discovery may lead to new insights and spur new ideas but require caution before application in teaching and learning practice, as correlation patterns do not necessarily reflect causes and effects.

Another data-related problem concerns a challenge in terms of our understanding of what type of previously unavailable data we need to collect, combine, and analyse in order to bring novel insights into students' learning processes. This requires a thorough understanding of the nature of educators' teaching practices and specific teaching-associated problems that the teacher might need help with.

Conclusions

The review presented here can be summarized by a set of recommendations to learning analytics practice, discussed in various ways in the papers reviewed. Following the Human-Centered Learning Analytics approach, inspired by the user-centered approach since decades taken in the field of human-computer interaction, learning analytics must focus more on understanding of users and use contexts.

- LA development must start with teaching and learning problems and goals. Do not start with data.
- Identify data needs based on goals and practice. Do not rest with what is easily available.
- In order to make sense of data for improving teaching and learning processes, it is important to engage both data professionals and teaching professionals. Inspiration to improvement can come both from data and from practice, but the decisions in learning processes that are to be supported rest with practitioners.
- Including different data sources and different kinds of data may be necessary so as to capture not only performance but also students and learning contexts and processes, which are all diverse. However, as this includes both complex situations and qualitative data, it is important to tread cautiously and make sure the data analysis used within LA systems is triangulated with empirical studies of use.
- Involve teachers and students and analyze their role in using the data.

Moreover, to be able to scale up LA research and support teachers in their data-driven decision-making processes, there is a critical need to develop a *responsible* approach to student data use in education. Even though the LA research community has been for some time interested in the ethics of data-driven practices (e.g., Ferguson, 2019; Tsai et al., 2019), most of this work has been performed in conceptual terms (Arnold & Sclater, 2017). As highlighted by Cerrato-Pargman et al. (2021), research on *applied ethics* has not become pervasive in LA practice. Scholars suggest the so-called 'socially sympathetic' design approach to LA systems (Selwyn, 2019). This approach—sometimes referred to as 'user-respectful' design as opposed to 'user-centered' only—implies designing LA systems and applications in ways that consider different social contexts in which they are intended to be used and the different needs and rights of the users. It also requires ensuring informed engagement concerning issues related to privacy, security, and user rights of individuals interacting with these systems (Selwyn, 2019).

References

Arnold, K., and Sclater, N. (2017). Student perceptions of their privacy in learning analytics applications. In: *Proceedings of the 17th international learning analytics and Knowledge Conference,* 66–69. https://doi.org/10.1145/3027385.3027392

Baker, R., and Hawn, A. (2021). *Algorithmic bias in education. Pre-print.* https://doi.org/10.35542/osf.io/pbmvz. Retrieved from https://edarxiv.org/pbmvz/ 2021-05-12

Bakharia, A., Kitto, K., Pardo, A., Gašević, D., and Dawson, S. (2016). Recipe for success: Lessons learnt from using xAPI within the connected learning analytics toolkit. In: *Proceedings of the Sixth International Conference on Learning Analytics and Knowledge,* 378–382. https://doi.org/10.1145/2883851.2883882

Beerwinkle, L. (2021). The use of learning analytics and the potential risk of harm for K-12 students participating in digital learning environments. *Education Technology Research and Development, 69,* 327–330. https://doi.org/10.1007/s11423-020 -09854-6

Buckingham Shum, S., Ferguson, R., and Martinez-Maldonado, R. (2019). Human-centered learning analytics. *Journal of Learning Analytics, 6*(2), 1–9. https://doi.org/10.18608/jla.2019.62.1

Cerrato-Pargman, T., McGrath, C., Viberg, O., Kitto, K., Knight, S., and Ferguson, R. (2021). Responsible learning analytics: creating just, ethical, and caring LA systems. *11ᵗʰ Learning Analytics and Knowledge Conference.* https://www.solaresearch.org/wp -content/uploads/2021/04/LAK21_CompanionProceedings.pdf, April.

Datnow, A., and Park, V. (2018). Opening or closing doors for students? Equity and data use in schools. *Journal of Educational Change, 19*(2), 131–152. https://doi.org/10.1007 /s10833-018-9323-6.

Davis, D., Jivet, I., Kizilcec, R. F., Chen, G., Hauff, C., and Houben, G. J. (2017, March). Follow the successful crowd: Raising MOOC completion rates through social comparison at scale. In: *Proceedings of the Seventh International Learning Analytics and Knowledge Conference (LAK'17)*, 454–463. https://doi.org/10.1145/3027385.3027411

Deahl, E. (2014). *Better the Data you Know: Developing Youth Data Literacy in Schools and Informal Learning Environments*. M.S. Thesis, Massachusetts Institute of Technology. https://cmsw.mit.edu/wp/wp-content/uploads/2016/06/233823808-Erica -Deahl-Better-the-Data-You-Know-Developing-Youth-Data-Literacy-in-Schools-and -Informal-Learning-Environments.pdf

Dodero, J., Conzáles-Conjero, E., Cutuérrez-Herrera, G., Peinado, S., Tocino, J., and Ruiz-Rube, I. (2017). Trade-off between interoperability and data collection performance when designing an architecture for learning analytics. *Future Generations Computer Systems, 68*, 31–37. https://doi.org/10.1016/j.future.2016.06.040

Ferguson, R. (2019). Ethical challenges for learning analytics. *Journal of Learning Analytics, 6*(3), 25–30. https://doi.org/10.18608/jla.2019.63.5

Gašević, D., Dawson, S. and Siemens, G. (2015). Let's not forget: Learning analytics are about learning. *Tech Trends, 59*, 64–71. https://doi.org/10.1007/s11528-014-0822-x

Gummer, E., and Mandinach, E. (2015). Building a conceptual framework for data literacy. *Teachers College Record, 117*(4), 1–22.

Hakami, E., and Hernández-Leo, D. (2020). How are learning analytics considering the societal values of fairness, accountability, transparency and human well-being?: A literature review. In: Martínez-Monés A, Álvarez A, Caeiro-Rodríguez M, and Dimitriadis Y. (Eds.), LASI-SPAIN 2020: Learning Analytics Summer Institute Spain 2020: Learning Analytics. Time for Adoption?; 2020 June 15–16; Valladolid, Spain. Aachen: CEUR, 121–141. http://ceur-ws.org/Vol-2671/paper12.pdf

Hao, K. (2020). AI still doesn't have the common sense to understand human language. *MIT Technology Review*. https://www.technologyreview.com/2020/01/31/304844 /ai-common-sense-reads-human-language-ai2/2021-05-12.

Henderson, R., and Corry, M. (2020). Data literacy training and use for educational professionals. *Journal of Research in Innovative Teaching and Learning*. https://doi .org/10.1108/JRIT-11-2019-0074

Holstein, K., and Doroudi, S. (2019). Fairness and equity in learning analytics systems (FairLAK). In: *Companion Proceeding of 9th International Conference on Learning Analytics and Knowledge (LAK 19)*. http://kenholstein.com/FairLAK_proceedings.pdf

Holstein, K., Wortman Vaughan, J., Daumé, H., Dudik, M., and Wallach, H. (2019). Improving Fairness in Machine Learning Systems: What Do Industry Practitioners Need? In: *Proceedings of the 2019 CHI Conference on Human Factors in Computing Systems*, 1–16. https://doi.org/10.1145/3290605.3300830

Ifenthaler, D., Gibson, D., Prasse, D., Shimada, A., and Yamada, M. (2020). Putting learning back into learning analytics: Actions for policy makers, researchers and practitioners. *Educational Technology Research and Development*. https://doi.org/10.1007 /s11423-020-09909-8

Jivet, I. (2021). *The Dashboard That Loved Me: Designing Adaptive Learning Analytics for Self-Regulated Learning.* Doctoral dissertation. Open University. ISBN/EAN: 978-94-93211-25-4

Kitchin, R. (2021). *Data Lives: How Data Are Made and Shape Our World.* Bristol UP.

Kizilcec, R. and Cohen, G. L. (2017). Eight-minute self-regulation intervention raises educational attainment at scale in individualist but not collectivist cultures. In: *Proceedings of the National Academy of Sciences, 114*(17), 4348–4353.

Klein, C. (2021). Privacy-by-design for responsible and equitable LA systems, policies, and practices. In: *Companion Proceeding of the 11th International Conference on Learning Analytics and Knowledge (LAK21), 336–341.* https://www.solaresearch.org/wp-content/uploads/2021/04/LAK21_CompanionProceedings.pdf

Knight, S., Gibson, A., and Shibani, A. (2020). Implementing learning analytics for learning impact: Taking tools to tasks. *The Internet and Higher Education, 45.* https://doi.org/10.1016/j.iheduc.2020.100729

Livingstone, S. (2020). Realizing children's rights in relation to the digital environment. *European Review.* Retrieved from http://eprints.lse.ac.uk/103563/ 2021-05-01

Long, P., and Siemens, J. (2011). Penetrating the fog: Analytics in learning and education. *Educause Review, 46*(5), 31–40. https://er.educause.edu/articles/2011/9/penetrating-the-fog-analytics-in-learning-and-education

Mandinach, E., and Gummer, E. (2016). *Data literacy for educators: Making It Count in Teacher Preparation and Practice.* New York, NY: Teacher College Press.

Mandinach, E., and Schildkamp, K. (2021). Misconceptions about data-based decision making in education: An exploration of the literature. *Studies in Educational Evaluation.* https://doi.org/10.1016/j.stueduc.2020.100842

Ochoa, X., Knight, S., and Wise, A. (2020). Learning analytics impact: Critical conversations on relevance and social responsibility. *Journal of Learning Analytics, 7*(3), 1–5. https://dx.doi.org/10.18608/jla.2020.73.1

Orlikowski, W., and Iacono, S. (2001). Research commentary: Desperately seeking the "IT" in IT research—A call to theorizing the IT artifact. *Information System Research, 12*(2), 121–134.

Samuelsen, J., Chen, W., and Wasson, B. (2019). Integrating multiple data sources for learning analytics—review of literature. *Research and Practice in Technology Enhanced Learning, 14*(1). https://doi.org/10.1186/s41039-019-0105-4.

Samuelsen, J., Chen, W., and Wasson, B. (2021). Enriching context descriptions for enhanced LA scalability: A case study. *Research and Practice in Technology Enhanced Learning, 16*(6). https://doi.org/10.1186/s41039-021-00150-2

Schildkamp, K. (2019). Data-based decision-making for school improvement: Research insights and gaps. *Education Research, 61*(3), 257–273. https://doi.org/10.1080/00131881.2019.1625716

Selwyn, N. (2019). What's the problem with learning analytics? *Journal of Learning Analytics, 6*(3), 11–19. http://dx.doi.org/10.18608/jla.2019.63.3

Tsai, Y., Poquet, O., Gašević, D., Dawson, S., and Pardo, A. (2019). Complexity leadership in learning analytics: Drivers, challenges and opportunities. *British Journal of Educational Technology, 50*(6), 2839–2854. https://doi.org/10.1111/bjet.12846

van Leeuwen, A., van Wermeskerken, M., Erkens, G., and Rummel, N. (2107). Measuring teachers sense-making strategies of learning analytics: A case study. *Learning Research and Practice, 3*(1), https://doi.org/10.1080/23735082.2017.1284252

Viberg, O., Andersson, A., Kolkowska, E., and Hrastinski, S. (2021). Calling for a more responsible use of student data in K-12 education. In: *Companion Proceedings of the 11th International Conference on Learning Analytics and Knowledge.* 357–362, https://www.solaresearch.org/wp-content/uploads/2021/04/LAK21_Companion Proceedings.pdf

Viberg, O., Hatakka, M., Bälter, O., and Mavroudi, A. (2018). The current landscape of learning analytics in higher education. *Computers in Human Behavior, 89,* 98–110. https://doi.org/10.1016/j.chb.2018.07.027

Viberg, O., Khalil, M., and Baars, M. (2020). Self-regulated learning and learning analytics in online learning environments: A review of empirical research. In: *Proceedings of the 10th International Conference on Learning Analytics and Knowledge (LAK20).* https://doi.org/10.1145/3375462.3375483

Wise, A., Sarmiento, J., and Boothe, M. (2021). Subversive learning analytics. In: *Proceedings of 11th International Learning Analytics and Knowledge Conference* (LAK21), April 12–16, 2021, Irvine, CA, USA. ACM, New York, NY, USA, 7 pages. https://doi .org/10.1145/3448139.3448210

Yu, Z. (2021). A literature review on MOOCs integrated with learning analytics. *Journal of Information Technology Research, 14*(2). https://doi.org./10.4018/JITR.2021040104

Chapter 3

Designing for Insights

An Evidenced-Centered Approach to Learning Analytics

Kara N. McWilliams, Kristen Herrick, K. Becca Runyon, and Andreas Oranje[1]

Abstract

The vast amount of data captured in digital learning experiences enable learning analytics that hold the potential not only to understand more deeply how people learn, but also to improve their learning experience. However, the nascent stage of learning and measurement theory, particularly in digital environments, raises concerns about the use of learning analytics. In this chapter, we discuss considerations associated with the validity and reliability of inferences made from learning analytics, illustrate the importance of data ethics, and suggest that learning analytics are most productively approached within the reasoning and architecture of evidence-centered design. We argue that a Theory of Change, Theory of Action, and Learning Model should undergird an intentional learner data footprint in learning systems so that analytics can reliably be used to provide insights and interventions; develop algorithms to power automated systems; understand implementation, engagement, and user behavior; and measure effectiveness and

---

[1] Educational Testing Service

efficacy. To ground the argument, we offer an example throughout that provides practical recommendations for applying an evidence-centered design to the research and development of technology-enhanced learning tools.

Keywords: technology-enhanced learning tools, Theory of Action, Theory of Change, technology-enhanced learning tools, learner data footprint, learner outcomes and models, learning design, learning model, human-centered learning analytics, evidence-centered approach, evidence-centered design, digitalization of education, digital learning, data footprint

Introduction

The proliferation of technology-enhanced learning tools and the data captured when used has the potential to unlock a wealth of learner insights. Behavioral, tool-interaction, and performance data can provide a window into learning processes within a digital learning experience and enable claims about how people learn, what they know, where they have gaps, and the ways in which they can best be supported to close those gaps. However, the meaningfulness and reliability of those inferences depend on the veracity of the validity argument developed for the use of the tool and the data being collected and analyzed. Considerations such as clearly articulated outcomes; a robust, theory-driven data collection design; the quantity and quality of data captured; the context in which they are analyzed; and how they are reported will all affect the reliability and validity of the inferences made from analyzing learner data and the usefulness of decisions, actions, and claims that are made subsequently.

Many stakeholders are interested in leveraging the vast amount of data available from digital learning tools to advance learning. We suggest that unless we consistently adopt an evidence-centered approach to learning experience development and analytics, we risk missing critical insights, or worse, drawing inappropriate inferences about what learners know, how they learn, and how we can take action to improve learning outcomes. In order to make the most meaningful claims based on learning analytics, learning scientists should work closely with research scientists, user-experience researchers and designers, and developers to intentionally design and implement a solution that enables appropriate and meaningful insights. While we are certainly not the first to point out the importance of using an evidence-centered design approach, the use in practice is still sparse. Therefore, our aim is to provide several practical steps toward proactively addressing challenges that inevitably arise when designing and implementing a digital learning experience to yield accurate and actionable insights about learning and the efficacy of a learning experience.

Current Issues in Learning Analytics

Culminating during a worldwide pandemic, the past decade has experienced a surge in the use of digital tools for learning and, increasingly, the use of analytics to make inferences about learning. Yet, the cognitive and learning sciences theories that undergird those inferences remain very much in their infancies (Knight et al., 2014). Scientists contend with many issues that extend beyond the fidelity of the data itself and the robustness or appropriateness of the analyses being applied to those data (e.g., solution usability or intentional data capture). In fact, many challenges exist, because learning analytics are routinely considered in isolation from the experience of the learner and the context in which the tool is being used. Measuring human cognition and behavior is a socio cognitive (Mislevy, 2020) endeavor that carries no meaning without increasingly refined contextual understanding. Hence, reliance on mostly passive data leads to significant contextual gaps in understanding, which at best results in lost opportunities of insights and at worst leads to poor decision making.

The core thesis of this chapter is that learning analytics are most productively approached within the reasoning and architecture of evidence-centered design (Mislevy et al., 2003). Conversely, omitting key evidence-building steps tends to elicit a range of issues associated with most learning analytics. In this section, we will discuss those issues, including several associated with data design and availability, contextual gaps, and ethics. We will subsequently offer a broader set of practical recommendations illustrated by examples. In order to facilitate collective understanding of the points outlined with these sections, we will begin by introducing some terminology and definitions.

Learning Theory and Learning Analytics

The field of learning and measurement theory has not developed uniformly across domains and constructs of interest. Unsurprisingly, learning and measurement theory of academic subjects is relatively mature, whereas other constructs typically of interest in learning analytics (e.g., persistence, problem solving, metacognitive ability) have not matured to the point that they can support similar levels of reliable analyses and inferences. The importance of learning theory underpinning digital learning applications is well documented (e.g., Branch & Merrill, 2012; Bransford et al., 2000; West, 2018), and common educational technology theories exist (e.g., the SAMR model; Puentedura, 2006, and the TPACK model; Mishra & Koehler, 2006). Still, examples of technology-enhanced educational tools that lack such a foundation are plentiful. Absence of a grounding theory results in solutions with ambiguous outcomes, post hoc construct operationalization, no evidentiary chain of reasoning, and misaligned instruction, assessment, and intervention.

Since learning analytics are quite broadly used, it is important to provide some definitional guardrails. Learning analytics are a set of processes and measures of critical aspects of learning (1st International Conference on Learning Analytics and Knowledge, 2011). At a very basic level, this can mean simple analytics for which the inferential distance is relatively short, such as number of times logging in or time spent in a learning environment to make inferences about behaviors only. At a more abstracted level where the inferential distance is larger, this can entail, for example, a sequence of clicks to make an inference about alternative solution strategies that the learner followed, some of which may be more appropriate or successful in finding a correct solution. At the highest level, those inferences may entail more complex constructs, such as persistence, where several behaviors together could be indicative of a certain level of proficiency. Learning analytics always rest heavily on the context of a practical application that is the basis for making the inference and mechanisms—for instance, Theories of Action and Theories of Change, Learner Outcomes and Models, and Learner Data Footprints are important to make those connections.

Complicating the consideration of learning theories driving analytics is the need for this fledgling field to equally develop theory. Teaching and learning are incredibly complex and made even more so when instruction and learning occurs digitally. Yet, most of the currently published learning theories, such as cognitive, behaviorism, constructivism, humanism, and connectivism, were derived based on traditional, face-to-face learning and are sometimes applied directly to the digital learning space. It is through the analysis of user data that existing learning theories can be validated in the digital space, and robust and reliable theories focused specifically on the digital environment can be developed (Knight et al., 2014). Scientists should remain aware that there may not be an existing theory driving their analyses, and that claims made based on inferences derived from their analyses should be tempered to reflect that gap. And, importantly, learning analytics should be used to validate, extend, and develop new learning theory.

Availability and Validity of Learner Data

In order to conduct meaningful analytics, data availability is an important consideration. The perceived wealth of data available to scientists contributes to a risk of considering data to be free byproducts of the solution in which they were collected, as opposed to something that requires careful design. Yet, data scientists are not typically core members of a solution's development team, and learning analytics are not typically considered until after a tool has been built and deployed. As a result, scientists are often forced into analyses that are possible using "free" data and may not be able to conduct the analyses appropriate to test the intended research hypotheses, make corollary and contextual inferences, or further build learning models.

A probable lack of learning theory contributes to the consideration of data availability. If a solution is built on established learning theory, the development of an intentional data architecture is more feasible. When this is the case, developers will have a better sense of how scientists hope to trace learning, the events or interactions captured by data, or "data hooks" that will need to be analyzed to evaluate learning and inform learning theory. Void of learning and measurement theory, however, developers are more likely to build in data hooks based on convenience or intuition. Unintentional data capture may have implications not only for the claims scientists can make, but also for the development of analytics-led learning theories. That is, if important interactions, processes, or outcomes are not captured, it can leave consequential gaps in a learning model developed from exploratory analytics.

In sum, the potential lack of a comprehensive learning and measurement theory functioning as the foundation for a solution and data-evidence architecture, and dependency on whatever data are captured, does little to contribute to the validity or value of data.

Contextual Gaps in Data Footprints

Each of the considerations discussed previously—convenient access to data, lack of driving learning and measurement theory, potential for inappropriately collected data, or gaps in a data footprint—lend themselves to the importance of contextualizing analyses conducted on data that are captured in a tool.

As learning systems collect increasingly voluminous data, the temptation of relying on those data sets for observational trends and inferential statistics becomes greater. Yet, it is the learning context that is the basis for actionable insights about learning pathways, key product performance indicators, and breadth of use. Understanding the context of how a solution was implemented, who the learners were engaging with, how they typically engage, what barriers to access exist, among other inputs, are critical when characterizing relationships between use and learning and the impact on outcomes. In the absence of context, scientists miss insight into important factors, such as whether a tool is accessible, culturally biased, or promotes diversity.

Ethical Considerations

As scientists grapple with these considerations, at the center of the discussion should be ethics related to data capture and usage. By increasing the amount and types of data available to organizations, digitally enhanced learning solutions offer opportunities to support learners in more meaningful ways while at the same time increasing risk in the form of (mis)use of data against their interests (e.g., due to exposure of PII and personal data generally). To combat risks associated with digital learning solutions, scientists and developers need to consider how they can offer transparency to users about what data are being captured and why, how they will be stored and handled and by whom, and if, when, and under what conditions they will be destroyed. Organizations and the scientists that represent them may also consider the ethics of their learning experience design processes and level of transparency around the analyses that were conducted on the data captured throughout, how they mitigated bias, and how the inferences based on the analyses were used.

Conclusion

With the intention of contextualizing the recommendations and examples for an evidence-centered design approach to learning analytics provided in the remainder of this chapter, this section discussed some key considerations when planning for and conducting learning analytics derived from digital learning solutions. While the considerations outlined here are not exhaustive, they do represent the areas that represent ongoing concerns for scientists making claims based on inferences derived from learning analytics. The next section of this chapter offers a practical approach to learning analytics that enables valid and reliable claims about learning and how we might best support learners to achieve their learning goals.

An Evidenced-Centered Design Approach to Yielding Valid and Reliable Learning Analytics

Meaningful learning analytics are enabled through the design and development of an effective and broadly usable digitally enhanced learning solution. A large body of research speaks to the benefits of applying a user-centered approach when building educational technology (e.g., Hassenzahl, 2010; Vrendenburg et al., 2002; Interactive Design Foundation, 2021). The approach helps development teams form a deep understanding of the individuals who will be using their solution, work collaboratively to co-design it, apply an evaluation-based design, and continue to optimize it in partnership with users. The successful execution of a user-centered design approach requires the appropriate composition of a development team.

A diverse, self-contained, cross-functional agile team is the most effective method for building a solution that meets user needs, has a high degree of usability, and has an impact on the intended outcome (Fowler et al., 2001; Manifesto of agile software development, 2021). Bringing various areas of expertise together enables rapid development and deployment, but, more importantly, ensures each component of the solution is working together to yield meaningful insights about learners and learning. For example, a data scientist can work directly with a developer to identify specific areas where data hooks should be built, while a user-experience designer can ensure the data are captured in a way that doesn't negatively impact the learning experience. Because of the importance of the composition of the development team, we outline the recommended roles and responsibilities in Table 3.1.

Table 3.1 Roles and Responsibilities of a Cross-Functional Agile Research and Development Team

Role	Responsibilities
Data scientist	Data scientists develop and build the user data footprint, conduct the preprocessing of structured and unstructured data, and lead on the research and development of statistical models and algorithms to glean meaningful insights.
Data architect	Data architects plan the implementation of solutions, identify the right technologies to meet user needs, and direct and oversee the development of data ingestion and data transformation infrastructure.
Product owner	Product owners ensure the voice of the user is represented in the team's backlog and serve as liaisons between the project team, the business, and the market to align needs and priorities.
Research/learning scientist	Research/learning scientists apply foundational research principles to the theory-driven solutions and apply learning science principles, learning design principles, and user-centered research to development processes.
Software developer	Software developers lead on the technical component of translating wireframes into engaging, interactive, and highly functioning solutions.
User-experience designer	User experience designers lead on the UI/UX aspects of the user experience, building needs into sketches and lo- and hi-fidelity prototypes.
User-experience researcher	User experience researchers engage with users in interviews, observations, focus groups, and other data-collection activities to understand their needs and translate them into features and capabilities that will be designed by a user-experience designer.

Each of the roles described in Table 3.1 represent a unique area of expertise, but only the cross-functional collaboration coordinated by the product owner will lead to an impactful solution. To that end, the team will be more successful it they sprint together through all phases of the design and development process, from discovery through optimization. To be clear, every project is different, and the exact mix of roles will change as projects pivot and mature.

User-centricity will not only support the development of a solution that meets user needs but will also inform a data architecture that supports meaningful learning analytics. At the core of learning analytics is a robust data strategy that should be considered through all stages of design and development. User needs should drive not only a solution's intended outcomes and composition of instructional and assessment content, but also what data are collected, how they are stored, and the insights that are shared back with users. Much like features built into a solution, data collection and analytics should be conceptualized and tested with users throughout development.

The following sections offer a discussion of key considerations when applying user-centered design and additional recommendations for applying it. To ground the recommendations, we offer examples from the research and development of a new learning solution, ELAborate.

ELAborate

ELAborate is a literacy-learning tool designed for seventh-grade English Language Arts students and teachers. The prototype meets teachers' needs by providing automated scaffolding of reading comprehension to aid students in identifying important themes and establishing thoughtful connections among reading concepts. Insights provided to teachers via ELAborate enable efficiencies, helping them make decisions about how to direct their instruction and which learners require additional supports. The interactive environment meets students' needs of closing skills gaps through the development of mental models of characters, their goals, sequence of events, and event cause and effect. It also meets student's needs for improved reading motivation and engagement, which, in turn, impacts ability and willingness to read independently. Students set goals and work to meet their intended outcomes through a set of activities aligned to an instructional model. ELAborate is currently in development, and the activities conducted by the team and planned for future development will be used as examples throughout this section as we describe the various stages of user-centered design.

User-Centered Design in Discovery

Discovery is the initial phase in user-centered design, where teams research user needs with the goal of identifying the problem to solve. Throughout discovery, a series of user-experience research methods are employed to empathize with users and gain an understanding of their values, beliefs, and experiences. Building empathy helps development teams identify user pain points, which leads to a prioritized list of problems to be solved. To provide a concrete example of the activities in this phase, the ELAborate development team initiated their discovery efforts by constructing a survey to send to a broad set of sixth to eighth grade ELA teachers with the goals of achieving a general understanding of the middle school ELA teacher experience, identifying the most common challenges or pain points of those teachers, and further refining their target user group. The survey provided initial user insights and helped the team construct more targeted questions to probe during four subsequent user focus groups. Using the data collected from their research, the great need was identified among seventh-grade teachers and constructed journey and empathy maps of their experiences. The discovery phase culminated in a set of prioritized and validated problem statements aligned to teaching literacy to seventh-grade students.

Learning Outcomes, Theory of Action, Theory of Change, and a Learning Model

Based on validated problem statements, program theory (Bickman, 1987), and evidence-centered design (ECD) (Mislevy et al., 1999, 2003, 2006; Arieli-Attali et al., 2019), frameworks should be leveraged to build learning models and drive learning experience design. We recommend that cross-functional teams work collaboratively on the learning model, given they will lay the foundation for creating the learner data footprint and subsequent feature and experience design.

Learning Outcomes

Driven by the problem statement(s) and reflected in the constructs a learning solution will address, the team can begin to articulate learner and learning outcomes for their solution. Outcome definition should include establishing the competencies the solution will address (e.g., what knowledge, skills, and/or attributes does the solution impact, why, and to what degree?) and occur at two levels: proximal and distal (Pope et al., 2019; Smith & Finney, 2020). Proximal outcomes are narrower, shorter-term, more easily measured outcomes, while distal outcomes are typically broader, longer-term outcomes that may be more challenging to measure.

For example, ELAborate currently has the following as one proximal outcome:

- Students will identify/extract themes and meanings of text;

and the following as one distal outcome:

- Students apply themes/meanings of text to understand their own social worlds.

Note, the proximal outcome is narrower, falls more directly within the purview of the learning solution, and as such, better lends itself to measurement. Although the distal outcome is broader, learning science research provides frameworks for linking the distal to the proximal outcome such that as students achieve proximal outcomes, it contributes to their achievement of more distal outcomes.

To align defined outcomes with the proposed activities, the team should work collaboratively to operationalize each of the competencies or constructs the solution aims to impact. The instructional content, assessment, and interventions that have been shown to positively affect those competencies can then be identified (Smith & Finney, 2020) and appropriate Learning Design Principles (LDPs) applied. The LDPs will underlie the solution, inform the ToA and the ToC, and be leveraged to construct a learning model (Novak, 2016; Meyer et al., 2014).

Theory of Action (ToA) and Theory of Change (ToC)

Learning models typically combine a Theory of Action (ToA) and a Theory of Change (ToC) components. A ToA may detail the intervention, solution, or capabilities that have been designed to "activate" change (e.g., *what* are the intervention components or capabilities?). A ToC conveys the intended process through which change occurs (*why* and *how* should the intervention components or capabilities work to bring about the desired change in knowledge, skill, attributes?). Within the expanded ECD (Arieli-Attali et al., 2019), the ToA is part of the Task-Support Model, while the ToC is part of the Transitional-Evidence Model and the Intended KSA-Change Model. Within Program Theory (Bickman, 1987), the ToA is the Programming or Educational Inputs component of the logic model, and ToC is found within the evidence-based research, linking the inputs to the proximal outcomes and the proximal outcomes to the distal outcomes.

For example, one feature of ELAborate is student annotation. The associated ToA includes learning supports, strategies, or inputs (i.e., the Task-Support Model from e-ECD), such as the ability to collaboratively annotate with peers, encouraging more active reading via annotating behaviors, the ability of annotations to slow down students' automated thought processes and help them engage in more deliberative thought processes, etc. These kinds of inputs can help students achieve the proximal learning outcomes, such as being able to identify/extract themes and meanings from text (i.e., the Transitional-Evidence Model from e-ECD). Next, the ToC includes the instructional and behavioral processes through which students should start to change their behaviors related to the proximal learning outcome.

Consider a seventh-grade student who has been struggling with reading and begins using ELAborate. The student will have both support engaging in a more deliberative process while reading via the use of annotations and help increasing their motivation to read via strengths-based feedback. The student will also receive appropriate strategies and nudges to help scaffold them through the reading and remembering processes and encouragement to collaborate with peers as they give and receive feedback on annotations. The ToA brings in research-based instructional practices and LDPs (e.g., active reading, collaborative learning, reading motivation, scaffolding), while the ToC conveys how and why those practices and principles can be combined to help improve the competencies or constructs of interest (e.g., the KSAs). Taken together, the ToA and ToC combine to form the theoretical and empirical core of a learning model.

A Learning Model

Whether or not a development team is applying ECD, the ToA and ToC should come together to form a Learning Model. A learning model articulates not only the desired impact on student outcomes but also the theoretical and empirical evidence underpinning solution capabilities and the interventions they enable. That is, the learning model specifies an evidence-based arrangement of instructional, assessment, and noncognitive components, which, when implemented with fidelity, are expected to impact learner outcomes.

Following the ELAborate example, in addition to consulting theoretical and empirical research, the team received feedback from subject matter experts (SMEs) and users to validate their learning model. To illustrate this process, Table 3.2 (beginning on next page) offers a high-level outline of the ELAborate learning model and the corresponding learning activities/components that were derived based on the LDPs, ToA, and ToC.

Learner Data Footprint

The learner data footprint can be thought of as an extension of the discovery and ideation phase. More specifically, it is the data architecture created to support the research foundation of the learning experience established within the Learning Model, Theory of Change, and Theory of Action.

An Intentional Learner Data Footprint

The operationalization of constructs and establishment of learning paths are key to informing the learner data footprint, which is required for meaningful learning analytics. Constructs and user flows come together to provide the blueprint for mapping out user data to collect and store at key points in the learning experience. Together, these data can yield valid and reliable insights that create a holistic view of learners, learning, interventions, and the solution's efficacy.

Table 3.2 High-Level Example of the Learning Model for the Annotation Capability Included in ELAborate

		Theory of Action/LDPs	Theory of Change	
Inputs/ Task-Support Model (Aligned Learning Strategies/ Activities/Supports)	Instructional Models	EXAMPLE: Short-Term Learning Outcomes (e.g., KSAs)	EXAMPLE: Theoretical & Empirical LINKS From Short- to Long-Term Learning Outcomes (Transitional Evidence Model)	EXAMPLE: Long-Term Learning Outcomes (e.g., KSAs)
Students learn about the objectives and highlight the purpose/benefit/VALUE of annotations (goals/outcomes) as a way to improve reading comprehension; students set their own goals for reading; students reflect on and start to develop their own identities as readers.	ARCS Model (Keller, 1987) Gain attention of the learner (Gagne, 1965); Task-centered (Merrill, 2002)	Students report that they value reading skills. Students will develop a reading identity.	Expectancy Value Theory (Eccles, 1984, Eccles et al., 1983, Wigfield, 1994); Intrinsic Motivation to Read (McRae & Guthrie, 2009); Self-Regulated Learning (Panadero, 2017, Zimmerman, 2000).	Students are better readers.
Ask students to describe previous annotation experience—what worked well for them in the past; ask students to reflect on what they already know about the reading topic or materials; students complete a diagnostic test to help them gauge their current understanding and prime or bring to mind what they already know about topic at hand.	Stimulate recall/ prior knowledge (Gagne, 1965); Knowledge activation (Merrill, 2002); Strengths-based (Saleeby, 1996)	Students will identify and extract themes and meanings of text	Strengths-based pedagogy (Seligman, 2012, Dept of Ed and Early Childhood Development, 2012); Self-Regulated Learning; Metacognition (Brandsford & Cocking, 2000)	Students are better readers.

Students see scaffolded work examples (pictures/images); teacher engages in think-aloud reading to model to students how they would read and annotate—models effective annotating behaviors, helps students start to see the value in annotating, etc.	Provide guidance for learning (Gagne, 1965); Task-centered (Merrill, 2002); Demonstration (Merrill, 2002)	Students will identify and extract themes and meanings of text	Modeling to promote learning (Bandura, 1986)	Students are better readers.
Students annotates while reading; students refine previous annotations; Smart Nudges (AI-enabled) help students stay on-track, also help students stop and think about their thinking (metacognitive checks).	Present content and elicit performance (Gagne, 1965); Practice (Merrill, 2002)	Students will identify and extract themes and meanings of text	Annotations to support improve reading comprehension (Novak, et al, 2012, Tseng, et al, 2015, Johnson et al., 2010)	Students are better readers.
Student experience Notice & Note question prompts; (fiction/non-fiction) and Critical Reading prompts (Tomasek, 2009); students answer reading comprehension questions to help them gauge their knowledge while reading.	Practice (Gagne, 1965); Practice (Merrill, 2002);	Students will identify and extract themes and meanings of text Students will increase their reading self-efficacy	Self-Regulated Learning (Pandero, 2017, Zimmerman, 2000); Metacognition (Bransford et al., 2000); Formative feedback (Nicol & Macfarlane-Dick, 2006)	Students are better readers.
Students engage with peers and teachers through collaborative annotations; students refine/review/reconsider their own annotations after compare/contrasting with peer or teacher annotations, etc.	Practice (Gagne, 1965); Provide feedback (Gagne, 1965); Practice (Merrill, 2002);	Students will identify and extract themes and meanings of text Students will increase their reading self-efficacy	Collaborative learning (Dewey, 1938, Vygotsky, 1962, Vygotsky, 1978); Active learning	Students are better readers.

(continues on next page)

Table 3.2 High-Level Example of the Learning Model for the Annotation Capability Included in ELAborate (cont.)

Students receive strengths-based, real-time formative feedback after completing metacognitive and/or comprehension check questions.	Provide feedback (Gagne, 1965); Strengths-based (Saleeby, 1996); Formative feedback (Wray, 2011)	Students will increase their reading self-efficacy.	Strengths-based pedagogy (Seligman, 2012, Dept of Ed and Early Childhood Development, 2012); Self-Regulated Learning; Metacognition (Bransford & Brown, 2000)	Students are better readers.
Students complete a more summative assessment of their reading comprehension skills; students receive formative feedback	Assess performance (Gagne, 1965); Provide feedback (Gagne, 1965); Strengths-based (Saleeby, 1996); Formative feedback (Wray, 2011); Practice (Merrill, 2002)	Students will identify and extract themes and meanings of text. Students will increase their reading self-efficacy.	Metacognition (Bransford & Brown, 2000); Strengths-based pedagogy; Formative feedback (Nicol & Macfarlane-Dick, 2006)	Students are better readers.
System offers tips for ways to use annotation processes for future tasks; students are provided annotation tips to help them plan, monitor, regulate, and reflect while reading in the future; students reflect on how what they learned can be applied to a future experience or the present lives; students reflect/refine their identities as readers.	Skill retention and transfer (Gagne, 1965); Strengths-based (Saleeby, 1996); formative feedback (Wray, 2011); Apply (Merrill, 2002)	Students will increase their reading self-efficacy. Students will develop a reading identity.	Self-regulated Learning (Panadero, 2017, Zimmerman, 2000); Intrinsic Motivation to Read (McRae & Guthrie, 2009)	Students are better readers. Students apply themes/ meanings of texts to understand their own social worlds.

Because the learner data footprint should be informed by user needs, the blueprint can also be leveraged to facilitate additional user research. Interviews and focus groups can help determine whether the right data are being captured at the right points to enable the inferences users want to make and the actions they may want to take.

Learning analytics to enable user insights will likely be only one of the uses of the data captured in a learning solution. It is critical that early in the development cycle teams collaboratively identify and clearly articulate each of the intended applications of the user data. The ELAborate development team identified five primary uses of data which informed the learner data footprint:

1. Analytics to provide user insights about individual, cohort, and class-wide outcomes and recommended interventions
2. The development of interpretable and explanatory algorithms to power automation and personalization in the system
3. Analytics to understand implementation, engagement, and user behavior for purposes of solution optimization
4. Learning analytics that support research of capabilities and components to generate new knowledge of educational technology
5. Learning analytics that support research on the effectiveness and efficacy of ELAborate to validate the learning model and help users understand what works, for whom, and in what context

Scientists should leverage both learning and measurement theory-driven as well as user-focused approaches when constructing the learner data footprint. Scientists should also work closely with user-experience researchers and designers as well as developers to ensure data architecture can translate appropriately within the user's experience in the system. The work that the ELAborate team had previously done on the needs assessment, operationalization of constructs, and articulation of a learning model illustrated in Table 3.2 enabled them to efficiently overlay and communicate a clear and robust data footprint for developers to construct.

Construct Validity and Meaningful Insights

A robust learner data footprint tied to development efforts can support a data architecture that enables valid insights and combats threats to construct validity (Messick, 1994; Cook & Campbell, 1979; Cronbach & Meehl, 1955). A construct validation approach suggests that teams should outline various threats to an evidentiary argument and attempt to address them within the design and development of technology-enhanced learning solutions (Huggins-Manley et al., 2019). Efforts can include building appropriate data hooks to understand the user journey, capturing data that are used to adequately and accurately *assess* constructs of interest, and creating opportunities to enable holistic insights.

First, developers should build hooks (i.e., triggers, interactions, events) into the system to capture checkpoint data that accurately represent a learner's journey and whether their journey is aligned to the Theory of Action. If appropriate hooks are not built, scientists will have difficulty measuring whether the solution is being used with fidelity. For example, the ELAborate team will need data that describe how, where, when, and what students annotated; the accuracy or quality of their annotations; how they used hashtags to make connections; refine their thinking about a text; build mental models of texts via graphic organizers like concept maps, etc. An understanding of how ELAborate was used will build the foundation for reliable learning analytics that enable valid inferences about effectiveness and efficacy.

Continuing the ELAborate example, the team will need to build enough aligned annotation and comprehension items that allow them to make appropriate inferences about students' understanding of text themes and meanings. The development team doesn't want to overburden learners with too many assessment items but at the same time needs to ensure that there is appropriate coverage of reading comprehension to make a valid inference and help the learner learn. To combat this threat, the team will gather multiple data points: which words or phrases a student annotates, the hashtags they use, as well as a small set of reading comprehension items. By aggregating across those data points and triangulating the findings, scientists can make more appropriate inferences about whether a student comprehends text themes and meanings.

Finally, it would benefit development teams to capture data across relevant affective, behavioral, *and* cognitive data points to glean holistic insights. A triangulation of these data can provide more robust, meaningful, and actionable insights about learners and how to support them. In ELAborate, for example, the team will want to be intentional about collecting data from learner goal setting and reflection activities and analyze them together with annotation and hashtag usage data as well as learner performance on comprehension questions. Aggregating and synthesizing across these distinct, yet related, data points will enable learners and instructors using ELAborate to better understand metacognitive ability and learning strategy implementation and how this impacts progress and performance. Such insights enable more targeted, effective intervention (e.g., informing focused intervention on goal setting/reflection vs. annotation or hashtag usage, etc.).

Experiential and Contextual Considerations

Often difficult to observe, experiential and contextual factors lead to a larger inferential distance between behaviors and demonstrated proficiency of outcomes (Oranje et. al, 2016). The usability of a solution is an important factor to consider when interpreting learning analytics. In thinking about ELAborate, when the team is interpreting the analysis of usage data, they must consider things such as whether the five steps it takes to apply an annotation (i.e., the usability of the system) influenced the average number of annotations applied across learners. Similarly, if analyses suggest that learners were not making comprehension connections daily (i.e., using the system with fidelity), the team will have to consider whether teacher implementation factored into this behavior or if the insight reflects a lack of student engagement.

Other experiential considerations that may impact the validity of learning analytic claims include issues of access (particularly if engagement with the solution requires a specific technology), requiring users to have a high degree of data literacy (particularly if interventions require interpretation of data-heavy insights or interventions), and requiring users to have a high degree of technology literacy (particularly if they have to manipulate technology in a way that may not be common to them in order to demonstrate their proficiency). The cultural relevancy and inclusiveness of learning and assessment materials or tasks can also contribute to experiential considerations that can affect validity of claims.

If a tool has low levels of usability or a generally poor overall user experience, user behaviors may not reflect how they would otherwise engage, and performance data may be invalid because learners could not demonstrate what they know or are able to do in a meaningful way. The ELAborate team is engaging in early and ongoing moderated and unmoderated testing with a representative sample of end users to provide qualitative (e.g., observational) and quantitative (e.g., system usability scale scores) data that offer insight into the user experience and usability. Iterative testing and regular evaluation during the design process will help to mitigate experiential threats.

Unobservable contextual factors are also likely to impact the validity of the claims that can be made based on learning analytics. It is extremely challenging to design a learning solution and create a data collection strategy that captures a full, comprehensive view of a learner's context, as well as that in which the solution was used. In some cases, qualitative data that provide insight into context, motivation, perceptions, etc. can be captured in the tool. However, overburdening the learning experience with data collection mechanisms may negatively impact student engagement with the learning content. If contextual data are going to be captured within an experience, user-experience researchers and designers, along with instructional designers, should advise on when such data collection is appropriate, and the flow should be iteratively tested with users.

By conducting targeted studies with representative samples of users, scientists can pair "off-platform" qualitative and quantitative data with "on-platform" checkpoint and process data. Although the findings may not be generalizable to the entire population of users, such studies can provide deep insight into contextual factors influencing behaviors and performance observed in the system. The ELAborate team, for example, has a long-term testing plan that enables them to triangulate checkpoint, process, experiential, and contextual data. The team is conducting an in-context beta test during which they will gather qualitative data about the context in which ELAborate is being used (e.g., what is the educational ecosystem, etc.); how teachers implemented it (e.g., is it being assigned for credit, as supplemental learning, or some mix of both, etc.); student perceptions of ELAborate and whether those perceptions influenced how they used it; among other contextual and perception data. Individual data will be matched to behavioral and process data to understand whether there are mediating factors confounding the measurement of outcomes.

Ethics-Informed Learning Analytics

As discussed throughout this chapter, the wealth of data available from digitally enhanced learning solutions offers scientists and development teams immense opportunity to understand how people learn and support their learning experience. With that opportunity comes the responsibility to weave principles of ethics throughout the design and development process. In this section we discuss three considerations aligned to designing for and conducting ethics-informed learning analytics. These considerations include representative design and development, transparency in data collection and use, and reducing bias in AI and ML.

Critical to the success of user-centered design is the acknowledgement of who is conducting that research and with what participants. Intentionally building a diverse development team made up of experts with different backgrounds, perspectives, and experiences will support the development of a solution that is more representative of the needs and perspectives of the end users. Similarly, recruiting co-design participants from disparate backgrounds will further support the design of a solution that will resonate with a broader group of users. For example, in addition to having a diverse development team, the ELAborate team recruited teachers from different school types in different geographical locations who teach students from uniquely diverse backgrounds to co-design the solution with them.

Transparency in data collection and use is both ethical and can build trust with users, making them more likely to engage with a solution. The ELAborate team, for example, developed clear and concise active, informed consent documents that outline why a co-design session or study was being conducted, what the data would be used for, and how the data would be stored and destroyed following the study. Other opportunities for transparency include making data management and storage policies publicly available and allowing users to access their data upon collection.

Transparency lends itself to considerations associated with the use of machine learning, as well. Teams should be explicit about how data are being processed in a solution and how algorithms are programmed. Possibly more critical is transparency around how inferences are derived based on the analysis conducted and how those inferences translate to claims about a learner. Key components of this consideration are acknowledging the research foundation that the algorithms were developed on and being transparent about the models that they were built on. It is impossible to completely remove bias in the development of ML models, making transparency of efforts and limitations necessary.

Conclusion

Advances in the learning sciences paired with the vast amount of data captured in digital learning experiences enable learning analytics that hold the potential not only to understand more deeply how people learn, but to improve their learning experience. As we've suggested in this chapter, however, scientists must acknowledge and account for the many limitations of inferences drawn from analyses of learning data. Particularly when learning tools were neither designed on the foundation of a learning theory nor developed with an intentional learner data footprint, scientists risk missed observations, or worse, inappropriate inferences. In this chapter, we've discussed considerations when developing learning analytics, suggested an evidence-centered design architecture, provided practical recommendations grounded in examples derived from the development of a new learning tool, and discussed important ethical considerations related to developing learning tools and examining the data they collect.

There are several issues to consider in the development of learning analytics. The often nascent stage of learning and measurement theory, particularly for non-academic, non-traditional domains and specifically in digital environments, raises additional concerns. In the absence of established theory driving the identification of outcomes and the development of learning models, data scientists risk architecting data capture based on convenience or intuition. Scientists may then continue to see data as ostensibly free byproducts of the solution in which they were collected rather than something that needs careful design. These issues make it critical that development teams demonstrate discipline when designing and building for insights.

The core thesis is that learning analytics are most valid, and can be most useful, if they are derived from data captured in learning solutions designed with user-centricity, following an evidence-centered design approach. Fundamental to a user-centered approach is building deep empathy for teachers and learners, understanding their needs from their perspectives, and co-designing and iteratively testing a solution to meet those needs. User-validated problem statements enable learning theory, supporting outcome definition and the articulation of competencies and attributes to demonstrate those outcomes. Clear operationalization of constructs helps create a solution learning model within the evidenced-centered design, which will then lead to a Theory of Change and, finally, the Theory of Action. Once the capabilities and features of a learning solution are articulated through the Theory of Action, scientists can architect an intentional learner data footprint that will allow them to validate their learning theory and make important inferences about learners and their learning processes.

Scientists will have to consider threats to construct validity and the experiential and contextual factors that can confound the insights derived from data analytics. To combat threats to construct validity, we offered three recommendations. First, we argued for the importance of mapping and developing appropriate data hooks to illustrate through data how users engage with a solution. Next, we noted the importance of capturing data that appropriately and accurately assess constructs of interest. We also recommended identifying various behavioral and cognitive activities that could provide more holistic insights into a learner's proficiency. Importantly, scientists must remember the highly socio cognitive nature of measuring learner cognition and the gaps that will exist in even the most intentional and robust learner data footprint. Experiential factors, such as a system's usability, and contextual factors, such as how a tool is implemented, will inevitably influence insights derived from learning analytics. In this chapter, we discussed the importance of pairing data collected inside a learning tool with contextual evidence.

We ended this chapter with a discussion of ethical considerations when designing and developing digitally enhanced learning tools and conducting analyses of the data captured within them. We touched on the importance of building a diverse development team and engaging a representative sample of co-design partners to reduce bias in design. The need for clear communication with users about data capture and use was also discussed. And finally, we discussed the importance of transparency around how algorithms are programmed, how inferences are derived, and, importantly, how those inferences translate to claims about learners.

Much of this chapter focused on considerations scientists should be aware of when making inferences based on learning analytics. Nevertheless, there is much to be learned from how people engage with learning tools and how they demonstrate what they know and can do. By employing a user-centered approach to design, applying an evidenced-centered design to development, and building an intentional data architecture based on theory, scientists can build effective and efficient learning solutions that support users and enable learning analytics that drive the advancement of learning theory.

References

1st International Conference on Learning Analytics and Knowledge, Banff, Alberta, February 27–March 1, 2011, as cited in George Siemens and Phil Long, Penetrating the fog: Analytics in learning and education. *EDUCAUSE Review, 46*(5).

Arieli-Attali, M., Ward, S., Thomas, J., Deonovic, B., and von Davier, A. A. (2019). The expanded evidence-centered design (e-ECD) for learning and assessment systems: A framework for incorporating learning goals and processes within assessment design. *Frontiers in Psychology, 10,* 1–17.

Bandura, A. (1986). *Social Foundations of Thought and Action: A Social Cognitive Theory.* Prentice-Hall, Inc.

Bickman, L. (1987). The functions of program theory. *New Directions for Program Evaluation, 33,* 5–17.

Branch, R. M., and Merrill, M. D. (2012). Characteristics of instructional design models. In: R. A. Reiser and J. V. Dempsey (Eds.), *Trends and Issues in Instructional Design and Technology* (3rd ed.), 8–16. Boston: Pearson.

Bransford, J. D., Brown, A. L., and Cocking, R. R. (2000). *How People Learn: Brain, Mind, Experience, and School.* Washington, DC: National Academy Press.

Cook, T. D., and Campbell, D. T. (1979). *Quasi-Experimentation: Design and Analysis Issues for Field Settings.* Houghton Mifflin.

Cronbach, L. J., and Meehl, P. C. (1955). Construct validity in psychological tests. *Psychological Bulletin, 52,* 281–302.

Department of Education and Early Childhood Development. (2012). *Strength-Based Approach. A Guide to Writing Transition Learning and Development Statements.* Melbourne, Australia: State of Victoria.

Dewey, J. (1938). *Experience and Education.* New York: Macmillan.

Eccles, J. S. (1984). Sex differences in achievement patterns. In: T. Sonderegger (Ed.), *Nebraska Symposium on Motivation, 32,* 97–132. Lincoln, NE: University of Nebraska Press.

Eccles J. S., Adler, T. F., Futterman, R., Goff, S. B., Kaczala, C. M., Meece, J. L., and Midgley, C. (1983). Expectancies, values, and academic behaviors. In: J. T. Spence (Ed.), *Achievement and Achievement Motivation,* 75–146. San Francisco, CA: W. H. Freeman.

Fowler, M., Martin, J., and Highsmith, J. (2001). The agile manifesto. *Software Development 9.8,* 21–65.

Gagne, R. M. (1965). The analysis of instructional objectives for the design of instruction. *Teaching Machines and Programmed Learning II: Data and Directions,* 21–65.

Hassenzahel, M. (2010). *Experience Design: Technology for All the Right Reasons.* Morgan and Claypool Publishers.

Huggins-Manley, A. C., Beal, C. R., D'Mello, S. K., Walter, W. L., Cetin-Berber, D. D., Kim, D., and McNamara, D. S. (2019) A commentary on construct validity when using operational virtual learning environment data in effectiveness studies. *Journal of Research on Educational Effectiveness, 12*(4), 750–759.

Interactive Design Foundation. (2021, April 23). *User Centered Design.* https://www.interaction-design.org/literature/topics/user-centered-design

Johnson, T., Archibald, T., and Tenenbaum, G. (2010). Individual and team annotation effects on students' reading comprehension, critical thinking, and meta-cognitive skills. *Computers in Human Behavior, 26,* 1496–1507.

Keller, J. M. (1987). Development and use of the ARCS model of instructional design. *Journal of Instructional Development, 10*(3), 2–10.

Knight, S., Shum, S. B., and Littleton, K. (2014). Epistemology, assessment, pedagogy: Where learning meets analytics in the middle space. *Journal of Learning Analytics, 1*(2), 23–47.

Lockyer, L., Heathcote, E., and Dawson, S. (2013). Informing pedagogical action: Aligning learning analytics with learning design. *American Behavioral Scientist, 57*(10), 1439–1459.

McRae, A., and Guthrie, J. T. (2009). Promoting reasons for reading: Teacher practices that impact motivation, 55–76. In: E. H. Hiebert (Ed.), *Reading More, Reading Better.* Guilford Press.

Manifesto of Agile Software Development. (2021, April 23). Retrieved April 23, 2021, from https://agilemanifesto.org/

Merrill, M. D. (2002). First principles of instruction. *Educational Technology Research and Development, 50*(3), 43–59.

Meyer, A., Rose, D. H., and Gordon, D. (2014). *Universal Design for Learning: Theory and Practice.* Wakefield MA: CAST.

Messick, S. (1994). The interplay of evidence and consequences in the validation of performance assessments. *Educational Research, 23*(2), 13–23.

Mishra, P., and Koehler, M. J. (2006). Technological pedagogical content knowledge: A new framework for teacher knowledge. *Teachers College Record, 108*(6), 1017–1054.

Mislevy, R. J. (2020). Statistical theoreticians and educational assessment: Comments on Shelby Haberman's NCME Career Contributions Award. *Journal of Educational Measurement, 57*(3), 386–396.

Mislevy, R. J., and Haertel, G. D. (2006). Implications of evidence-centered design for educational testing. *Educational Measurement: Issues and Practice, 25*(4), 6–20.

Mislevy, R. J., Steinberg, L. S., Breyer, F. J., Almond, R. G., and Johnson, L. (1999). A cognitive task analysis with implications for designing simulation-based performance assessment. *Computers in Human Behavior, 15*(3–4), 335–374.

Mislevy, R. J., Steinberg, L. S., and Almond, R. G. (2003). On the structure of educational assessments. *Measurement: Interdisciplinary Research and Perspectives, 1,* 3–66.

Nicol, D. J., and Macfarlane-Dick, D. (2006). Formative assessment and self-regulated learning: A model and seven principles of good feedback practice. *Studies in Higher Education, 31*(2), 199–218.

Novak, K. (2016). UDL *Now!: A teacher's Guide to Applying Universal Design for Learning in Today's Classroom.* Wakefield, MA: CAST Professional Publishing.

Novak, E., Razzouk, R., and Johnson, T. (2012). The educational user of social annotation tools in higher education: A literature review. *Internet and Higher Education, 15,* 39–49.

Oranje, A., Keehner, M., Persky, H., Cayton-Hodges, G., and Feng, G. (2016). The role of cognition in the design, development, and reporting of educational survey assessments. In: A. A. Rupp and J. Leighton (Eds.), *Handbook of Cognition and Assessment*. New York: Wiley.

Panadero, E. (2017). A review of self-regulated learning: Six models and four directions for research. *Frontiers in Psychology, 8(422)*, 1–28.

Pope, A. M., Finney, S. J., and Barre, A. K. (2019). The essential role of program theory: Fostering theory-driven practice and high-quality outcomes assessment in student affairs. *Research & Practice in Assessment, 14,* 5–17.

Puentedura, R. (2006). *Transformation, technology, and education*. Presentation given August 18, 2006, as part of the Strengthening Your District Through Technology Workshops. Maine, USA.

Saleebey, D. (1996). The strengths perspective in social work practice: Extensions and cautions. *Social Work, 41*(3), 296–305.

Seligman, M. E. (2012). *Flourish: A Visionary New Understanding of Happiness and Well-Being*. Simon and Schuster.

Tomasek, T. (2009). Critical reading: Using reading prompts to promote active engagement with text. *International Journal of Teaching and Learning in Higher Education, 21*(1), 127–132.

Tseng, S., Yeh, H., and Yang, S (2015) Promoting different reading comprehension levels through online annotations. *Computer Assisted Language Learning, 28*(1), 41–57.

Shibani, A., Knight, S., and Shum, S. B. (2019). Contextualizable learning analytics design: A generic model and writing analytics evaluations. *Proceedings of the 9th International Conference on Learning Analytics & Knowledge*, 210–219.

Smith, K. L., and Finney, S. J. (2020). Elevating program theory and implementation fidelity in higher education: Modeling the process via an ethical reasoning curriculum. *Research & Practice in Assessment, 15,* 1–13.

Vredenburg, K., Mao, J.-Y., Smith, P. W., and Carey, T. (2002). A survey of user-centered design practice. *CHI'02: Proceedings of the SIGCHI Conference on Human Factors in Computing Systems*, 471–478. New York: ACM.

Vygotsky, L.S. (1978). *Mind in Society*. Cambridge, MA: Harvard University Press.

Vygotsky, L.S. (1962). *Thought and Language*. Cambridge, MA: MIT Press.

Wigfield, A. (1994). Expectancy-value theory of achievement motivation: A developmental perspective. *Educational Psychology Review, 6,* 49–78.

West, R. E. (2018). *Foundations of Learning and Instructional Design Technology: The Past, Present, and future of Learning and Instructional Design Technology* (1st ed.). EdTech Books.

Wray, E. (2011). *RISE model for peer feedback*. Retrieved April 21, 2021, from https://static1.squarespace.com/static/502c5d7e24aca01df4766eb3/t/5c4e71ecf950b77130df9756/1548644844456/RISE-Model-Peer-by-Emily-Wray-2018.pdf.

Zimmerman, B. J. (2000). Attaining self-regulation: A social cognitive perspective. In: Boekaerts M., Pintrich P. R., and Zeidner M. (Eds.), *Handbook of Self-Regulation*, 13–40. San Diego, CA: Academic Press.

Chapter 4

Implementing Learning Analytics at Scale in an Online World

Lessons Learned from the Open University UK

Bart Rienties[1]

Abstract

While many "brick-and-mortar" universities had to rapidly shift online provision during the pandemic, a range of online and distance-learning universities have been teaching in blended and online formats for years. The Open University UK has been trailblazing innovative and effective learning designs for diverse learners across the globe for 50 years, and learning analytics in particular since 2014. This chapter explores two large-scale implementations (i.e., Analytics4Action, learning design) as a multiple case-study to illustrate how educators and institutions might make sense of meaningful learning analytics at scale. The findings indicate that active engagement by educators with learning analytics can positively improve the chances of learners to get support early and

---

[1] Institute of Educational Technology, Open University UK, Milton Keynes, UK

to set them up for success. However, more needs to be done to actively support our educators to make sense of learning data.

Keywords: Learning analytics, Open University, case study, Analytics4Action, learning design

Introduction

With COVID-19 and the rapid shift to blended and online provision, the way educators and learners engage with each other has dramatically changed since March 2020. A range of studies have started to explore the impact of COVID-19 on how the roles of educators and learners are changing over time (Gherheș, Simon, & Para, 2021; Haras, Calhoun, Olson, & Rosenberg, 2021; Naffi, 2020), as many institutions had to shift "over night" to online provision. Over half a billion students and thousands of educators were disrupted by the sudden shift to online education (Crawford et al., 2020; Gonzalez et al., 2020; Naffi, 2020).

In a review of educational reactions to COVID-19 in 20 countries, Crawford et al. (2020) found a vast range of strategies and practical solutions by higher education institutions (HEIs) to deal with the new situation. Furthermore, in a Spanish context, Gonzalez et al. (2020) found that confinement led to a significant positive effect on academic performance. However, in a medical context, Haras et al. (2021) found that most medical institutions were not equipped to teach online, and that a mindful teaching approach was needed that "creates presences that set climate and support discourse, establish routines that build practice, model professional expectations, and challenge but support learners." Naffi (2020) found a similar renewed interest in pedagogy to move towards online education, but at the same time a risk in anxiety and stress amongst educators.

While many "brick-and-mortar" universities had to rapidly shift online provision during the pandemic, a range of online and distance learning universities have been teaching in blended and online formats for years (Lucena, Díaz, Reche, & Rodríguez, 2019; Tait, 2018), and some, like the Open University UK (OU), even for decades. The OU has been trailblazing innovative and effective learning designs for diverse learners across the globe for 50 years. In the last 15 years, the OU has been on the forefront of providing innovative learning design approaches, frameworks, and trainings to its learners online across the globe. Furthermore, since 2014, the OU has started to implement learning analytics approaches to help support their students and educators (Calvert, 2014; Clow, 2014; Open University UK, 2014; Rienties, Olney, Nichols, & Herodotou, 2020; Wolff, Zdrahal, Herrmannova, Kuzilek, & Hlosta, 2014).

Designing effective and engaging learning activities for learners in blended and online learning environments traditionally has been regarded as an art and a skill, primarily embedded in technology-focussed system thinking and strongly influenced by educator beliefs of what is "good" learning (Neelen & Kirschner, 2020). With the advance of technological affordances of learning systems and increased digitalisation of learning activities, the OU has developed a range of approaches to map which learning activities might be useful for learners and how institutions could systematically capture common learning design approaches (Conole, 2012; McAndrew, Nadolski, & Little, 2005) and learning analytics approaches in particular (Rienties et al., 2016; Rienties & Toetenel, 2016). In this chapter, I will review the lessons learned from implementing learning analytics and learning design at scale at the OU with its 170,000 students and around 7,000 educators.

Making Use of Learning Analytics Data

While some higher education institutions (HEIs) are starting to use data to make sense of what may be happening with their students, in comparison to most contemporary companies and the wider public sector, the use of data is mostly retrospective. Until recently, most HEIs primarily collated two types of data, often in an isolated manner (Phillips, 2013; Viberg, Hatakka, Bälter, & Mavroudi, 2018). One type of data, *academic learner data*, mainly consists of relatively static data about registered learners (e.g., demographics, prior education, progress/completion data) (Matz et al., 2021; Tempelaar, Rienties, & Giesbers, 2015). Most of these data are collated and managed to award grades and degrees, often maintained for formal quality assurance and quality enhancement processes. Often these academic learner data are mainly used by "non-educators" (e.g., administrators, managers, policy makers).

The second type of data, *learning data* about what learners are (not) doing in a module, is increasingly becoming available to educators (Herodotou et al., 2019; Tempelaar et al., 2015). In particular, with the rise of virtual learning environments (VLEs), many educators in the last 10–20 years have gained access to behavioural and cognitive learning data of their learners (Herodotou et al., 2019; Matz et al., 2021; Tempelaar et al., 2015), occasionally supplemented with affective learning data (Fan, Saint, Singh, Jovanovic, & Gašević, 2021; Kia, Hatala, Baker, & Teasley, 2021; Tempelaar, Nguyen, & Rienties, 2020).

These VLEs often provide standardised metrics of how a learner has, for example, engaged within the VLE, when the last log-in was, and how long a learner has spent on the VLE in the last week. However, most educators do not actively use these data. Educators may think that there is no need to use them (Herodotou, Rienties, et al., 2020), the data are too complex to understand (Rienties, Herodotou, Olney, Schencks, & Boroowa, 2018), or the data stored in these dashboards are not necessarily relevant (Kaliisa, Mørch, & Kluge, 2021).

The Rise of the Learning Analytics Community

In the last ten years, an incredible body of research has become available under the umbrella term of *learning analytics,* which aims to apply the outcomes of analysing data from learners and affect their learning behaviour. A wide breadth of systematic literature reviews have found that learning analytics can help to identify which learners are potentially at risk using learning analytics dashboards (Bodily & Verbert, 2017), who might need more/less support (Ifenthaler & Yau, 2020), which interventions might be more effective for which learner (Ferguson & Clow, 2017; Knobbout & van der Stappen, 2020; Viberg et al., 2018), and how to identify which part of a learning design may (not) be effective (Mangaroska & Giannakos, 2019). While many of these reviews provide strong evidence and support of the power of learning analytics, most of these learning analytics applications were implemented in single-module or small-scale settings (Ferguson & Clow, 2017; Viberg et al., 2018). Few institutions have implemented learning analytics at scale and across its institution.

A notable exception is the OU, who since 2014 has gradually moved from small-scale experimentation to large-scale adoption of learning analytics throughout all 400+ modules and qualifications available within the OU for its 170,000+ online learners. In part, this is also evidenced by the wide body of research on learning analytics coming from the OU, as it has led the publication output table in Web of Science on the topic of learning analytics for years. At the OU, two specific learning analytics systems are currently used; one focused on risk-assessment and longitudinal progression over time (Calvert, 2014; Herodotou, Naydenova, Boroowa, Gilmour, & Rienties, 2020), while the other focused more on predicting whether (or not) a student will make and pass the next assessment based upon VLE behaviour (Hlosta, Papathoma, & Herodotou, 2020; Wolff et al., 2014).

In parallel to developing predictive learning analytics approaches, substantial investment is made in supporting educators to make sense of these data and to design interventions where needed. Based upon dozens of studies at the OU and elsewhere, educators are essential for effective development, implementation, and evaluation of learning analytics approaches at scale. This chapter will focus on two large-scale implementations (i.e., Analytics4Action project, learning design) as a multiple case study to illustrate how educators and institutions might want to consider making sense of meaningful learning analytics at scale. Both these cases received substantial support from senior management at the initiation stage of development, as well as continued support when these innovations were main-streamed and implemented as business as usual.

Case Study 1: The Analytics4Action Project

In Analytics4Action (Hidalgo & Evans, 2020; Rienties et al., 2016; Rienties & Herodotou, 2021), we realised from 2014 that developing and implementing any dashboard for educators with learning and learner data, let alone a state-of-the-art learning analytics dashboard, requires involvement of a wide range of stakeholders. As indicated by Rienties et al. (2016, p. 4), in Analytics4Action, "the first step is to bring together the key stakeholders in the module, such as educators, learning analysts and administrators for the purpose of presenting, unpacking and understanding learning data available taken from various VLE and related systems. This is termed a data touch point meeting [now labelled data support meetings] and the project held four of these with each module over a one-year period".

Typically within an academic year, the Analytics4Action team will be working with teams of academics responsible for 40+ modules (Hidalgo & Evans, 2020). As indicated in Figure 4.1 (Rienties et al., 2016), in the Analytics4Action framework, there are six (potential) steps that educators and institutions might want to take to make sense of data about learners and their learning. Note that we are not

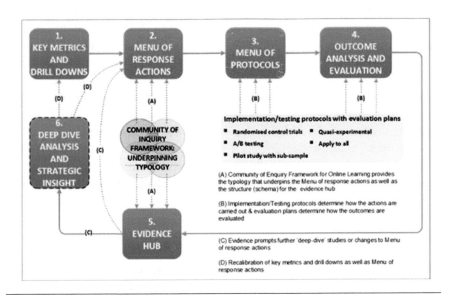

Figure 4.1 Analytics4Action Framework (*Source:* Rienties et al., 2016) JIME (Creative Commons license)

expecting all educators to go through all six Analytics4Action steps, or in any specific order. For some educators, just starting with the first step of "what is known about your students" might already lead to substantial new insights. For others, it might be already a common practice to look deeply at data, but perhaps there is no evidence hub yet to store and collate these insights. In this case study, we will focus only on the first step in the Analytics4Action framework. In other publications, more detailed examples of fully-worked-out examples are provided (Hidalgo & Evans, 2020; Rienties & Herodotou, 2021).

Key Metrics and Drill Downs: What Is Known About Your Students?

Typically, during three or four data support meetings within one module, educators will work with other stakeholders and data experts from the Analytics4Action team through a range of dynamic and static dashboards provided by the OU. These dashboards have been organically developed and further fine-tuned over time based upon feedback from educators and other stakeholders. By iteratively revising dashboards together with educators, a co-constructed approach was adopted to make sense of the emerging data.

An example learning analytics dashboard is shown in Figure 4.2, which presents a range of visualisations from a medium-size introductory module on engineering of 546 learners who started in October 2020. In OU Analyse (Herodotou et al., 2019; Herodotou, Rienties, et al., 2020; Wolff et al., 2014), educators can compare how engaged (in terms of average VLE clicks) their learners on average are (orange line) relative to the previous cohort of students attending the same engineering course (blue line). Furthermore, the bar charts indicate the average assessment scores of the various module assessments (orange bar) relative to the previous cohort (blue bar). It also shows when learners have to pay the next part of their study fee (i.e., Fee Liability Point). In the first week of the course, students were more active relative to previous cohort(s), similar in week 2, slightly below in week 3, etc., until the first two assignments in week 7 (one so-called Computer Marked Assessment, and one Tutor Marked Assessment). Furthermore, the dashboard illustrates that in week 10, 521 students were still registered, and 320 students were active in the VLE in the previous week.

As illustrated in Figure 4.3, educators at the OU also have access to detailed predictions of their learners through the OU Analyse dashboard. Used in a traffic-light-like visualisation, OU Analyse predicts whether (or not) a learner is going to submit (and pass) the next assignment. After 10 weeks in this (anonymised) example list of 10 learners, only one learner (we gave her the name "Camren") did not submit the first assignment (in OU jargon this is called Teacher Marked Assignment, TMA). Furthermore, one learner (named as "Stacy") was indicated as amber after the first assignment in week 7 due to a below-average engagement. An

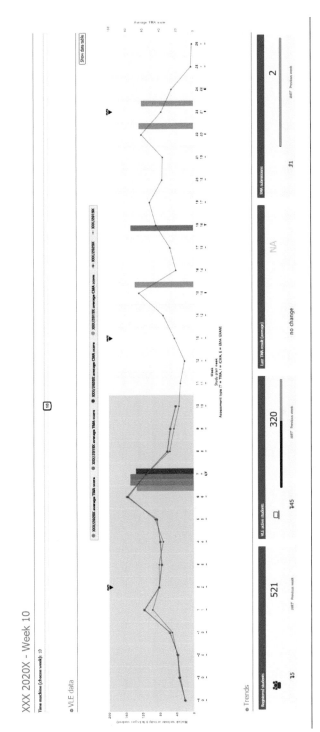

Figure 4.2   OU Analyse Module Overview

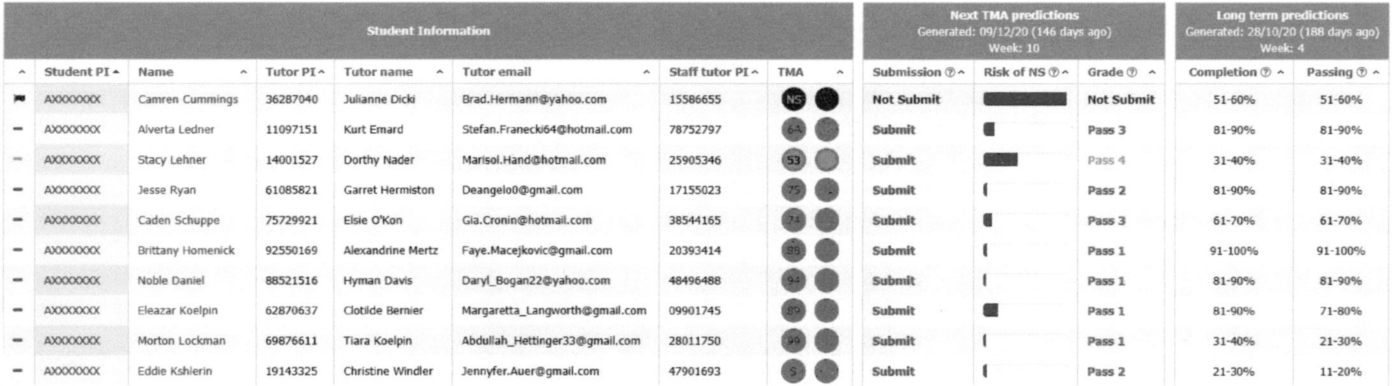

	Student Information						Next TMA predictions Generated: 09/12/20 (146 days ago) Week: 10			Long term predictions Generated: 28/10/20 (188 days ago) Week: 4	
Student PI	Name	Tutor PI	Tutor name	Tutor email	Staff tutor PI	TMA	Submission	Risk of NS	Grade	Completion	Passing
A0000000X	Camren Cummings	36287040	Julianne Dicki	Brad.Hermann@yahoo.com	15586655	NS	Not Submit		Not Submit	51-60%	51-60%
A0000000X	Alverta Ledner	110971151	Kurt Emard	Stefan.Franecki64@hotmail.com	78752797	64	Submit		Pass 3	81-90%	81-90%
A0000000X	Stacy Lehner	140001527	Dorthy Nader	Marisol.Hand@hotmail.com	25905346	53	Submit		Pass 4	31-40%	31-40%
A0000000X	Jesse Ryan	61085821	Garret Hermiston	Deangelo0@gmail.com	17155023	75	Submit		Pass 2	81-90%	81-90%
A0000000X	Caden Schuppe	75729921	Elsie O'Kon	Gia.Cronin@hotmail.com	38544165	74	Submit		Pass 3	61-70%	61-70%
A0000000X	Brittany Homenick	92550169	Alexandrine Mertz	Faye.Macejkovic@gmail.com	20393414	88	Submit		Pass 1	91-100%	91-100%
A0000000X	Noble Daniel	88521516	Hyman Davis	Daryl_Bogan22@yahoo.com	48496488	94	Submit		Pass 1	81-90%	81-90%
A0000000X	Eleazar Koelpin	62870637	Clotide Bernier	Margaretta_Langworth@gmail.com	09901745	89	Submit		Pass 1	81-90%	71-80%
A0000000X	Morton Lockman	69876611	Tiara Koelpin	Abdullah_Hettinger33@gmail.com	28011750	96	Submit		Pass 1	31-40%	21-30%
A0000000X	Eddie Kohlerin	19143325	Christine Winder	Jennyfer.Auer@gmail.com	479001693	5	Submit		Pass 2	21-30%	11-20%

Figure 4.3 Individual Predictive Learning Analytics in OU Analyse

educator can subsequently zoom into the dashboard details of a learner like Stacy, as illustrated in Figure 4.4, and perhaps consider taking an action.

A strong feature of OU Analyse is that it knows which learning activities are key for successful completion of an assessment, and which ones are not. Based upon thousands of (un)successful learner paths, OU Analyse gives information to the educator whether (or not) key learning activities have been undertaken by Stacy (Herodotou, Rienties, et al., 2020; Hlosta et al., 2020). Unfortunately, Stacy did not successfully complete the module, as she did not submit her second assignment. Of the 10 learners in this example, three learners (Alverta, Camren, Stacey) did not pass this engineering course. In a range of studies, we have shown that active engagement by educators with learning analytics can positively improve the chances of learners to get support early (Herodotou, Naydenova, et al., 2020) and to set them up for success (Herodotou, Rienties, et al., 2020).

At the same time, not all educators will engage with learning analytics (Herodotou, Rienties, et al., 2020). In part this is explained by the type of contract that associate lecturers are currently on at the OU, which do not require them to look at learning analytics data, and they are not financially rewarded to do so either. Furthermore, our research (Herodotou, Rienties, et al., 2020; Kaliisa, Gillespie, Herodotou, Kluge, & Rienties, 2021; Rienties et al., 2018) indicates that whether (or not) educators actively use learning analytics is dependent upon respective faculty's engagement, embedding educators as "champions", helping with evidence generation and dissemination, digital literacy, and conceptions about teaching online. The Analytics4Action approach shows that when educators are intensively supported to make sense of learning analytics, they are not only more inclined to use learning analytics data, but they also become advocates to their peers of using learning analytics (Hidalgo & Evans, 2020; Rienties & Herodotou, 2021).

Case Study 2: Learning Design to Understand Learning Analytics

While learning analytics dashboards such as OU Analyse provide an engaging and integrated perspective on behaviour and cognitive engagement of learners, our experience at the OU indicates that without a deep understanding of the underlying learning design of a particular course, it is difficult to understand the peaks and troughs in such systems.

Learning Design is a structured design, specification, and review process (Conole, 2012; McAndrew et al., 2005; Rienties & Toetenel, 2016; Toetenel & Rienties, 2016a; Wasson & Kirschner, 2020). In the Open University Learning Design Initiative (OULDI), learning activities are categorised according to seven main types of what learners do (i.e., assimilative, finding and handing information, communicative, productive, interactive, experiential, assessment), as indicated in Table 4.1. OULDI is

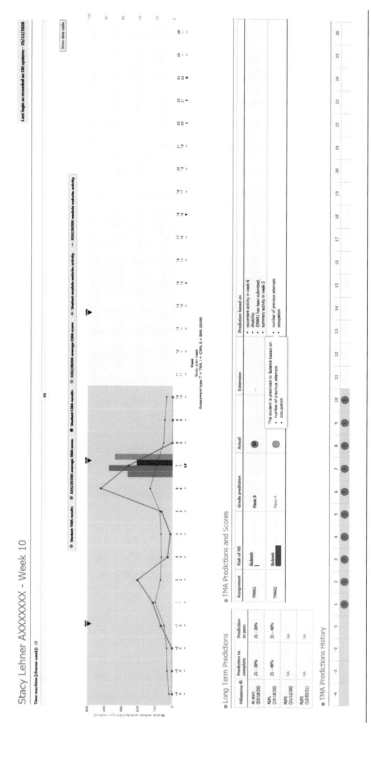

Figure 4.4   Predictive Learning Analytics Overview of Stacey

Table 4.1 OULDI Learning Design

	Assimilative	Finding and handling information	Communication	Productive	Experiential	Interactive/ Adaptive	Assessment
Type of activity	Attending to information	Searching for and processing information	Discussing module related content with at least one other person (student or tutor)	Actively constructing an artefact	Applying learning in a real-world setting	Applying learning in a simulated setting	All forms of assessment, whether continuous, end of module, or formative (assessment for learning)
Examples of activity	Read, watch, listen, think about, access, observe, review, study	List, analyse, collate, plot, find, discover, access, use, gather, order, classify, select, assess, manipulate	Communicate, debate, discuss, argue, share, report, collaborate, present, describe, question	Create, build, make, design, construct, contribute, complete, produce, write, draw, refine, compose, synthesise, remix	Practice, apply, mimic, experience, explore, investigate, perform, engage	Explore, experiment, trial, improve, model, simulate	Write, present, report, demonstrate, critique

supported by a simple set of tools and resources that enable a student-activity-based approach that puts the student experience at the heart of curriculum design.

By embedding learning design with state-of-the-art learning analytics approaches since 2014, the OU has been trailblazing research on the OULDI framework (1) how 1541 educators are designing blended/online modules; (2) how these designs are impacting 170K+ learners' behaviour and academic performance; and (3) how learning designs could be effectively adjusted based upon learning process data of students and effective practice from peer educators.

1) How Are Educators Designing Online Learning Activities?

For example, Toetenel and Rienties (2016a) analysed 157 learning designs developed in the OU using OULDI. Results revealed that the majority of educators used two types of learning activities most widely—namely, assimilative activities (M = 39%, SD = 17%: reading, watching videos, and listening to audio), and assessment activities (M = 22%, SD = 15%). The categories of productive (M = 13%, SD= 10%), communicative (M = 8%, SD = 7%), finding information (M = 7%, SD = 7%), experiential (M = 6%, SD = 8%), and interactive (M = 5%, SD = 7%) were relatively little used on average. However, as is visible by the relatively large standard deviations, substantially different practices were found where some educators did integrate substantially more productive and communicative learning activities, while others mainly focussed on assimilative and assessment activities.

In order to encourage educators to consider more student-centred designs, an interactive dashboard and online tool was developed that allows educators to directly map their own learning design and compare and contrast their own designs with other designs from colleagues. Figure 4.5 illustrates the learning design of the Introduction to Engineering course previously mentioned in case study 1, in which 41% of learning activities were labelled as assimilative in total, whereby for example in week 16, 6 hours was pencilled in by the educators for students to work on assimilative activities. In week 19, a range of productive and experiential activities were included, while the last three weeks were designed for preparation for the final assessment. By mapping and visualising the learning activities, educators can ensure that appropriate workload balancing is introduced and communicated to students.

The OULDI tool has been made available online using a Creative Commons license (Van Ameijde, 2015). The use of the OULDI model has resulted in an impact on the understanding, learning, and practice of 1541 university educators over a dozen countries, including Belarus (Olney, Endean, & Banks, 2020), China (Olney, Li, & Luo, 2021), Kenya (Mittelmeier et al., 2018), South Africa (Greyling, Huntley, Reedy, & Rogaten, 2020), and the UK by shaping their understanding and implementation of learning design.

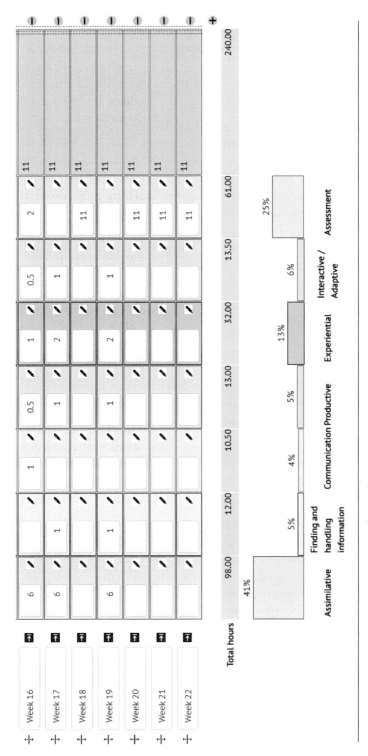

Figure 4.5   Learning Design Mapping of Introduction to Engineering Course

2) How Is Learning Design Impacting Learner Behaviour and Academic Performance?

Obviously, it is one thing being able to map how educators design and implement online learning activities, but another is whether (or not) learning design influences learners' behaviour and academic outcomes. In one of the first large-scale empirical studies finding a strong link between learning design and academic outcome, Rienties and Toetenel (2016) used multiple regression models to link 151 modules taught in 2012–2015 at the OU and studied by 111,256 students with students' behaviour.

Findings indicated that the primary predictor of academic retention was the relative amount of communication activities (e.g., student-to-student interaction, student-to-educator interaction). The findings indicated that a 1% increase in learning activities related to communication would increase pass rates of modules with 0.5%. Furthermore, the way educators designed the online activities had a significant impact on student engagement and student satisfaction (Rienties & Toetenel, 2016).

Follow-up temporal analyses by Nguyen, Rienties, Toetenel, Ferguson, and Whitelock (2017) on a week-by-week basis of how educators' learning activities designed for, say, week 1 influenced students' behaviour in week 1, with 72,377 students showing that 69% of how students engage on a weekly basis is a direct result of how educators design courses. In other words, two-thirds of study engagement and success of students is directly related to how educators design online learning activities. This is a tremendously important finding, as how educators create, design, and implement learning activities has a substantial impact on learners' success.

3) How Can Learning Designs Be Effectively Adjusted Based upon Learning Process Data of Students and Effective Practice from Peer Educators?

By using both OULDI dashboards and student engagement data from Analytics 4Action and OU Analyse, educators are actively (re)designing their learning activities in an evidence-based manner. For example, Toetenel and Rienties (2016b) showed that giving educators early access to visualisations of other learning design options could actively encourage educators to change their learning design approaches by incorporating more communicative and interactive activities relative to assimilative activities. Herodotou, Rienties, et al. (2020) showed that 1159 associate lecturers at the OU in 231 courses over a period of four years were successfully able to intervene to support students who were struggling with the learning design.

Furthermore, in a mixed-effect logistic-regression study on 123K undergraduate students in 205 modules at the OU, Nguyen, Thorne, and Rienties (2018) showed a positive association between providing so-called study breaks (i.e., a week without any scheduled learning activities) and the odds of passing a course, while there was no statistically significant effect in relation to the number of assessment preparation and revision weeks (i.e., a week to study for assessment/exam). Many educators at the OU assumed that providing assessment preparations and revision weeks before an assessment would have a positive impact on study success. However, the analysis showed that a higher proportion of passed students remained active during preparation and exam revision weeks compared to failed students (Nguyen et al., 2018). This study helped to shift the learning design thinking of educators by giving learners regular study breaks to catch up during a module, rather than collating them all at the end of a module.

In a recent study looking at learning designs in Massive Open Online Courses (MOOCs), Rizvi, Rienties, Kizilcec, and Rogaten (2021) used process-mining techniques to inspect trace data for 49K learners enrolled in 10 large FutureLearn MOOCs (massive open online courses). They examined whether (or not) differences regarding the number of assimilative activities (articles and videos), communication activities (discussions), and assessment activities (quizzes) within a MOOC could be used to predict learners' persistence and why learners engaged differently. The quantitative and qualitative findings indicated that learning design decisions made by Western educators were mainly beneficial for Western learners, while learners from other geo-cultural regions either had to adopt a new learning approach or were more likely to drop out. As argued by Rizvi et al., (2021) "[u]ntil we reach the (difficult yet attainable) milestone of a flexible, culturally adaptive MOOC LD, we recommend taking a balanced approach by combining different types of learning activities, not just video-based, or reading MOOCs."

Discussion

By closing the loop between what educators are designing and how learners are engaging with blended and online learning activities, both fundamental and theoretical advances have been made on how to effectively support online learning in a wide range of publications at the Open University UK (OU), which have been applauded and recognised widely by both the research community (Mangaroska & Giannakos, 2019; Neelen & Kirschner, 2017; Wasson & Kirschner, 2020) and practice (Greyling et al., 2020; Mittelmeier et al., 2018; Olney et al., 2020; Olney et al., 2021).

In this multiple case study, we illustrated how the OU is facilitating educators to make sense of data and learning analytics, in particular by two large-scale implementations of Analytics4Action and learning design. One main lesson learned from large-scale implementation in organisations such as the OU is that innovation takes substantial time to grow, develop, mature, and embed into an organisation. For example, the initial seeds of the learning design approach were already developed in 2005 (McAndrew et al., 2005) and received a substantial push in 2010–2012 when some funding was received to work together with six UK institutions (Conole, 2012). Nonetheless, the actual large-scale adoption and "maturation" of learning design only started after 2014, when substantial strategic effort was placed in mapping the learning designs of each new module and recruitment of a range of learning designers bringing in new ideas (Toetenel & Rienties, 2016a, 2016b; Van Ameijde, 2015). Similarly, with Analytics4Action, it probably took three to four years before the process matured and was sufficiently embedded as business as usual.

Linked with the first lesson, our second lesson is that without clear senior management support it would be extremely difficult to reach a critical mass to implement innovations such as learning analytics at scale. As these innovation projects are complex and take up a lot of time on educators, strong buy-in from senior management is needed to prioritise these innovations (Dawson et al., 2018; Rienties et al., 2020).

Thirdly, as evidenced by a range of technological adoption failures over the years, without bottom-up support from educators and researchers who are willing to take a risk, any educational innovation is probably doomed to fail (Herodotou et al., 2019; Kaliisa, Gillespie, et al., 2021; Kaliisa, Mørch, et al., 2021). In both Analytics4Action and learning design, we specifically worked with a relatively small group of educators in the initial first two years. This allowed us to test-and-learn what works for them, learn and develop a better understanding of their needs, and also allow us to fine-tune our approach(es) afterwards when we went mainstream. Another main advantage of starting small is that these educators became champions in their own disciplines/departments and were probably more able to sell the innovation than were the actual innovators (Kaliisa, Gillespie, et al., 2021).

Fourthly, evidence-based research can gradually change perspectives and narratives in an organisation, and throughout both case studies, we continuously conducted scholarly research together with key stakeholders to understand what was working and what was not. By bringing educators and researchers together, we developed a rich, detailed understanding of why certain elements in an innovation were working, which afterwards helped new educators joining later to get more buy-in, as we could signpost evidence of a particular approach.

Fifthly, our experience indicates that you quickly forget about the small/medium/large successes you make in your innovation project and often fail to realise that you are making a real impact. It is extremely tempting to focus on bug fixing, error chasing, and continuous tinkering of particular approaches, but it takes courage and insight to let an innovation run for some time and appreciate how much ground you have already covered.

Finally, if there is one thing both case studies have in common, it is all about people. While both case studies have some substantial technical and technological elements, the key drivers for success and failure have nothing to do with the next algorithm or machine learning approach but how we work with people to make sense of what makes them tick. Therefore, any institution thinking about learning analytics is encouraged to bring different people together from a range of disciplines and perspectives.

References

Bodily, R., and Verbert, K. (2017). Review of research on student-facing learning analytics dashboards and educational recommender systems. *IEEE Transactions on Learning Technologies, 10*(4), 405–418. doi: 10.1109/TLT.2017.2740172

Calvert, C. (2014). Developing a model and applications for probabilities of student success: a case study of predictive analytics. *Open Learning: The Journal of Open, Distance and E-Learning, 29*(2), 160–173. doi: 10.1080/02680513.2014.931805

Clow, D. (2014). Data wranglers: Human interpreters to help close the feedback loop. Paper presented in the *Proceedings of the Fourth International Conference on Learning Analytics and Knowledge,* Indianapolis, Indiana.

Conole, G. (2012). *Designing for Learning in an Open World.* Dordrecht: Springer.

Crawford, J., Butler-Henderson, K., Rudolph, J., Malkawi, B., Glowatz, M., Burton, R., . . . Lam, S. (2020). COVID-19: 20 countries' higher education intra-period digital pedagogy responses. *Journal of Applied Learning & Teaching, 3*(1), 1–20.

Dawson, S., Poquet, O., Colvin, C., Rogers, T., Pardo, A., and Gasevic, D. (2018). Rethinking learning analytics adoption through complexity leadership theory. Paper presented in the *Proceedings of the 8th International Conference on Learning Analytics and Knowledge,* Sydney, New South Wales, Australia.

Fan, Y., Saint, J., Singh, S., Jovanovic, J., and Gašević, D. (2021). *A Learning Analytic Approach to Unveiling Self-Regulatory Processes in Learning Tactics.* Paper presented at the LAK21: 11th International Learning Analytics and Knowledge Conference, Irvine, CA. doi: 10.1145/3448139.3448211

Ferguson, R., and Clow, D. (2017). Where is the evidence? A call to action for learning analytics. Paper presented in the *Proceedings of the 6th Learning Analytics Knowledge Conference,* Vancouver.

Gherheş, V., Simon, S., and Para, I. (2021). Analysing students' reasons for keeping their webcams on or off during online classes. *Sustainability, 13*(6), 3203. doi: 10.3390/su13063203

Gonzalez, T., de la Rubia, M. A., Hincz, K. P., Comas-Lopez, M., Subirats, L., Fort, S., and Sacha, G. M. (2020). Influence of COVID-19 confinement on students' performance in higher education. *PLOS One, 15*(10), e0239490. doi: 10.1371/journal.pone.0239490

Greyling, L. E., Huntley, B., Reedy, K., and Rogaten, J. (2020). Improving distance learn-ing mathematics modules in South Africa: A learning design perspective. *South African Journal of Higher Education, 34*(3), 89–111.

Haras, C., Calhoun, A., Olson, A. P. J., and Rosenberg, M. (2021). Mindful medical edu-cation online. *Medical Science Educator*. doi: 10.1007/s40670-021-01253-7

Herodotou, C., Hlosta, M., Boroowa, A., Rienties, B., Zdrahal, Z., and Mangafa, C. (2019). Empowering online teachers through predictive learning analytics. *British Journal of Educational Technology, 50*(6), 3064–3079. doi: 10.1111/bjet.12853

Herodotou, C., Naydenova, G., Boroowa, A., Gilmour, A., and Rienties, B. (2020). How can predictive learning analytics and motivational interventions increase student retention and enhance administrative support in distance education? *Journal of Learning Analytics, 7*(2), 72–83. doi: 10.18608/jla.2020.72.4

Herodotou, C., Rienties, B., Hlosta, M., Boroowa, A., Mangafa, C., and Zdrahal, Z. (2020). The scalable implementation of predictive learning analytics at a distance learning university: Insights from a longitudinal case study. *The Internet and Higher Education, 45*, 100725. doi: 10.1016/j.iheduc.2020.100725

Hidalgo, R., and Evans, G. (2020). Analytics for action: Assessing effectiveness and impact of data informed interventions on online modules. *Revista Iberoamericana de Educación a Distancia, 23*(2), 23. doi: 10.5944/ried.23.2.26450

Hlosta, M., Papathoma, T., and Herodotou, C. (2020). *Explaining Errors in Predictions of At-Risk Students in Distance Learning Education*, Cham.

Ifenthaler, D., and Yau, J. Y.-K. (2020). Utilising learning analytics to support study suc-cess in higher education: A systematic review. *Educational Technology Research and Development*. doi: 10.1007/s11423-020-09788-z

Kaliisa, R., Gillespie, A., Herodotou, C., Kluge, A., and Rienties, B. (2021). Teachers' perspec-tives on the promises, needs and challenges of LA visualizations: Insights from a blended and distance learning institution. In: D. Ifenthaler and M. Sahin (Eds.), *Visualizations and Dashboards for Learning Analytics*. Cham: Springer International Publishing.

Kaliisa, R., Mørch, A. I., and Kluge, A. (2021). 'My point of departure for analytics is extreme skepticism': Implications derived from an investigation of university teach-ers' learning analytics perspectives and design practices. *Technology, Knowledge and Learning*. doi: 10.1007/s10758-020-09488-w

Kia, F. S., Hatala, M., Baker, R. S., and Teasley, S. D. (2021). *Measuring Students' Self-Regulatory Phases in LMS with Behavior and Real-Time Self Report*. Paper presented at the LAK21: 11th International Learning Analytics and Knowledge Conference, Irvine, CA. doi: 10.1145/3448139.3448164

Knobbout, J., and van der Stappen, E. (2020). Where is the learning in learning analyt-ics? A systematic literature review on the operationalization of learning-related constructs in the evaluation of learning analytics interventions. *IEEE Transactions on Learning Technologies*, 1–1. doi: 10.1109/TLT.2020.2999970

Lucena, F. J. H., Díaz, I. A., Reche, M. P. C., and Rodríguez, J. M. R. (2019). A tour of open universities through literature. *The International Review of Research in Open and Distributed Learning, 20*(4). doi: 10.19173/irrodl.v20i3.4079

Mangaroska, K., and Giannakos, M. N. (2019). Learning analytics for learning design: A systematic literature review of analytics-driven design to enhance learning. *IEEE Transactions on Learning Technologies, 12*(4), 516–534. doi: 10.1109/TLT.2018 .2868673

Matz, R., Schulz, K., Hanley, E., Derry, H., Hayward, B., Koester, B., . . . McKay, T. (2021). *Analyzing the Efficacy of ECoach in Supporting Gateway Course Success Through Tailored Support.* Paper presented at the LAK21: 11th International Learning Analytics and Knowledge Conference, Irvine, CA, USA. https://doi.org /10.1145/3448139.3448160

McAndrew, P., Nadolski, R., and Little, A. (2005). Developing an approach for learning design players. *Journal of Interactive Media in Education, 2005*(1). doi: 10.5334/2005-14

Mittelmeier, J., Long, D., Melis Cin, F., Reedy, K., Gunter, A., Raghuram, P., and Rienties, B. (2018). Learning design in diverse institutional and cultural contexts: Suggestions from a participatory workshop with higher education leaders in Africa. *Open Learning, 33*(3), 250–266. doi: 10.1080/02680513.2018.1486185

Naffi, N. (2020). *Disruption in and by Centres for Teaching and Learning During the COVID-19 Pandemic Leading the Future of Higher Ed.* Quebec: Universite Laval.

Neelen, M., and Kirschner, P. (2017). Where are the learning sciences in learning analytics research? Retrieved from https://3starlearningexperiences.wordpress.com/2017/10/17 /where-are-the-learning-sciences-in-learning-analytics-research/

Neelen, M., and Kirschner, P. A. (2020). *Evidence-Informed Learning Design: Creating Training to Improve Performance.* London, UK: Kogan Page Publishers.

Nguyen, Q., Rienties, B., Toetenel, L., Ferguson, F., and Whitelock, D. (2017). Examining the designs of computer-based assessment and its impact on student engagement, satisfaction, and pass rates. *Computers in Human Behavior, 76*(November 2017), 703–714. doi: 10.1016/j.chb.2017.03.028

Nguyen, Q., Thorne, S., and Rienties, B. (2018). How do students engage with computer-based assessments: Impact of study breaks on intertemporal engagement and pass rates. *Behaviormetrika, 45*(2), 597–614. doi: 10.1007/s41237-018-0060-1

Olney, T., Endean, M., and Banks, D. (2020). Evaluating the impact of the learning design and course creation (LDCC) workshop on the participants of the enhancement of lifelong learning in Belarus (BELL) project. Paper presented in the *Proceedings of the Final Conference on the Erasmus+ Project.*

Olney, T., Li, C., and Luo, J. (2021). Enhancing the quality of open and distance learning in China through the identification and development of learning design skills and competencies. *Asian Association of Open Universities Journal* (ahead-of-print). doi: 10.1108/AAOUJ-11-2020-0097

Open University UK. (2014). Ethical use of student data for learning analytics policy. Retrieved 23 June 2016, from http://www.open.ac.uk/students/charter/essential-documents/ethical-use-student-data-learning-analytics-policy

Phillips, E. D. (2013). Improving advising using technology and data analytics. *Change: The Magazine of Higher Learning, 45*(1), 48–55. doi: 10.1080/00091383.2013.749151

Rienties, B., Boroowa, A., Cross, S., Kubiak, C., Mayles, K., and Murphy, S. (2016). Analytics4Action evaluation framework: a review of evidence-based learning analytics interventions at Open University UK. *Journal of Interactive Media in Education, 1*(2), 1–12. doi: 10.5334/jime.394

Rienties, B., and Herodotou, C. (2021). Making sense of learning data. In: R. Sharpe, S. Bennett, and T. Varga-Atkins (Eds.), *Handbook for Digital Higher Education*. New York: Edward Elgar Publishing.

Rienties, B., Herodotou, C., Olney, T., Schencks, M., and Boroowa, A. (2018). Making sense of learning analytics dashboards: A technology acceptance perspective of 95 teachers. *The International Review of Research in Open and Distributed Learning, 19*(5). doi: 10.19173/irrodl.v19i5.3493

Rienties, B., Olney, T., Nichols, M., and Herodotou, C. (2020). Effective usage of learning analytics: What do practitioners want and where should distance learning institutions be going? *Open Learning, 35*(2), 178–195.

Rienties, B., and Toetenel, L. (2016). The impact of learning design on student behaviour, satisfaction and performance: A cross-institutional comparison across 151 modules. *Computers in Human Behavior, 60*, 333–341. doi: 10.1016/j.chb.2016.02.074

Rizvi, S., Rienties, B., Kizilcec, R., and Rogaten, J. (2021). Culturally-adaptive learning design—A mixed-method study of cross-cultural learning design preferences in MOOCs. In: B. Rienties, R. Hampel, E. Scanlon, and D. Whitelock (Eds.), *Open World Learning: Research, Innovation and the Challenges of High-Quality Education* (in press). London: Routledge.

Tait, A. (2018). Open universities: The next phase. *Asian Association of Open Universities Journal, 13*(1), 13–23. doi: 10.1108/AAOUJ-12-2017-0040

Tempelaar, D. T., Nguyen, Q., and Rienties, B. (2020). Learning feedback based on dispositional learning analytics. In: M. Virvou, E. Alepis, G. Tsihrintzis, and L. Jain (Eds.), *Machine Learning Paradigms. Intelligent Systems Reference Library, 158*, 69–89. Cham: Springer.

Tempelaar, D. T., Rienties, B., and Giesbers, B. (2015). In search for the most informative data for feedback generation: Learning analytics in a data-rich context. *Computers in Human Behavior, 47*, 157–167. doi: 10.1016/j.chb.2014.05.038

Toetenel, L., and Rienties, B. (2016a). Analysing 157 learning designs using learning analytic approaches as a means to evaluate the impact of pedagogical decision-making. *British Journal of Educational Technology, 47*(5), 981–992. doi: 10.1111/bjet.12423

Toetenel, L., and Rienties, B. (2016b). Learning design—Creative design to visualise learning activities. *Open Learning, 31*(3), 233–244. doi: 10.1080/02680513.2016.1213626

Van Ameijde, J. (2015). Jisc student workload tool. https://github.com/IET-OU/jisc-workload. Retrieved from https://github.com/IET-OU/jisc-workload

Viberg, O., Hatakka, M., Bälter, O., and Mavroudi, A. (2018). The current landscape of learning analytics in higher education. *Computers in Human Behavior, 89* (December 2018), 98–110. doi: 10.1016/j.chb.2018.07.027

Wasson, B., and Kirschner, P. A. (2020). Learning design: European approaches. *Tech-Trends*, 1–13.

Wolff, A., Zdrahal, Z., Herrmannova, D., Kuzilek, J., and Hlosta, M. (2014). *Developing Predictive Models for Early Detection of At-Risk Students on Distance Learning Modules.* Workshop: Machine Learning and Learning Analytics. Paper presented at Learning Analytics and Knowledge (2014), Indianapolis.

Chapter 5

Realising the Potential of Learning Analytics

Reflections from a Pandemic

Mohammad Khalil,[1] Paul Prinsloo,[2] and Sharon Slade[3]

Abstract

This chapter presents a conceptual exploration of the potential of learning analytics to inform teaching and learning during extraordinary contextual events such as the recent and continuing impact of COVID-19. In reflecting on the potential of learning analytics to ameliorate teaching in the dark, we first share some empirical evidence of how learning analytics has been considered and applied during the pandemic since it has started. We then consider the implications and potential of learning analytics in a time of pandemic, concluding with an initial list of recommendations. The value contribution of this chapter is mapping of the conceptual operations in need of consideration in realising the potential of learning analytics going forward during emergency movements to online learning.

Keywords: Learning analytics, COVID-19, pandemic, privacy, technology, education, digital learning, emergency

---

[1] University of Bergen, Norway; [2] University of South Africa, South Africa; [3] Earth Trust, UK

Introduction

Educators may sometimes feel that they are teaching blind—not really knowing whether students understand key concepts, are making sufficient progress, or are needing additional support or stimulation. In residential (higher) education, educators use observations, engagement with students, and formative and summative assessment to determine student progress and to identify students at risk or those needing extra support. In distance and online contexts, the experience of teaching 'in the dark' can be amplified, given a lack of physical cues and engagement. In online environments, educators must rely on their observations of student engagement patterns and on a range of other behavioural data to get a sense of student progress. Since the emergence of learning analytics in 2011 (Joksimović, Kovanović, & Dawson, 2019; Siemens, 2013), the collection, analysis, and use of student data in support of learning has evolved into a mature research field and practice. Evidence suggests that learning analytics provides insight for instructional design (Macfadyen, Lockyer, & Rienties, 2020); impacts positively on student success and retention (Ifenthaler & Yau, 2020); increases teacher understanding of students' work and cognitive load (Curum & Khedo, 2021); and provides educators, student-support teams, and students with insights into progress and learning needs and with estimations of students' probabilities of failing or attrition (Verbert, Ochoa, De Croon, Dourado, & De Laet, 2020).

In response to the global pandemic, an estimated 1.5 billion students and counting have been affected by the rapid, emergency move to online learning (Anderson, 2020, par. 4). As education has moved to remote online modes of delivery, educators, administrators, and student-support teams have faced a sudden loss of direct contact with students and have experimented with different ways to maintain contact and respond to students' emotional, cognitive, and administrative needs. There is a growing range of literature citing institutional responses to the pandemic and the resulting implications, such as the adoption of Intelligent Personal Assistants (IPAs) (Sáiz-Manzanares, Marticorena-Sánchez, & Ochoa-Orihuel, 2020); the integration of Artificial Intelligence (AI) and machine learning components into educational systems (Bañeres, Rodríguez, Guerrero-Roldán, Karadeniz, 2020; Choi & McClenen, 2020); the use of big data as a tool (Villegas-Ch, Roman-Cañizares, Jaramillo-Alcázar, & Palacios-Pacheco, 2020); the use of mobile apps and virtual case studies (Machado, Bonan, Perez, da Cruz, & Martelli Jr., 2020); and the use of asynchronous online discussion forums (Eryilmaz, Thoms, Ahmed, & Lee, 2021).

As higher education has moved online, institutions have had access to more student data than ever. Where Learning Management Systems (LMSs) had once functioned primarily as digital repositories for resources, they now became indispensable aspects of teaching and learning. "LMSs have taken on an enhanced infrastructural role, moving from a background position to being a dominant medium through which institutions, staff, and students interact" (Williamson & Hogan, 2021, p. 28). In the process, LMS providers "built interoperable integrations with third-party platform plug-ins to enable data mining at scale from the increasing participation of students in digitally-mediated education" (Williamson & Hogan, 2021, p. 28). Fonseca, García-Peñalvo, and Camba (2020) observe that "Educational data usability and accessibility is even more relevant in the context of the global pandemic" (p. 1).

In reflecting on the potential of learning analytics to ameliorate teaching in the dark, we first share some empirical evidence of how learning analytics has been considered and applied during the pandemic in its first year or so. We then consider the implications and potential of learning analytics in a time of pandemic, concluding with an initial list of recommendations.

Some Notes on the Nature of Conceptual Exploration

This chapter presents a conceptual exploration of the potential of learning analytics to inform teaching and learning during extraordinary contextual events, such as the recent and continuing impact of COVID-19. We are cognisant of the suggestion made by Hirschheim (2008) that conceptual work should "emphasise assumptions, premises, axioms, assertions, etc.; and these need to be made as explicit as possible so they can be evaluated" (p. 435). According to Hirschheim, the essential components of conceptual papers are claims, grounds, and warrants. *Claims* are statements that authors want the reader to accept as true, while *grounds* are constituted by the methods and data authors use as evidence to their claims. *Warrants* "are the assumptions or presuppositions underlying the argument. They are often unstated or implied, and typically not debated" (p. 345). Whetten (1989) suggests that theoretical and conceptual papers should "challenge and extend existing knowledge, not simply . . . rewrite it. Therefore, authors should push back the boundaries of our knowledge by providing compelling and logical justifications for altered views" (p. 491). He points out that it is not the addition or listing of new variables that add value, but how those new variables change relationships in existing frameworks. He refers to Poincare (1983, in Whetten, 1989, p. 492), who notes that "Science is facts, just as houses are made of stone . . . But a pile of stones is not a house, and a collection of facts is not necessarily science."

Following Hirschheim (2008) and Whetten (1989), the following claims, grounds, and warrants are central to this chapter:

- We *claim* that learning analytics has potential to be an essential tool for institutions, educators, and student-support teams during disruptive macro-societal events.

- The *grounds* for this claim are based on empirical evidence that learning analytics has provided insights into student learning behaviours (albeit under normal circumstances).
- The *warrants* of our claim are based around the assumption that as institutions moved to Emergency Online Remote Teaching (EORT), they have had access to digital traces of student behaviour that could be used to support students and inform pedagogical strategies and which may also be used in future events.

The next section explores evidence that has emerged regarding uses of learning analytics during the pandemic, and, with this as a basis, we discuss the implications and the (un)realised potential of learning analytics. The chapter concludes with tentative recommendations.

Glimpses of Learning Analytics During the Pandemic

Recent research from Prinsloo, Khalil, and Slade (2021) adopted a systematic review exploring citations of applications of learning analytics since the start of the pandemic. Perhaps surprisingly, only 18 articles were found to specifically mention or address the potential and/or practice of learning analytics in this context. Prinsloo et al. (2021) suggest that, despite this apparent lack of reported research, we should not conclude that learning analytics or research into learning analytics has missed an opportunity to appropriately and ethically engage with student data at this time. It is likely that further findings and more detailed analyses of the response of learning analytics to the pandemic will emerge over time.

Flowing from their review, Prinsloo et al. (2021) identify the following dominant themes:

- **Multimodal analytics.** Research covering multimodal learning analytics has increased in recent years (Blikstein & Worsley, 2016). With a move away from fixed, traditional places of learning, multimodal learning analytics was identified as having potential to overcome many of the issues facing educators and students operating at a distance, such as providing a flexible means to offer real-time feedback to students and to support and foster greater collaboration.
- **Student perceptions and student privacy.** Perhaps understandably, given the haste with which many institutions, educators, and students responded to the rapid move to online teaching and learning, issues around ethical uses of student data and privacy emerged as another key theme. For many, the need to adopt emergency approaches meant that there was little time to consider the wider implications of a significant increase in generated data trails.

- **Adaptive learning.** In the absence of time to translate learning materials created with classroom delivery in mind, adaptive learning emerged as one approach flagged as potentially helpful in enabling the creation of customised resources and learning activities to address the unique needs of learners.
- **Artificial intelligence (AI), machine learning and predictive analytics.** The potential, challenges, and implications of AI, machine learning and predictive analytics were key themes. AI offers the potential to support a personalised, student-centred approach to learning, with big data facilitating improved engagement and reduced drop out. Learning analytics has supported understanding assessment, enriching views on learners' motivation, and participation during the pandemic.
- **Student behaviour and engagement.** Learning analytics has offered a unique opportunity to explore student engagement and behaviours, as well as their perceptions of engagement strategies during emergency online learning. Specific approaches, such as social network analysis, offer potential to better understand learners' paths during the pandemic. Additionally, the ability to self-regulate learning is key in the light of a rapid transition to online learning—learning analytics was identified as one means to support effective self-regulated learning.
- **Data literacy.** Data literacy has always been a key component for effective applications of learning analytics. In the context of the increased collection, analysis, and use of data during the pandemic, data literacy becomes even more vital. The concept of "pandemic pedagogies" (Barbour et al., 2020) comes to the fore, as educators scrambled to make sense of unfamiliar conditions. Concerns exist around the ways that educators have sought to make sense of student data whilst lacking sufficient data literacy skills and in the broader datafication of education resulting from the adoption of third-party technologies.
- **Teacher development.** Although data literacy is flagged as a possible shortcoming of moves to online teaching; there was also recognition of the potential of learning analytics to facilitate improved teacher performance—for example, by enabling comparisons of teacher performance and through the adoption of smart learning environments.

Since this study (Prinsloo et al., 2021), a number of later articles focusing on learning analytics during the pandemic have emerged, such as Zhang, Taub, and Chen (2020), Xu and Wilson (2021), Wood-Harper (2021), as well as Hilliger, Miranda, Schuit, Duarte, Anselmo, and Parra (2021). Though it falls outside the scope of this chapter to provide an overview of all of the relevant published research, we have sought to include references to several recent publications in the following discussion.

Implications and (Un)Realised Potential of Learning Analytics

We mentioned earlier that the move to teaching and learning in online environments during the pandemic had caused educators, administrators, and student support to feel the loss of direct student contact, with the result that they were 'teaching in the dark'. This may appear to contradict the notion that the move of teaching and learning to online yielded access to a greater quantity, variety, granularity, and velocity of behavioural data than before. However, there has emerged a greater understanding of the digital divide, with many students and staff not having regular, sustainable, and affordable access to the internet as might have been assumed before the pandemic (Czerniewicz et al., 2020). The assumption that educators have had access to more student data than before does not perhaps reflect reality. Even if we assume an increase in the availability of student data, many institutions did not have the data infrastructures, data expertise, as well as policies and processes to optimise the analysis of that data.

Prinsloo, Khalil, and Slade (2021) also posit that during the pandemic, some students and educators opted for alternative ways of communications outside of the institutional LMS—for example, by using WhatsApp®, Telegram®, or Signal™, as well as Zoom®, Google® Hangouts, and a variety of other social media. Educators also looked for different software and apps to facilitate teaching and learning, and many of these were not linked to the institutional LMS. Most learning analytics approaches rely on a combination of institutional registration and administrative systems in combination with data from the LMS to analyse and use student data (Khalil, 2018). As learning has moved outside of the LMS, the potential for learning analytics to provide insights into student progress, needs, potential, and risk may have been impacted.

Brown (2021) claims that COVID-19 has upended "data analytics practices, side lining predictive analytics, and driving firms to external data and other economic indicators". While predictive analytics has dominated evidence-based research in recent years, the pandemic led to many companies moving instead toward descriptive analytics and pausing machine learning initiatives, "taking the time to figure out what information is still relevant". There have also been organisational moves to consider external data as indicators, offering insight on how COVID might impact. As such, the role of data has not changed, but the value of past data and external data has been revaluated.

The themes identified by Prinsloo, Khalil, and Slade (2021), make clear how crucial learning analytics can be to institutions, instructional teams, and students in order to adapt in extraordinary circumstances. As artificial intelligence (AI) and machine learning depend on the availability of data to operationalise adaptive teaching and learning as well as predictive analytics, the changing behaviours of

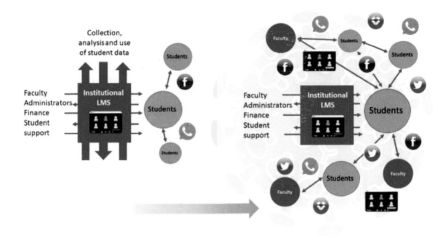

Figure 5.1 Distributed Learning in a Time of Pandemics

both students and educators during the pandemic and the resulting data trails have important implications. How learning analytics responds to these changes, the quantity, variety, granularity, and velocity of data and the integration of different social media into the learning platform remains to be seen. Figure 5.1 illustrates how teaching and learning became increasingly unbundled as a result of faculty and students adopting a range of tools to communicate during the pandemic.

While the figure above illustrates how teaching and learning became, in a sense, disaggregated during the pandemic, this was not the only change. We should also consider changes in assessment strategies, pedagogy, and student support, as well as the disruption to students' reliance on campus-based support and resources. A more pertinent question for this chapter is to consider the implications for learning analytics during (and following) a pandemic. In the following section, we consider mapping a number of distinctive, but interrelated, concepts and operations as enabling conditions for the potential of learning analytics to be fully realised.

Conceptual Operations

The pandemic has not only affirmed the importance and potential of learning analytics but also provided pointers for realising its potential. In this section, we discuss six interrelated and often overlapping conceptual operations that we believe provide the enabling conditions for reconsidering learning analytics. Figure 5.2 provides an overview.

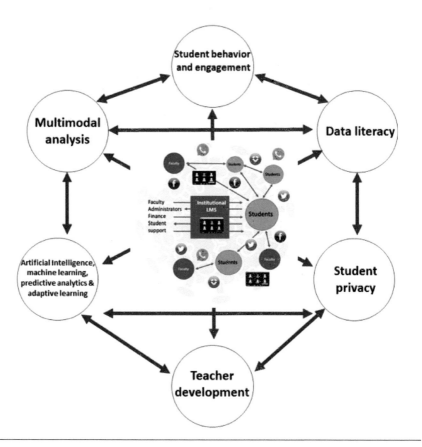

Figure 5.2   Lessons from a Pandemic: Six Conceptual Operations for Realising the Potential of Learning Analytics

It is crucial to reiterate that the six conceptual operations should be read as interlinked and interdependent. For example, one cannot talk about student behaviour and engagement without also considering multimodal learning analytics and student privacy.

- **Student behaviour and engagement.** Learning analytics can help in examining student behaviour in the times when extraordinary events such as COVID-19 significantly affect education as a system, from administration to student support, finances, ICT, teaching, and learning. There has not been an event affecting education on such a global level for many decades. The pandemic has not only raised the importance of self-regulated learning and engagement but also reiterated the need to look afresh at the data we have access to and at our assumptions about those data and what such data can tell us about student behaviour and engagement during extraordinary times. A providential example is the study by Zhang, Taub, and Chen (2021). This sought to measure the impact of COVID-19 on student engagement and self-regulated learning processes by analysing log data and flagging issues appearing to affect student planning and progress in completing their studies. Learning analytics has a clear role to play in informing a variety of stakeholders (including but not limited to students, teachers, and higher management) about the impact of disruptive events such as the pandemic. It can provide useful overviews of evolving trends of learning behaviour and facilitate timely and effective interventions. In the example of Zhang et al. (2021), the observations and the analyses of clickstream data provided an excellent mapping of the rate of student attempts, identifying those falling behind and guessing, and yielded to a view of how students responded with changing strategies during the pandemic.

- **Multimodal.** As the move to EORT and the resulting 'unbundling' of teaching and learning during the pandemic has shown (refer to Figure 5.1), it became more difficult to use visual, auditory, and kinaesthetic sensors (i.e., multimodal) away from local settings and in remote learning setups. The pandemic has raised important questions pertaining to multimodal learning analytics as students and teachers have moved to more disaggregated learning spaces, both formal and informal, outside of the 'normal' catchment data collection networks traditionally associated with multimodal learning analytics. An example of the reconfiguration of multimodal learning analytics is research from Cornide-Reyes et al., (2020) who developed a multimodal learning analytics platform for remote learning situations. Their real-time feedback platform captures, stores, analyses, and visualizes spoken interactions between individuals participating in remote group activities. This is one example of how the pandemic has accelerated the operationalisation of new features such as hybrid models of web and mobile data sources. Earlier work by Antoniadou (2017) has explored applications of multimodality which "may include image, sound, music, gestures, posture, even the use of space, which is nowadays virtual or blended. Meaning is multimodal, conveyed by image, text, interaction, sound, and music in unique and complementary ways, each adding a particular value to the whole; this added value cannot be deduced or obtained from any of the other modalities" (p. 436). Through a mixture of auditory input, dashboards, and log files, multimodal learning analytics offers opportunities to review and recommend expanding the use of technologies to support academic activities during periods of disruptive change.
- **AI, machine learning, predictive analytics, as well as adaptive learning.** How can AI, machine learning, and adaptive learning within the context of learning analytics help in a time of pandemic? As stated previously, institutions have had access to a greater range of data from a broader

range of sources. While few may have doubted the potential of AI, machine learning, and predictive analytics prior to the pandemic, authors such as Brown (2021) alert us to the ways in which the pandemic has changed the data and data analytics landscape. A greater focus on understanding broader societal changes external to the organisation and how these might impact on performance has emerged. Data professionals are increasingly acting like 'epidemiologists' and trying to make sense of what might happen by employing current data and external indicators. Brown (2021) suggests that the nature and role of data analytics have changed as a result of the pandemic. We should then consider any parallel impact on learning analytics, given the move to EORT. Villegas-ch et al. (2020) state that "face-to-face models went virtual . . . the change was so abrupt that both resources and learning activities designed in a face-to-face education model were not adjusted to the new needs of the students" (p. 2). We do not doubt that computer and data-driven (e.g., AI, machine learning) methods will continue to operationalise adaptive learning to more fully deliver student-centred learning but wonder whether there will be a renewed appreciation of descriptive analytics. Brown (2021) warns of the risks of using existing machine learning models, despite the preponderance of student data as a result of learning and teaching online. A relatively sudden change in data (type, quantity, etc.) may decay the performance of predictive models built on AI and machine learning models. This is known as 'concept drift' (Xu & Wilson, 2021), whereby "the problem that how and whether data is collected and how it relates to outcomes changes over time" (p. 505). The pandemic has led to major disruptions, refashioning educational data collection, which in turn has altered the quality and potentially the meaning of education data gathered. In this context, the call for action is to re-examine whether current AI and machine learning modules function similarly post-pandemic to the pre-pandemic era. Xu and Wilson (2021) suggest the inclusion of a socio-political dimension.

- **Teacher development.** In the context of the Prinsloo et al. (2021) systematic review, teacher development refers to the potential of analytics to flag areas for teacher training, rather than to the development of analytics skills for teachers (partially covered under data literacy, below). Although some feel that evaluating teaching performance is key to improving teaching quality (see, for example, Chena, Hsieha, & Do, 2015), it is fair to say that the use of analytics to assess teacher performance remains complex and contentious. At the institutional level, any such measure must be defensible as a "specific quantitative or qualitative representation of a capacity, process or outcome deemed relevant to the assessment of performance" (Molefe, 2010). Amongst the complexities associated with the use of teacher analytics, Dean (2014) suggests the need for context to be considered (different subject areas, levels of student experience, etc. may all impact on outcomes or instructor perceptions) and for any data-driven performance snapshots to be both valid and complete—that is, not skewed by a minority of very negative or positive results. This is not to say that teacher analytics do not or should not have a role, but that any system must be first agreed with recognised teaching representatives as fair and representative for a particular role and context (taking account of, for example, other institutional responsibilities). Performance analytics should be robust in that they are driven by statistically significant datasets and interpreted correctly, should be transparent and meaningful to both teacher and institution, and available to students only if formally agreed. In the context of short-term, rapid changes to teaching practices brought about by the pandemic, it will be particularly challenging to ensure that standards for analytics intended to drive improvements in teaching are well considered before implementation.

- **Student privacy.** Issues around privacy have long been part of the conversation around ethical uses of student data for learning analytics (e.g., Slade and Prinsloo, 2013; Khalil & Ebner, 2016). However, the rapid move to online learning has perhaps exacerbated privacy issues. In the haste to adapt traditional teaching to an online setting, many institutions will undoubtedly have opted for technologies which promote availability and ease of use and, at the same time, minimise cost, rather than selecting products or platforms with clear privacy protections in mind (Duball, 2020). Whilst educational institutions will have internal data-protection policies in place, the use of third-party technologies opens the door to the additional collection and potential use of students' personal information. In certain cases—for example, for school age learners—such uses may contravene laws, such as the US Family Educational Rights and Privacy Act. Certainly within the US, many education technology providers are built around their capacity to monetise student data and to extend the surveillance of students' learning experiences before, throughout, and after higher education.

  For those institutions adopting external products, the impacts of any loosening of privacy principles may only reveal themselves long after the event. For others, there may yet be time to more fully assess the appropriateness of external technologies. Whilst the onus is on the institution to ensure continued protections of student data, technology companies should also take some responsibility when interacting with the education sector, particularly where that involves school-age learners. In such cases, privacy policies should be made more transparent, with potential risks highlighted (Duball, 2020).

- **Data literacy.** While understanding data—its collection, analysis, and use—has always been thought to be the purview of data analysts, researchers, and departments of institutional research, there is recognition that a broader range of stakeholders, including students, faculty, and student-support staff needs to be data literate (Raffaghelli & Stewart, 2020). With an increasing use of student and instructor-facing dashboards, data literacy is no longer a luxury but an essential component of learning analytics (Ifenthaler, Gibson, Prasse, Shimada, & Yamada, 2020; Verbert, Ochoa, De Croon, Dourado, & De Laet, 2020). There is a need to connect the dots in making sense not only of data but also of its analysis and application, and this is as important for students and faculty as it is for researchers and data analysts (Tsai, Kovanović, & Gašević, 2021). Indeed, it is part and parcel of responsible learning analytics (Jaakonmäki, vom Brocke, Dietze, Drachsler, Fortenbacher, Helbig, . . . & Yun, 2020).

The pandemic has destabilised many of our assumptions about data categories—for example, understanding patterns of login data during these extraordinary times, when pedagogies and student behaviours have changed and when concerns about the increasing surveillance of students have reached all-time highs (Chin, 2021; Doffman, 2020). It is to be expected that our pre-pandemic understanding of data literacy will be an evolving issue.

Conclusions

In this chapter, we worked from an assumption that the COVID-19 pandemic created an opportunity to interrogate assumptions around student data and specifically learning analytics as a basis for (re)considering its potential. As the pandemic unfolded and disrupted education on a global scale, many educators have felt that they were teaching in the dark, not knowing whether or how students were engaging and coping. To compound matters, the pandemic unbundled the primary role of the institutional LMS as teachers and students adopted apps and tools outside of the LMS. Where once the LMS had facilitated the collection of student learning and behavioural data as a feed for machine learning and AI, the feed was disrupted. This has impacted on the capacity of many institutions to predict student behaviour and provide personalised feedback, weakening what we know about how students learn and engage during extraordinary events or major changes, scaling back the usefulness of predictive analytics and machine learning (e.g., Brown, 2021).

This chapter has taken a broad look at how learning analytics was used during the pandemic, using a range of published papers. As a conceptual paper, we have employed Hirschheim's (2008) claims, grounds, and warrants. We had claimed that learning analytics is an essential tool for institutions, educators, and student-support teams during pandemics or disruptive macro-societal events. The grounds for this were based on historical empirical evidence that learning analytics has provided insights into the learning behaviour of students (albeit under normal circumstances).

The warrant for our claim was that institutions moving to Emergency Online Remote Teaching (EORT) had resulted in increased digitalisation of teaching and learning, which was then datafied on a scale previously unheard of. Educators and institutions had access to digital traces of student behaviour that could be used to support students and inform pedagogical strategies and which might also be used in future events. However, as learning during COVID became unbundled (as illustrated in Figure 5.1), a number of assumptions informing learning analytics also evolved, such as the nature and sources of data, the potential of AI and predictive analytics, and concerns about student privacy, to mention but a few. The value contribution of this chapter is in our tentative mapping of the conceptual operations in need of consideration in realising the potential of learning analytics going forward.

References

Anderson, J. (2020). *The Coronavirus Pandemic Is Reshaping Education*. Quartz. https://qz.com/1826369/how-coronavirus-is-changing-education/.

Antoniadou, V. (2017). Collecting, organizing and analyzing multimodal data sets: The contributions of CAQDAS. In E. Moore and M. Dooly (Eds), *Qualitative Approaches to Research on Plurilingual Education*, 435–450. Research-publishing.net

Bañeres, D., Rodríguez, M. E., Guerrero-Roldán, A. E., and Karadeniz, A. (2020). An early warning system to detect at-risk students in online higher education. *Applied Sciences. 10*(13):4427. https://doi.org/10.3390/app10134427

Barbour, M. K., LaBonte, R., Hodges, C., Moore, S., Lockee, B. B., Trust, T., Bond, M. A., Hill, P., and Kelly, K. (2020). *Understanding Pandemic Pedagogy: Differences Between Emergency Remote, Remote, and Online Teaching*. https://doi.org/10.13140/RG.2.2.31848.70401.

Blikstein, P., and Worsley, M. A. B. (2016). Multimodal learning analytics and education data mining: Using computational technologies to measure complex learning tasks. *The Journal of Learning Analytics, 3*(2), 220–238. http://learning-analytics.info/journals/index.php/JLA/article/view/4383

Brown, S. (2021). How COVID-19 is disrupting data analytics strategies. MIT Sloan. Retrieved from https://mitsloan.mit.edu/ideas-made-to-matter/how-covid-19-disrupting-data-analytics-strategies

Chena, J-F., Hsieha, H-N., Do, Q. (2015). Evaluating teaching performance based on fuzzy AHP and comprehensive evaluation approach. *Applied Soft Computing, 28*, 100–108.

Chin, M. (2021). University will stop using controversial remote-testing software following student outcry. *The Verge*. Retrieved from https://www.theverge.com/2021/1/28/22254631/university-of-illinois-urbana-champaign-proctorio-online-test-proctoring-privacy

Choi, Y., and McClenen, C. (2020). Development of adaptive formative assessment system using computerized adaptive testing and dynamic Bayesian networks. *Applied Sciences, 10*(22), 8196. doi:10.3390/app10228196

Cornide-Reyes, H., Riquelme, F., Monsalves, D., Noel, R., Cechinel, C., Villarroel, R., Ponce, F., and Munoz, R. (2020). A multimodal real-time feedback platform based on spoken interactions for remote active learning support. *Sensors, 20*(21), 6337.

Curum, B., and Khedo, K.K. (2021). Cognitive load management in mobile learning systems: Principles and theories. *Journal of Computers in Education, 8,* 109–136. https://doi.org/10.1007/s40692-020-00173-6

Czerniewicz, L., Agherdien, N., Badenhorst, J., Belluigi, D., Chambers, T., Chili, M., De Villiers, M., Felix, A., Gachago, D., Gokhale, C., Ivala, E., Kramm, N., Madiba, M., Mistri, G., Mgqwashu, E., Pallitt, N., Prinsloo, P., Solomon, K., Strydom, S., … Wissing, G. (2020). A wake-up call: Equity, inequality and COVID-19 emergency remote teaching and learning. *Postdigital Science and Education, 2*(3), 946–967.

Dean, K. L. (2014, January). It's not just Rate My Professor anymore! Ethical issues with student evaluations of teaching (SET). *Academy of Management.* Weblog retrieved from https://connect.aom.org/blogs/kathy-lund-dean/2014/01/21/its-not-just-rate-my-professor-anymore-ethical-issues-with-student-evaluations-of-teaching-set.

Doffman, Z. (2020). Exam monitoring webcam tech meets student outrage. *Forbes.* Retrieved from https://www.forbes.com/sites/zakdoffman/2020/04/24/no-lockdown-exams-sorry-kids-this-creepy-webcam-tech-lets-you-sit-them-at-home/?sh=28207ef25cc5

Duball, J. (2020). Shift to online learning ignites student privacy concerns. Retrieved from https://iapp.org/news/a/shift-to-online-learning-ignites-student-privacy-concerns/

Eryilmaz, E., Thoms, B., Ahmed, Z. et al. (2021). Effects of recommendations on message quality and community formation in online conversations. *Education and Information Technologies, 26,* 49–68. https://doi.org/10.1007/s10639-020-10364

Fonseca, D., García-Peñalvo, F. J. and Camba, J. D. (2020). New methods and technologies for enhancing usability and accessibility of educational data. *Universal Access in the Information Society.* https://doi.org/10.1007/s10209-020-00765-0

Hilliger, I., Miranda, C., Schuit, G., Duarte, F., Anselmo, M., and Parra, D. (2021, April). Evaluating a learning analytics dashboard to visualize student self-reports of time-on-task: A case study in a Latin American university. In *LAK21: 11th International Learning Analytics and Knowledge Conference,* 592–598.

Hirschheim, R. (2008). Some guidelines for the critical reviewing of conceptual papers. *Journal of the Association for Information Systems, 9*(8), 432–441.

Ifenthaler, D., Gibson, D., Prasse, D., Shimada, A., and Yamada, M. (2020). Putting learning back into learning analytics: Actions for policy makers, researchers, and practitioners. *Educational Technology Research and Development,* 1–20.

Ifenthaler, D., and Yau, J. Y. K. (2020). Utilising learning analytics to support study success in higher education: A systematic review. *Educational Technology Research and Development, 68*(4), 1961–1990.

Jaakonmäki, R., vom Brocke, J., Dietze, S., Drachsler, H., Fortenbacher, A., Helbig, R., . . . & Yun, H. (2020). Responsible cooking with learning analytics. In: *Learning Analytics Cookbook,* 15–30. Springer, Cham.

Joksimović, S., Kovanović, V., and Dawson, S. (2019). The journey of learning analytics. *HERDSA Review of Higher Education*, 6, 27–63.

Khalil, M., and Ebner, M. (2016). De-identification in learning analytics. *Journal of Learning Analytics*, 3(1), 129–138.

Khalil, M. (2018). *Learning Analytics in Massive Open Online Courses*. arXiv preprint arXiv:1802.09344.

Macfadyen, L. P., Lockyer, L., and Rienties, B. (2020). Learning design and learning analytics: Snapshot 2020. *Journal of Learning Analytics*, 7(3), 6–12. https://doi .org/10.18608/jla.2020.73.2

Machado, R. A., Bonan, P. R. F., Perez, D. E. da Cruz, and Martelli Junior, H. (2020). COVID-19 pandemic and the impact on dental education: Discussing current and future perspectives. *Brazilian Oral Research, 34*, e083. Epub June 29, 2020. https:// dx.doi.org/10.1590/1807-3107bor-2020.vol34.0083

Molefe, G. (2010). Performance measurement dimensions for lecturers at selected universities: An international perspective. *SA Journal of Human Resource Management, 8*(1), Art. #243, 13 pages. DOI: 10.4102/sajhrm.v8i1.243

Prinsloo, P., and Slade, S. (2019). Mapping *responsible* learning analytics: A critical proposal. In: B. H. Khan, R. Corbeil, and M. E. Corbeil (Eds.), *Responsible Analytics and Data Mining in Education*, 63–80. London: Routledge.

Prinsloo, P., Khalil, M., and Slade, S. (2021). Learning analytics in a time of pandemics: mapping the field. In: *Proceedings of the European Distance and E-Learning Network Annual Conference*, EDEN'21.

Raffaghelli, J. E., and Stewart, B. (2020). Centering complexity in 'educators' data literacy' to support future practices in faculty development: A systematic review of the literature. *Teaching in Higher Education*, 25(4), 435–455.

Sáiz-Manzanares, M. C., Marticorena-Sánchez, R., and Ochoa-Orihuel, J. (2020). Effectiveness of using voice assistants in learning: A study at the time of COVID-19. *International Journal of Environmental Research and Public Health*, 17(15), 5618. doi:10.3390/ijerph17155618

Siemens, G. (2013). Learning analytics: The emergence of a discipline. *American Behavioral Scientist, 57*(10), 1380–1400.

Slade, S., and Prinsloo, P. (2013). Learning analytics: Ethical issues and dilemmas. *American Behavioral Scientist, 57*(10), 1510–1529. https://doi.org/10.1177 /0002764213479366

Tsai, Y. S., Kovanović, V., and Gašević, D. (2021). Connecting the dots: An exploratory study on learning analytics adoption factors, experience, and priorities. *The Internet and Higher Education, 50*, 100794.

Verbert, K., Ochoa, X., De Croon, R., Dourado, R. A., and De Laet, T. (2020, March). Learning analytics dashboards: The past, the present and the future. In *Proceedings of the Tenth International Conference on Learning Analytics & Knowledge*, 35–40.

Villegas-Ch, W., Roman-Cañizares, M., Jaramillo-Alcázar, A., and Palacios-Pacheco, X. (2020). Data analysis as a tool for the application of adaptive learning in a university environment. *Applied Sciences, 10*(20), 7016.

Whetten, D. (1989). What constitutes a theoretical contribution? *Academy of Management Review, 14,* 490–495.

Williamson, B., and Hogan, A. (2021). Pandemic privatisation in higher education: Edtech & university reform. *Education International,* Brussels, Belguim. https://eprints.qut. edu.au/209029/

Wood-Harper, T. (2021). Emerging EdTechs amidst the COVID-19 pandemic: Cases in higher education institutions. *Fostering Communication and Learning with Underutilized Technologies in Higher Education,* 93–107.

Xu, Y., and Wilson, K. (2021). Early alert systems during a pandemic: A simulation study on the impact of concept drift. In *LAK21: 11th International Learning Analytics and Knowledge Conference,* 504–510.

Zhang, T., Taub, M., and Chen, Z. (2020). Measuring the impact of COVID–19 induced campus closure on student self-regulated learning in physics online learning modules. In: *Learning Analytics and Knowledge '21.* ACM, New York, NY, USA, 16 pages.

Chapter 6

Using Learning Analytics and Instructional Design to Inform, Find, and Scale Quality Online Learning

John Fritz, Mariann Hawken, and Sarah Shin[1]

Abstract

How do we improve the perception and experience of online learning? In this chapter, we use the COVID-19 pandemic teaching experience of the University of Maryland, Baltimore County (UMBC), as a case study in how institutions might leverage learning analytics and instructional design to inform, find, and scale the quality of the online learning experience and outcomes for both faculty and students. To do so, we offer a selected review of the research and practice about online learning quality generally (albeit before its largest implementation to date), followed by UMBC's thought leadership in learning analytics, which has helped create a foundation and culture of assessment. Then, using our Planning Instructional Variety in Online Teaching (PIVOT) initiative as a response to the pandemic, we focus especially on outcomes assessment baked into the planning process to show the impact faculty training can have on the perception and reality of online learning quality. However, to bring about lasting change

---

[1] University of Maryland, Baltimore County (UMBC)

beyond an immediate crisis, we also need to change the culture. We need to win the hearts and minds of faculty by clearly showing the benefits of quality design and delivery of online education.

Keywords: Learning analytics, instructional design, quality online learning, impact, pedagogical innovation

Introduction

During a recent panel presentation at an online learning leadership conference, moderator Tom Cavanagh, who is Vice Provost for Digital Learning at the University of Central Florida (UCF), asked a simple but profound question: "What are we going to do when the backlash against online instruction occurs after the pandemic?" (2021).

Cavanagh's question hits a nerve for several reasons. First, it is somewhat surprising coming from a leader at UCF, considered by many to be one of the largest and most experienced institutions to effectively use online learning for student success. Cavanagh's UCF colleagues, Kelvin Thompson and Patsy Moskal, even attempted to manage expectations early in the coronavirus pandemic by arguing that a rapid move to widespread remote instruction was not the same as intentionally designed online learning (2020). But if UCF can expect a backlash about online learning, chances are that most institutions should do so as well.

Second, Cavanagh's question speaks to a perception that may be widespread among many institutions: the pandemic caught higher ed by surprise, leaving faculty and students little time to prepare for or adjust to virtual instruction—indeed virtual institutions, too. As such, was this a mass improvement—by scaling—of online learning quality or a mass demonstration of the status quo when the Covid meteor hit? While higher ed's massive pandemic pivot to online learning rivals what the most ardent MOOC proponents could ever have hoped for, a new backlash could make it even harder to win long-term institutional investment in online learning as a strategic priority, as EDUCAUSE recently reported (McCormack, 2021). You can just hear it now, with accompanying eye rolls: "Oh, we tried online learning during the pandemic. It didn't work."

Finally, was the massive scale of online learning only "temporarily strategic," to get through a global health crisis? Or did something happen that will fundamentally transform teaching and learning going forward? Only time will tell, but given predictions about a looming "demographic cliff" projecting a dramatic decline in the number of traditional 18- to 22-year-old, college-aged students (Hoover, 2020), the pandemic pivot to online learning could be a rehearsal for more flexible forms of learning that will appeal to—and be required by—a wider group of adult degree seekers. At UMBC, we have even seen that play out through our Finish Line[2] near completer re-engagement initiative made possible by our new-found supply of online courses (Rous et al., 2021).

In this chapter, we wish to use the pandemic teaching experience of the University of Maryland, Baltimore County (UMBC) as a case study in how institutions might leverage instructional design and learning analytics to inform, assess, and scale quality of the online learning experience and outcomes for both faculty and students. To do so, we'll first provide a brief, selected review of the research and practice about online learning quality generally (albeit before the largest implementation to date), followed by UMBC's thought leadership in learning analytics that has helped create a foundation and culture of assessment. Then, using our Planning Instructional Variety in Online Teaching (PIVOT) initiative,[3] we'll focus especially on outcomes assessment baked into the planning process so we could report on the impact that faculty training can have on the perception and reality of online learning quality—even during a pandemic.

Selected Research and Practice About Online Learning Quality

Even before the pandemic, there has been an extensive body of research and practice exploring (and debating) the quality of online learning, especially compared to traditional, face-to-face (F2F) learning.[4] A few key themes are worth summarizing to help frame our discussion of post-pandemic online learning quality generally and the UMBC case study specifically.

First, QualityMatters™ (QM)[5] is one of the most highly respected, research-based[6] standards organizations for supporting and promoting quality in online

---

[2] https://undergraduate.umbc.edu/finishline/

[3] http://pivot.umbc.edu

[4] A good example is the No Significant Difference database (https://detaresearch.org/research-support/no-significant-difference) "first established in 2004 as a companion piece to Thomas L. Russell's book, The No Significant Difference Phenomenon (2001, IDECC, fifth edition), a fully indexed, comprehensive research bibliography of 355 research reports, summaries, and papers that document no significant differences (NSD) in student outcomes between alternate modes of education delivery. Redesigned in 2010 and provided as a service of WCET, (WICHE Cooperative for Educational Technologies), a division of the Western Interstate Commission for Higher Education, the database was designed to expand the offerings from the book by providing access to appropriate studies published or discovered after its publication."

[5] http://www.qualitymatters.org/

[6] https://www.qualitymatters.org/research

and hybrid course design. QM is subscription funded, but it actually began as MarylandOnline through a grant from the U.S. Department of Education's Fund for the Improvement of Postsecondary Education (FIPSE). UMBC has had an institutional license for years, and QM informed a 2014 redesign of our Alternate Delivery Program (ADP),[7] which was the basis for our PIVOT program during the coronavirus pandemic.

Currently used by more than 40,000 educators throughout the world (Adair & Shattuck, 2015), QM offers peer review of online and hybrid courses using its rubric.[8] Currently in its sixth edition, the rubric is available for higher education, K–12, and continuing/professional education. A central theme in the QM rubric and course review process is ensuring alignment where assessments, learner engagement, instructional materials, and course tools reinforce and support the course and unit-level learning objectives. As such, QM standards inform course *design* and not course *delivery,* which can also be less threatening when initially introducing a rubric of "quality standards" to faculty.

Second, in 2019, the e-Literate blog known for touting "what we're learning online about online learning" published an extensive, three-part review of seven rubrics (including QM) about online learning quality.[9] In Part 1, the series author, Kevin Kelly, states that, "Currently, the primary method to scale online course quality is through the use of rubrics that inform online course (re)design." In Part 2, Kelly specifically references the Quality Matters Research Library,[10] which "can be searched by standard or keyword and a set of Curated Resources"[11]:

Of these 25 curated studies, four studies . . . look at the end results, or to what extent redesigning a course based on the rubric affects students completing and/or passing a course. An equal number of studies investigate . . . changes in faculty behavior as a result of training and exposure to the rubric.

In Part 3 of the e-Literate series, Kelly critiques most online rubrics (including QM's) for not including student engagement or interaction data as part of the calculus for determining online learning quality. In other words, most rubrics look at the quality of an online or hybrid course *design* (before students ever see or participate in the course). But what happens if faculty design or intent does not match or satisfy the student expectations or experience? The result could be a mismatch in perceived vs. actual experience of online learning quality. As Kelly notes:

---

[7] https://doit.umbc.edu/itnm/adp/
[8] https://www.qualitymatters.org/rubric
[9] https://eliterate.us/online-course-design-rubrics-part-1-what-are-they
[10] https://www.qmprogram.org/qmresources/research/
[11] https://www.qualitymatters.org/research/curated-research-resources

If both the research literature and the accreditation bodies state that interaction, community, and the like are critical to online student persistence and success, then the online course design rubric providers should provide more criteria for and guidance about reviewing faculty-student and student-student interaction after the course has begun.

The continuous improvement process fostered by QM, however, supports additional reflection on both course design and instruction, encouraging faculty and institutions to explore and define what quality means to online learning (Martin et al., 2019). Additional metrics often leveraged to describe or identify quality in online learning include, but are not limited to, course evaluations and faculty peer feedback. Since many quality assurance rubrics do not assess delivery, including QM, extensive engagement indicators may also be useful for identifying quality (Southard & Mooney, 2015). Multidimensional checklists and engagement frameworks may encourage faculty and students to assess planned and actual engagement level as well as evidence of active learning (Bigatel & Edel-Malizia, 2018); however, these require frequent monitoring and reflection that may not be feasible with certain types of online courses.

Here is why combining instructional design with learning analytics may help by marrying course design (or intent) with user experience data and outcomes. In the section that follows, we'll first define learning analytics and then summarize how it has been applied to both student success interventions and faculty course design at UMBC. As we shall see, much of the infrastructure for evaluating the impact of UMBC's pandemic-related faculty training initiative was already in place beforehand, which is why we were able to quickly leverage it to roll out and assess the PIVOT program.

Learning Analytics in Higher Ed and at UMBC

Learning analytics (LA) is frequently defined as "the collection and analysis of usage data associated with student learning," the purpose of which is "to observe and understand learning behaviors in order to enable appropriate interventions" (Brown, 2011). Given the specific focus on *interventions,* not just *analysis,* learning analytics—like analytics or "business intelligence" generally—has also become known as "actionable intelligence." This is important because, while final grades in prerequisite courses are necessary for degree progression, they occur too late in the semester for actionable interventions that might help students while taking the course.

Accordingly, LA is often associated with students' use of digital tools such as the campus learning management system (LMS), the most widely used instructional technology in higher education, precisely because it may be possible to infer students' time, attention, effort, and even engagement earlier in a term. While grade point average (GPA) and course credits support a perspective of student success *across* terms—in order to complete graduation requirements—learning analytics typically tries to look at student engagement *during* a term, preferably as early as possible, when there may be more time to change a student's projected trajectory and outcome.

However, this is also important: student usage data in an IT system is not the same as student learning itself, which has led some researchers understandably to distinguish between "learner analytics" and "learning analytics" (Bishop, 2017). As such, it's best to look at students' "digital footprints" in campus IT systems as a *proxy* for engagement, which might be correlated with academic performance such as final grades and GPA. Many social science studies use proxies to operationalize concepts that may be inherently difficult to measure (e.g., social capital, standard of living, belonging, resilience, etc.), and LA is no different.

For well over a decade, UMBC has been a thought-leading institution in higher education's maturing use of learning analytics.[12] For example, consider the following, which we have observed as an institution through the use of LA:

- Since 2008, students earning a D or F typically use our Blackboard (Bb) LMS 40% less than peers earning higher grades. At the time, usage or activity simply meant "hits and clicks"—recorded when they log into Bb, access a course, click on content, post in a discussion board, or submit an assignment (Fritz, 2011).
- While we have developed a student-facing dashboard called Check My Activity (CMA)[13] to help raise student awareness and nudge help-seeking behavior (Fritz, 2017), given the relationship between student LMS activity and course outcomes, we and others also began looking at how faculty use an LMS course to express their pedagogy and course design (Campbell, 2007; Dawson et al., 2008; Fritz, 2011; Fritz & Whitmer, 2017; Macfadyen & Dawson, 2012; Whitmer, 2012).
- In fact, it is now commonly accepted that there are three main ways faculty use an LMS, and typically in order of wide-spread use: (1) user and document management, (2) interaction and communication, and (3) online assessments. Ironically, the latter, especially auto-graded quizzes, exams, and assignments that an LMS is purpose-built to provide, typically generate far more student LMS activity than simply posting content such as the syllabus, presentations, or readings, yet fewer numbers of faculty actually do this (Fritz, 2019).
- Also, based on a study by Blackboard (Whitmer et al., 2016), we've recently learned that the "strength of relationship" between student LMS usage and final course grades across our Fall '19, Spring '20, and Fall '20 terms was

---

[12] For more information, see doit.umbc.edu/analytics/publications
[13] For a brief demo, see https://youtu.be/rpU1GdvS_yc

highly correlated with five LMS course design "archetypes" established by Blackboard—based on analysis of more than 3,374,462 unique students, in 70,000 courses, from 927 institutions, hosted by Blackboard in North America in Spring 2016—ranging from "supplemental" to "holistic" courses (described below):

o Supplemental (content-heavy, low interaction)
o Complementary (one-way communication via content, announcements, and gradebook)
o Social (high peer-to-peer interaction through discussion board)
o Evaluative (heavy use of assessments)
o Holistic (high LMS activity, balanced use of assessments, content, and discussion).

- Specifically, we sorted all courses by "fit" (e.g., how well or poorly a course's activity correlates to final grade). Essentially, this is the slope of a line (covariance divided by variance of independent variables) from final grades of A to B to C to D to F. If the slope is zero, there's little to no difference in student LMS activity by grade. If the slope is large, then As are more active than Bs, which are more active than Cs, and so on (Fritz et al., forthcoming[14]).
- Finally, we recognize that some may have concerns about using "big data" to monitor students, let alone serve as the basis of nudges and interventions. However, in addition to acting on what we think we know or observe about our students, we take John Campbell's classic LA question to heart: "What is an institution's ethical obligation of knowing?" (Fritz & Whitmer, 2020).

With this LA experience in mind, let us now turn to how UMBC spent its pandemic, with a particular focus on assessing the impact of faculty training on student perceptions of online learning quality, course evaluations, and even faculty willingness to consider non-traditional alternatives to traditional (F2F) teaching after the pandemic ends.

UMBC's Pandemic PIVOT

Many faculty already know how to use available instructional technology tools to supplement most forms of classroom teaching. But planning and teaching courses entirely online requires technical training and integration of the tools into pedagogy, which takes time (Ward & Benson, 2010).

Fortunately, as mentioned above, we were able to build on prior experience from our Alternate Delivery Program (ADP), first offered in 2006 as a collaboration

---

[14] Anticipated publication is August 2021; preview of final draft is available at https://umbc.box.com/blrpch5vol3preview

between our Division of Information Technology (DoIT) and Division of Professional Studies (DPS). During the 14 years of its existence, nearly 90 faculty have participated in the ADP and were provided financial, technical, and pedagogical support as they developed hybrid and online courses for Winter/Summer delivery. Effective practices and peer feedback were critical components of ADP with the introduction of Quality Matters standards for course design into the program's curriculum revision in 2014.

Theory and Practice

Like the ADP, our PIVOT initiative was grounded in the evidence-based principles for how people learn and shares many of the best practices of teaching in face-to-face classrooms (Chickering & Gamson, 1987) but leverages those principles and adapts the practices to the online environment (Dayton & Vaughn, 2007; Rienties et al., 2013). Providing faculty with opportunities to work in an online environment from the student perspective was also a critical component, especially if they did not have prior online teaching experience (Benson & Ward, 2013). Quality Matters informed much of PIVOT's conception and delivery, both to effectively demonstrate key design principles in practice and to emphasize value to student success. We knew that faculty engagement in planning and delivering this important training was critical to forming peer relationships (Bain, 2004), adopting new technologies (Rogers, 1976), and building long-term networks for reducing the isolation associated with teaching online (Covington et al., 2005; Shapiro, 2006).

The formal PIVOT program was delivered in multiple pathways to support faculty schedules and preferred training formats. PIVOT Live was a synchronous model consisting of five webinars over five days; the first prototypes were offered before the Spring 2020 semester ended. This option was ideal for participants who had some experience with course development and online instruction. PIVOT topics were selected to focus on helping instructors achieve competency in areas related to pedagogy, course design, and development, as well as technical and administrative skills.

Offered after the Spring semester concluded, a more rigorous, two-week PIVOT+ program included two faculty mentors per cohort for pedagogical and technical facilitation. Twenty-five PIVOT mentors from our three colleges supported the faculty during the program and throughout the Summer, and in some cases into Fall 2020 and beyond. The PIVOT mentors logged in every day, hosted office hours, responded to their group questions, demonstrated course designs and tool usage. They were exemplary models of peer engagement during a time when many faculty needed this support.

Despite the pandemic, proactive support from the administration allowed and encouraged UMBC faculty to explore pedagogical innovation during a challenging period (Garrison Institute, 2013). Faculty received stipends to complete PIVOT programming, and mentors were compensated for their time and support. Funding was provided by the Provost's office under the Hrabowski Innovation Fund,[15] which was established in 2012 through substantial grants from the Carnegie Corporation of New York and the Heinz Awards to support initiatives for enhancing teaching and learning at UMBC.

Adoption

The scope and impact of PIVOT was apparent when the workshops were posted for online registration in Spring and Summer 2020. Expecting less than 50 participants for the prototypes offered during the first week of May, UMBC recorded more than 1,000 registrations, with 764 actual attendees during the week for one or more of the five-day PIVOT Live sessions.[16] Collectively, this demand represented more than 250 unique PIVOT Live participants engaged during the week, nearly half of whom were teaching online during the summer. The success of PIVOT Live resulted in two additional offerings in June and August.

Organized into college disciplines and communities or practice (e.g., labs, large enrollment), 275 faculty completed the more rigorous,10-day PIVOT Plus (+) program.[17] The College of Engineering and Information Technology (CoEIT) further coordinated peer-driven webinars and panels on STEM-specific topics, while the College of Arts, Humanities, and Social Sciences (CAHSS) organized smaller, department-based cohorts within its larger PIVOT+ training to facilitate deeper conversations on course-specific topics. All colleges leveraged peer faculty mentors.

Impact

Leveraging an approach that targeted an individual instructor's reflection on technology use, online pedagogies, and course content (Mishra & Koehler, 2006), the PIVOT program benefited faculty and students in the following ways:

---

[15] https://calt.umbc.edu/academic-innovation-competition
[16] https://pivot.umbc.edu/pivot-live. For context, as of Fall 2020, UMBC had 931 FT & PT faculty.
[17] https://pivot.umbc.edu/pivot+

Faculty

Around 77% of PIVOT Live participants and nearly 85% of PIVOT+ participants said the program was helpful for their shift to online teaching.

- Faculty found their role as students (78%) and access to peer mentors (77%) to be among the most valuable aspects of the PIVOT+ program. As one instructor wrote, "PIVOT brought together a very heterogeneous group of educators, from those with a deep skepticism about the online delivery of instruction to those that are fond of technology. Such diversity made the discussion very productive and enlightening."
- Faculty feedback suggested that the topics covered were highly valuable. Learning objectives and alignment, active learning and assessment, engagement and community building, and getting students started with a strong course introduction were among the popular sessions. Increased interest in supporting tools associated with student engagement and active learning drove further changes to training schedules.
- Results from a February 2021 survey about lessons learned from teaching online during Fall 2020 suggests a shift in the faculty's pre/post pandemic teaching preferences for Fall 2021 (Penniston & Hawken, 2021). While 81% of 204 faculty respondents said they preferred to teach in a traditional (F2F) format before the pandemic, only 50% said they preferred to teach F2F going forward (see Figure 6.1). The change in pre- vs. post-pandemic preference for

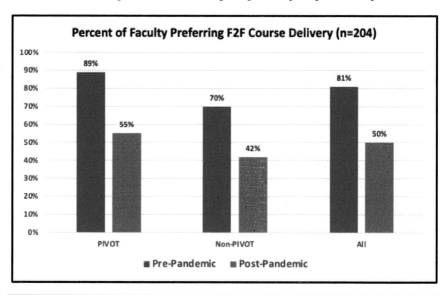

Figure 6.1   UMBC "Lessons Learned" Faculty Survey (Spring 2021)

F2F delivery was slightly greater for PIVOT-trained faculty (34%) vs. non-PIVOT faculty (28%). Across the board, all faculty cited learner engagement as an area of concern; however, non-PIVOT faculty cited learner engagement as a concern more often than PIVOT faculty who received specific pedagogical and technical support.

Students

- In a survey distributed to more than 500 courses taught by faculty who completed the PIVOT+ professional development program in Summer 2020, students said they enjoyed taking classes that were well organized and planned (Hawken, 2020). This underscores the importance of findability and aligns to student self-efficacy and motivation (Simunich et al., 2015).
- More than 85% of students who completed surveys said they agreed or strongly agreed that PIVOT+ courses flowed in a logical format. About 90% agreed or strongly agreed that requirements for the course were clear, while 83% agreed or strongly agreed that instructions for assignments were clear. This is consistent with research indicating that students value clear instructions for getting started, descriptive criteria for course activities and assignments, and consistent navigation (Ralston-Berg, 2014).
- Moreover, there is a statistically significant ($p < .001$) positive relationship between a faculty member completing PIVOT training and elevated course-level average values on Student Evaluation of Educational Quality (SEEQ) surveys ($p < .001$). For Fall 2020, student course evaluations improved by about .08 for those faculty who completed the training when compared with classes taught by instructors who did not (4.354 on a scale of 1–5) (Penniston, 2021).
- Courses taught by PIVOT-trained instructors also have increased Bb interactions, which are both indicative of improved engagement and can also be leveraged for more precise predictive modeling to inform student outreach (Penniston, 2019)
- DFW rates for PIVOT-instructed courses did not increase when compared with the pre-pandemic baseline.

Finally, it is worth noting that DoIT's Instructional Technology team—and our host of 25 faculty PIVOT peer mentors—recently won UMBC's 2021 "Job Well Done" Award[18] from the University's Human Resources office.

---

[18] https://hr.umbc.edu/job-well-done-award-program/job-well-done-award-recipients-spring-2021

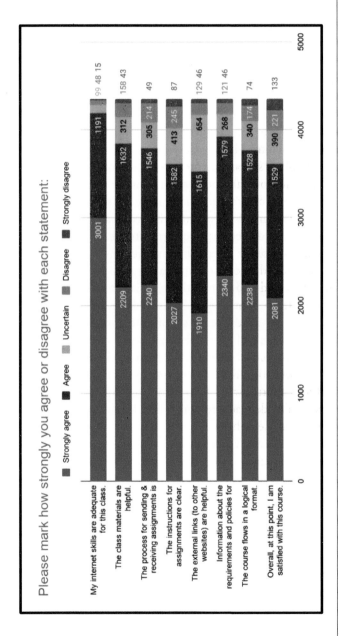

Figure 6.2   Fall 2020 UMBC Student Mid-term Survey About PIVOT Courses

Lessons Learned

As we reflect on UMBC's pandemic pivot to online learning—and complementary use of instructional design and learning analytics—a few observations may be useful for others who anticipate questions about the value and quality of online learning, let alone if and how it should be part of an institution's post-pandemic strategy.

First, there is a difference between equivalent course delivery and equivalent learning outcomes. When UMBC was first exploring alternate delivery formats in the early 2000s, some in our faculty senate raised concerns about traditional (F2F) undergraduate courses being redesigned for online or hybrid delivery. Our instructional technology support staff were even asked to appear before the faculty senate's undergraduate council, which approves all new undergraduate courses, to justify our support of faculty's proposing to design and deliver online or hybrid alternatives. Among other things, the senators asked how online or hybrid courses could offer equivalent "contact hours" or "seat time" compared to the traditional version of the same course.

Eventually, we leaned upon a little-known provision in the Code of Maryland (CoMAR) that had allowed our sister institution, University of Maryland University College (now known as University of Maryland Global Campus) to offer online courses for academic credit decades earlier—based on achieving "equivalent learning outcomes" and "when supervision is assured and learning is documented."[19] Subsequent federal requirements affecting financial aid, Title III, and the State Authorization Reciprocity Agreement (SARA), as well as regional and specialized accreditation standards, require consideration for quality assurance and measurement of student activity and learning.

The problem for online or hybrid learning has always been that few traditional, F2F courses actually have documented student learning outcomes, which makes the task of assessing or comparing "equivalency" very challenging indeed. Without articulated and measurable learning outcomes, the default assumption may be that traditional F2F delivery is inherently "better," which may be based (in part) on equivalent delivery measures of "seat time" or "contact hours" that can literally make alternate course delivery formats suffer by comparison. In other words, the burden of proof (and effort) can be even higher for redesigned online or hybrid courses if learning outcomes were never defined in their original F2F iterations.

The first step in designing any course is articulating what students should know, understand, or be able to do after completing it. Measurable learning outcomes drive the course and pedagogical design of instructional activities and assessments.

---

[19] See p. 30, section 16.D.(1)(a) https://mhec.maryland.gov/institutions_training/Docu ments/acadaff/acadproginstitapprovals/COMAR%2013B%2002%2002.pdf

Moreover, as we reflect on how course design may impact student learning, clustering Quality Matters course design standards helps isolate themes for future research questions on learning outcomes as well as retention, motivation, satisfaction, and more (Legon, 2015).

With the pandemic pivot to remote instruction and online learning, it is likely that many online (and probably synchronous) courses did not go through a thorough articulation of learning outcomes either, which makes "equivalency" with asynchronous online courses challenging, as well. So, if we don't have the traditional notion of "seat time" or "contact hours," perhaps this will become replaced with "direct [synchronous?] instruction."

What's worse, given the scale of likely rushed, synchronous virtual learning in 2020, these could be the majority of courses on which people base their "online learning doesn't work" sentiments. As such, online learning proponents may have won the battle—to scale virtual learning in a crisis—but be in jeopardy of losing the war to advance online learning as quality instruction and institutional strategic priority.

Second, without documented student learning outcomes across courses, let alone programs and degrees, it is difficult to connect and scale learning analytics to traditional student success metrics such as final grades, term and cumulative GPA, credits attempted/earned, student retention and persistence rate, progress toward degree, and four- or six-year graduation rates. While we may understandably assume that students who learn "more or better" in a course will eventually become successful graduates, how do we prove it, let alone intervene with students who we may project or even predict to be at risk of not succeeding? Research from the Education Advisory Board (EAB) has shown that about 45% of students who drop out of college do so after their second year, and with a GPA between 2.0 and 3.0 (Tyson, 2014; Venit, 2016). These so-called "Murky Middle" students leave college in "good academic standing" without a degree, the typical definition of "student success."

For this reason, we have not only been working hard to define and align learning outcomes across course, program, college, and the university—thanks largely to our Faculty Development Center[20]—but also to integrate them into our institutional data warehouse strategy. Two initiatives in particular are worth noting: (1) our development of what is often referred to as the Comprehensive Learner Record (CLR), a digital record that can be used to document a student's academic and co-curricular learning and accomplishments (*Comprehensive Learner Record*, n.d.; *Comprehensive Learner Record | IMS Global Learning Consortium*, n.d.; Shendy et al., 2019); and (2) a Learner Record Store (LRS), which is a learning/learner-specific data warehouse or data lake that can collect and curate massive amounts of student engagement data, not only in the LMS, but also from third-party extensions, e-Textbooks, publisher homework systems, and more (Learning Record Store, n.d.)

---

[20] https://fdc.umbc.edu/learning-assessment

Ideally, we ought to be able to view any aspect of a student's learner experience like an academic "core sample" of what is or could be occurring across the institution for similar peers. Imagine a student who initially struggled to understand the pH of a salt solution in general chemistry but eventually managed to demonstrate proficiency on a quiz, assignment, or test: Did they read the open educational resource (OER) textbook? Take advantage of practice problems before midterm exam? Attend tutoring, supplemental instruction, or even office hours? Is the student living on campus or a commuter? Is the course taught by an instructor who has sought training in active learning or online/hybrid course delivery? Are there other courses (perhaps pre-calculus or English composition) that, when combined with general chemistry, are more likely to be associated with students who are retained in STEM degrees? Yes, this sounds like a "kitchen sink" of data and variables, but if we can link student learning outcomes to the digital footprints of the student learning experience, the courses they enroll in, and the instructors who teach them, we may be able to help shine light on how quality course design can help students learn and succeed.

Finally, as UMBC's President Freeman A. Hrabowski likes to say, "If you want to change the culture, shine light on success, not failure." He's right, of course, and we need to define success and look for it. When it comes to quality teaching and learning (online or otherwise), we have to start with the end in mind, or "backward course design." What do we want students to know, understand, or be able to do after completing a course? Not only what grades or credits did they earn. What did they learn, and what did this knowledge allow them to understand or do next? Better still, what should these learning outcomes be a year after completing the course? Now we're moving from a short-term memorization to perhaps changing how people think critically to solve problems or even create new knowledge.

However, since most faculty teach the way they were taught, and most weren't taught online, how do we give faculty the time and opportunity to learn a new mode of instruction or course delivery to achieve their desired learning outcomes for students? Consequently, as we shift from being forced online to perhaps choosing to do so, what does online learning quality *and* student success look like?

Yes, faculty will need to know the basics of how to use specific tools and technologies, and we might even create financial incentives such as course development stipends. But what we're really striving for here is helping faculty use technology to reflect on and express their pedagogy or philosophy of learning in ways that can best help students achieve their desired learning outcomes. In our experience, faculty learn this best from other faculty, which is why our PIVOT and all forms of instructional technology support and training relies so heavily on identifying, supporting, and rewarding faculty peer mentors.

Here's where we can use learning analytics to help find and shine light on success in online learning precisely because our students and faculty leave digital footprints we can make inferences about, validate, and even reverse-engineer as effective practices others might wish to implement. Yes, user activity data are an indirect proxy for engagement, but they are also a plausible and reasonable place to start. If we know someone who teaches in ways we wish others would consider, we can see if and how their students have been successful in the next course that follows. Alternatively, we might also be intrigued by patterns of student engagement in one course that differ significantly from other courses. In both cases, we can use the data as a starting point for a conversation or interview with the instructor to find out "What's going on in your course?" or "What are you doing that leads to your students' success?" In this way, we can find both effective practices—and practitioners—who we can support and "shine light on."

Conclusion

What would make online learning more of a priority for the institution going forward? How can we scale online learning quality? For most higher education institutions whose course offerings have been primarily in person, this requires a fundamental shift in institutional culture. Instructional design and integrating learning analytics are key, but no amount of these improvements will bring about lasting change if faculty are not convinced of the value of online learning. In other words, we will need to work to win the hearts and minds of faculty by clearly showing the benefits of online education for the instructor and the students.

As Hrabowski, Rous, & Henderson (2019) point out in their book, *The Empowered University,* any proposed change at university that is perceived as top-down is likely to be dead on arrival for the faculty and staff who must implement it. Rather, the most effective ways to change the culture and practices of an institution are by clearly articulating a vision for the future through a collaborative process with others—faculty, staff, administrators, and students—who broadly embrace it and developing colleagues who align with the culture, mission, and work.

Moving the hearts and minds of faculty requires a multi-pronged approach. A method that works well for one group of faculty may not work as well with another group. For example, showing the concrete benefits of participating in our PIVOT training—better student course evaluation scores reported for faculty who completed the PIVOT training than those who did not—may help in winning the hearts and minds of some faculty. For others, demonstrating how a thoughtfully designed online course promotes student engagement and success may do the job. Still for others, incentives can help. With our PIVOT initiative, we developed a faculty award program with funds from the Hrabowski Innovation Funds to recognize faculty who participated. But incentives are not always necessary. As Hrabowski et al. (2019) point out, passion is a characteristic that is found in the context of change. What successful change and innovation often require are the people who lead. These leaders take the initiative, go "above and beyond" their normal work. There are obstacles, but they are passionate enough to move past those obstacles. We have been fortunate that UMBC has had more than its share of passionate and committed people who will roll up their sleeves and do the work. Our community is better for this broad set of leaders, and our students have benefited substantially from their commitment.

A big part of the success of our PIVOT program has come from a close partnership between our Division of Instructional Technology, the Faculty Development Center, and our Colleges, all of which collaborated closely to facilitate faculty peer learning communities. Tapping peer mentors from throughout the university was also key to the success of this program because faculty often learn best from other faculty. Many of our faculty peer mentors are full-time lecturers, but we have also been thrilled to hear some of our senior tenure-track faculty share that their teaching has benefited markedly from the peer learning communities. Senior faculty play a critical role in shaping departmental expectations for reviewing the performance of junior faculty, and we are seeing a shift in faculty's attitude toward online instruction more broadly.

It takes concerted effort over time and continuous vigilance to sustain these culture changes. We need to continuously monitor progress to ensure that it endures and, when new people join our campus community, be sure to educate them about our culture and approaches. Change is hard, and success is never final. But we can win the hearts and minds of our community members one person at a time.

References

Adair, D., and Shattuck, K. (2015). Quality Matters™: An educational input in an ongoing design-based research project. *American Journal of Distance Education, 29*(3), 159–165. https://doi.org/10.1080/08923647.2015.1057094

Bain, K. (2004). *What the Best College Teachers Do.* Harvard University Press. https://www.hup.harvard.edu/catalog.php?isbn=9780674013254

Bigatel, P. M., and Edel-Malizia, S. (2018). Using the "Indicators of Engaged Learning Online" framework to evaluate online course quality. *TechTrends, 62*(1), 58–70. https://doi.org/10.1007/s11528-017-0239-4

Bishop, M. (2017, March 29). Splitting hairs: Exploring learn-ing vs learn-er analytics (and why we should care). *The EvoLLLution.* https://evolllution.com/technology/metrics/splitting-hairs-exploring-learn-ing-vs-learn-er-analytics-and-why-we-should-care/

Brown, M. (2011). *Learning Analytics: The Coming Third Wave* [ELI Brief]. EDUCAUSE Learning Initiative. http://www.educause.edu/library/resources/learning-analytics-coming-third-wave

Campbell, J.P., DeBlois, P. B., and Oblinger, D. G. (2007). *Academic Analytics* (White Paper). https://er.educause.edu/articles/2007/7/academic-analytics-a-new-tool-for-a -new-era

Cavanagh, T. (2021, February 2). *The Pandemic Pivot (or Pendulum)—Growing and Sustaining Online Through Lessons Learned* [Panel]. 2021 SOLA+R (Summit for Online Leadership and Administration + Roundtable), https://conferences.upcea.edu /SOLAR21/index.html. https://conferences.upcea.edu/SOLAR21/generalsessions .html#reflections

Chickering, A. W., and Gamson, Z. F. (1987). Seven principles for good practice in undergraduate education. *American Association for Higher Education Bulletin, 39*(7), 3–7. http://eric.ed.gov/?id=ED282491

Comprehensive Learner Record. (n.d.). Retrieved April 7, 2021, from https://www.aacrao .org/signature-initiatives/comprehensive-learner-record

Comprehensive Learner Record | IMS Global Learning Consortium. (n.d.). Retrieved April 7, 2021, from https://www.imsglobal.org/activity/comprehensive-learner-record

Covington, D., Petherbridge, D., and Warren, S. E. (2005). Best practices: A triangulated support approach in transitioning faculty to online teaching. *Online Journal of Distance Learning Administration, 8*(1).

Dawson, S., McWilliam, E., and Tan, J. P. L. (2008). Teaching smarter: How mining ICT data can inform and improve learning and teaching practice. *Proceedings Ascilite Melbourne 2008.* http://ascilite.org.au/conferences/melbourne08/procs/dawson.pdf

Dayton, D., and Vaughn, M. M. (2007). Developing a quality assurance process to guide the design and assessment of online courses. *Technical Communication, 54*(4), 475–489. https://www.jstor.org/stable/43090959

Fritz, J. (2011). Classroom walls that talk: Using online course activity data of successful students to raise self-awareness of underperforming peers. *The Internet and Higher Education, 14*(2), 89–97. https://doi.org/10.1016/j.iheduc.2010.07.007

Fritz, J. (2017). Using analytics to nudge student responsibility for learning. *New Directions for Higher Education, 2017*(179), 65–75. https://doi.org/10.1002/he.20244

Fritz, J. (2019, November 25). Why CNMS student Bb use is so high [news]. *UMBC DoIT News.* https://doit.umbc.edu/news/?id=88786

Fritz, J., Penniston, T., Sharkey, M., and Whitmer, J. (*Forthcoming*). Scaling course design as learning analytics variable. In: *Blended Learning Research Perspectives* (Vol. 3). Taylor & Francis Group. https://ucf.qualtrics.com/jfe/form/SV_cOSPw4Ps9l8vpm5

Fritz, J., and Whitmer, J. (2017, February 27). Learning analytics research for LMS course design: Two studies. *EDUCAUSE Review Online.* http://er.educause.edu /articles/2017/2/learning-analytics-research-for-lms-course-design-two-studies

Fritz, J., and Whitmer, J. (2020). Ethical learning analytics: "Do no harm" versus "do nothing." *New Directions for Institutional Research, 2019*(183), 27–38. https://doi .org/10.1002/ir.20310

Garrison Institute. (2013, October 10). *Peter Senge: Systems Thinking and the Gap Between Aspirations and Performance*. https://www.youtube.com/watch?v=_PFo7zdiw34

Hawken, M. (2020, November 18). Students praise organized course designs from PIVOT+ faculty. *DoIT News*. https://doit.umbc.edu/news/?id=97557

Hoover, E. (2020, December 15). The demographic cliff: 5 findings from new projections of high-school graduates. *The Chronicle of Higher Education*. https://www.chronicle.com/article/the-demographic-cliff-5-findings-from-new-projections-of-high-school-graduates

Hrabowski III, F. A., Rous, P. J., and Henderson, P. H. (2019). *The Empowered University*. Johns Hopkins University Press. https://jhupbooks.press.jhu.edu/title/empowered-university

Learning Record Store: What Is an LRS?—SCORM. (n.d.). scorm.com. Retrieved April 7, 2021, from https://scorm.com/what-is-an-lrs-learning-record-store/

Legon, R. (2015). Measuring the impact of the Quality Matters Rubric™: A discussion of possibilities. *American Journal of Distance Education, 29*(3), 166–173. https://doi.org/10.1080/08923647.2015.1058114

Macfadyen, L. P., and Dawson, S. (2012). Numbers are not enough. Why e-learning analytics failed to inform an institutional strategic plan. *Journal of Educational Technology & Society, 15*(3), 149–163. http://www.ifets.info/index.php?http://www.ifets.info/issues.php?id=56. https://www.jstor.org/stable/jeductechsoci.15.3.149

Martin, F., Ritzhaupt, A., Kumar, S., and Budhrani, K. (2019). Award-winning faculty online teaching practices: Course design, assessment and evaluation, and facilitation. *The Internet and Higher Education, 42*, 34–43. https://doi.org/10.1016/j.iheduc.2019.04.001

McCormack, M. (2021). EDUCAUSE QuickPoll Results: Assessment and Learning Design (*EDUCAUSE Research Notes*) [Quick Poll]. https://er.educause.edu/articles/2021/4/educause-quickpoll-results-assessment-and-learning-design

Mishra, P., and Koehler, M. J. (2006). Technological pedagogical content knowledge: A framework for teacher knowledge. *Teachers College Record, 108*(6), 1017–1054. https://www.learntechlib.org/p/99246/

Penniston, T. (2019, September 25). Combining machine and human intelligences for interventions. *DoIT News*. https://doit.umbc.edu/analytics/analytics-news/?id=87052

Penniston, T. (2021, February 2). PIVOT and the student evaluation of FA20 courses. *DoIT News*. https://doit.umbc.edu/news/?id=98871

Penniston, T., and Hawken, M. (2021, February 24). Faculty survey suggests shift in pre/post-pandemic teaching. *DoIT News*. https://doit.umbc.edu/news/?id=99554

Ralston-Berg, P. (2014). Surveying student perspectives of quality: Value of QM rubric items. *Internet Learning*. https://doi.org/10.18278/il.3.1.9

Rienties, B., Brouwer, N., Carbonell, K. B., Townsend, D., Rozendal, A.-P., Loo, J., van der Dekker, P., and Lygo-Baker, S. (2013). Online training of TPACK skills of higher education scholars: A cross-institutional impact study. *European Journal of Teacher Education, 36*(4), 480–495. https://doi.org/10.1080/02619768.2013.801073

Rogers, E. M. (1976). New product adoption and diffusion. *Journal of Consumer Research, 2*(4), 290–301. https://www.jstor.org/stable/2488658

Rous, P. J., Mozie-Ross, Y., Shin, S. J., and Fritz, J. (2021, April 8). A pandemic silver lining: Helping former students finish degrees online. *EDUCAUSE Review.* https://er.educause.edu/articles/2021/4/a-pandemic-silver-lining-helping-former-students-finish-degrees-online

Shapiro, P. J. (2006). The evolution of peer driven training for teaching online courses. *Online Journal of Distance Learning Administration, 9*(3).

Shendy, J. E., Grann, J., Leuba, M., Green, T., and Parks, R. (2019). 7 things you should know about the comprehensive learner record (7 things you should know about) [Brief]. *EDUCAUSE Learning Initiative.* https://library.educause.edu/resources/2019/1/7-things-you-should-know-about-the-comprehensive-learner-record

Simunich, B., Robins, D. B., and Kelly, V. (2015). The impact of findability on student motivation, self-efficacy, and perceptions of online course quality. *American Journal of Distance Education, 29*(3), 174–185. https://doi.org/10.1080/08923647.2015.1058604

Southard, S., and Mooney, M. (2015). A comparative analysis of distance education quality assurance standards. *Quarterly Review of Distance Education, 16*(1), 55–68. http://proxy-bc.researchport.umd.edu/login?url=http://search.ebscohost.com/login.aspx?direct=true&db=aph&AN=108714693&site=ehost-live&scope=site

Thompson, K., and Moskal, P. (2020, May 26). Simultaneously supporting faculty for remote instruction and (actual) online teaching during covid-19. *OLC.* https://onlinelearningconsortium.org/simultaneously-supporting-faculty-for-remote-instruction-and-actual-online-teaching-during-covid-19/

Tyson, C. (2014, September 10). To maximize graduation rates, colleges should focus on middle-range students, research shows. *Inside Higher Education.* https://www.insidehighered.com/news/2014/09/10/maximize-graduation-rates-colleges-should-focus-middle-range-students-research-shows

Venit, E. (2016). *The Murky Middle Project* [White Paper]. Education Advisory Board. https://eab.com/technology/whitepaper/student-success/the-murky-middle-project/

Ward, C. L., and Benson, S. N. K. (2010). Developing new schemas for online teaching and learning. *TPACK, 6*(2), 9.

Whitmer, J. (2012). Logging on to improve achievement: Evaluating the relationship between use of the learning management system, student characteristics, and academic achievement in a hybrid large enrollment undergraduate course [University of California, Davis]. http://johnwhitmer.net/dissertation-study/

Whitmer, J., Nuñez, N., Harfield, T., and Forteza, D. (2016, October 27). Patterns in blackboard learn tool use: How Instructors actually use the lms. *Blackboard Bog.* https://blog.blackboard.com/patterns-in-course-design-how-instructors-actually-use-the-lms/

Chapter 7

Democratizing Data at a Large R1 Institution

Supporting Data-Informed Decision Making for Advisers, Faculty, and Instructional Designers

Chris Millet, Jessica Resig, and Bart Pursel[1]

Abstract

In this chapter, we share best practices for advancing learning analytics and establishing a data-informed decision-making culture in higher education based on over a decade of experience at The Pennsylvania State University. We include general principles for articulating learning analytics project goals and considerations for ensuring such projects align with institutional imperatives related to privacy, security, and ethics. We conclude with three examples of successful learning analytics implementations at Penn State that illustrate these principles.

Keywords: Learning analytics, instructional design, academic advising, learning engineering, higher education

---

[1] The Pennsylvania State University

Introduction

The Pennsylvania State University (Penn State) is a large land-grant Research 1 institution with 24 campuses distributed amongst the beautiful forests and mountains of the commonwealth. Penn State enrolls approximately 96,000 students, including 18,000 at the fully online World Campus.

Like many institutions of higher education, Penn State uses data extensively to inform many of its strategic decisions. However, only within the last decade has it begun to invest significantly in developing the capacity to use data to directly inform teaching and learning, otherwise known as *learning analytics*. Historically, querying, analyzing, and visualizing data has required niche skillsets and complex statistical software.

As new data interoperability standards have emerged and software such as R, Tableau®, and PowerBI® have become accessible and relatively inexpensive, and as the field of learning analytics has developed, the prospect of putting the power of data in the hands of faculty, instructional designers, and academic technology units has slowly become a reality. While Penn State has engaged with established third-party vendors to help establish key infrastructure and even to accelerate its learning analytics efforts, the latter has largely evolved over the past 10 years through a series of small experimental projects, each contributing new competencies and modernized policies that have prepared us for this new era.

In this chapter, we'll share some of our current projects and the lessons we've learned getting to this point. We hope you'll take away from this journey the idea that regardless of current buy-in or the maturity of your institution's analytics capability, you can move decisively from initial explorations to an established data-informed decision-making culture in a reasonable timeframe and with only a modest financial investment.

Dimensions of Learning Analytics

Learning analytics can serve a wide variety of purposes within an institution. At one end of the spectrum, it may support traditional institutional research functions. In this instance, large historical datasets are used by administrators and researchers, in part to inform enrollment management or the processes that "influence the size, shape, and characteristics of a student body by directing institutional efforts in marketing, recruitment, admissions, pricing, and financial aid" (Clagett, 1991).

While learning analytics' role in enrollment management or other macro-level institutional decision making may be limited, it can add another dimension to an institution's understanding about how large-scale effects correlate with individual student performance within a course. That in turn may affect an institution's decisions regarding what academic support services to bolster to best address the needs of their specific student population. For example, a well-placed math tutoring service targeting the right students may have a profound impact on long-term retention.

On the other end of the spectrum, learning analytics can be used to provide very fine-grained information to an individual instructor about a student who is struggling in a course and inform specific interventions to get that student back on track. At the heart of both of those very different decisions is a similar set of data and analytical techniques. However, considerations related to the purpose of each project, the intended audience, the scope of impact, and the nature of and risks associated with the data have direct bearing on approval, funding, timelines, personnel, and skillsets required. Understanding both how such projects differ and how they relate can lead to a much more efficient, integrated, and overall effective strategy. Careful categorization may also help identify misalignment between a project and institutional priorities and suggest different and more fruitful directions. In this section, we suggest an approach to describing the diversity of possible learning analytics projects and articulate discrete dimensions of project categorization that may be useful to you, whether you are proposing new projects, evaluating proposals, or simply looking to identify a more efficient approach to managing legacy projects.

Learning Analytics Project Dimensions

The following is not meant to be comprehensive, but rather to serve as an example of how you might systematically evaluate and categorize potential learning analytics projects. Each of these dimensions has implications related to ethics, security, difficulty of implementation, impact on learning, value to the institution, or costs and may help determine the overall viability of your project. For each category, we'll suggest framing questions to draw out critical details and then provide a series of representative examples and their related considerations.

Purpose

What problem is this project trying to solve? Have other approaches been considered or attempted that were not successful? How do data specifically help solve this problem? What expertise is required to support such a project? (See Table 7.1.)

Table 7.1 Project Purpose and Related Considerations

Purpose	Considerations
Predicting student performance	Requires significant historical data to develop predictive models. Potential for misuse introduces ethical risks.
Adaptive learning	Substantial research has been conducted that can guide design. Significant effort may be required to incorporate adaptive systems into courses.
Improving learning materials and tools	Usage logs and performance data are readily available in most cases. May require academic technology and instructional design expertise to interpret data and design improvements.

Audience

Who do you intend to utilize these analytics? What knowledge or skills are necessary for this audience to accurately interpret and act on these analytics? Are there policies specific to this audience accessing this data? Have you considered any unintended consequences of misuse of these analytics? (See Table 7.2.)

Table 7.2 Project Audience and Related Considerations

Audience	Considerations
Students	Student-facing analytics can support self-regulation and build metacognitive skills in students but can also inadvertently undermine self-confidence. Messaging should be constructive and not unnecessarily compare students. FERPA regulations must be strictly adhered to.
Instructors	Analytics can help instructors identify and intervene with at-risk students but can also be misused. Training and in-app scaffolding that reinforces intended usage can mitigate these issues.
Advisors	Advisors are trained to interpret data and translate this to students. They often have heavy workloads, so LA dashboards need to be intuitive and highly customized to advisor workflows.
Learning designers	Learning designers have deep knowledge of course designs and will typically understand drivers for specific student behaviors and performance issues. LA dashboards must allow them to drill down to granular details.
Administrators	Administrators seek to understand high-level trends. Predictive analytics that utilize large historical datasets visualized in dashboards that draw attention to the most salient insights are highly desirable to this audience.

Data Sources

What are the questions you are trying to answer? Do data currently exist to help answer these questions? Do you require additional data? How do the data you are requesting directly contribute to answering those questions? What are the policies governing access to these data? (See Table 7.3.)

Table 7.3 Data Sources and Related Considerations

Data Source	Considerations
Student Information System (SIS)	SIS's will likely contain far more data than you need. Individual data stewards may govern access to specific tables, so gaining access may be complicated. Consider if this is strictly necessary.
Learning Management System (LMS)	The LMS is a critical data source for many LA projects, as it contains comprehensive data about both student behaviors and performance. Some LMS vendors provide standardized formats such as Caliper® or xAPI.
Third-party learning environments	You may need to negotiate with a vendor to gain access to these data if you have not included data access in your contract. The data may not be in an easily usable format.

Risk

All learning analytics projects introduce some level of risk (including the security, ethics, and privacy considerations discussed later in this chapter). Is your risk level acceptable to your stakeholders? Does the expected value justify the potential risk? Are there strategies you can take to mitigate risks while still providing the same value? (See Table 7.4.)

An appropriately categorized learning analytics project is an excellent starting point for determining your next steps, including identifying critical stakeholders and gatekeepers across your institution who you should consult before beginning any implementation. We'll use these dimensions in our examples later in this chapter.

Organizational Considerations: Creating Conditions for Success

The Department of Education states that, "[U]sing data is now taken for granted as an essential component of any educational improvement process" (Murray, 2014, p. 1).

Table 7.4 Risk Factors and Related Considerations

Risk Factors	Considerations
Student data breach	This should be the primary concern for all LA projects, as it carries the greatest risk to harm students and the institution, particularly if you are using high-risk data sources such as student aid data. Project leaders should work closely with privacy and security offices to mitigate this risk.
Unethical use of analytics	Misuse of data may be deliberate or unintentionally introduced by poor design. Potential unethical uses should be enumerated by the project team during the planning phase.
Incorrect interpretation or unsupported claims	Incorrect data queries or flawed statistical methods can mislead users. Robust testing and user validation can mitigate this risk.

This use has evolved from a "data-driven" to a "data-informed" orientation (Shen, 2011), the distinction being a shift from the assumption that data itself contain the key insights that prescribe an optimal decision to the more measured expectation that data can, at best, narrow the set of optimal decisions and that humans must ultimately decide on a course of action. This orientation has a twofold benefit. First, it helps us avoid an overreliance on approaches that rely solely on quantitative data that can lead to an overconfidence in what those data alone can tell us (Jones & McCoy 2018). Second, we establish a firm basis of trust in the analysis itself when stakeholders are invited to draw on their personal knowledge and expertise to balance claims based on data alone. These stakeholders, including registrars, IT security professionals, faculty, students, library staff, and data stewards, can all be incorporated into the planning and validation phases of any analytics project. The trust that is developed when operating in this manner will help ensure downstream awareness and adoption of project outcomes.

Security, Privacy, and Ethics

The foundation of learning analytics projects often requires data. Sometimes these data can be innocuous, such as a sequence of courses that combine to create a degree program. Other times these data can contain personal information that individuals may be hesitant to share, such as financial aid details. In our experience, every learning analytics project will at some point need to balance the goals of a project with the security, privacy, and ethical responsibilities of working with different types of data.

Security

Whether dealing with learning analytics data, research data, health data, or other types of data, your institution likely has some form of policy or guidelines on how different types of data need to be secured. As the criticality of information and cybersecurity grows, most institutions have offices or individuals charged with ensuring certain types of data are secured in the appropriate manner. As learning analytics data often include data about individuals, understanding the offices that deal with personal data is important to get a learning analytics project off the ground.

At Penn State, the Office of Information Security[2] is responsible for ensuring University data are secured in a way that protects the interests of the University as well as individuals of which the University collects data. Similar offices exist for many higher education institutions, though where these offices reside in the organizational structure at each institution may differ.

Penn State currently defines four classifications of data and has procedures in place regarding how to secure the information based on each classification. The classifications are driven by the possible harm to individuals, communities, or the University if data were compromised in some way. At a high level, these classifications are:

- **Level 1.** Low-risk data that include publicly available information, as well as some non-public data. Examples include schedules of courses, published research data, and educational data.
- **Level 2.** Moderate-risk data include information such as personnel records and some components of identifiable student records. Important to note is how an institution defines Personally Identifiable Information (PII). For example, Penn State does not consider certain information that might be used to identify an individual as PII, such as a date of birth or an email address.
- **Level 3.** High-risk data, specifically data that are deemed PII. This includes data such as social security numbers, health data, and University identification numbers.
- **Level 4.** Restricted data that include various financial information such as credit card and bank account data, as well as data identified in the Federal Information Security Modernization Act (FISMA).

While these risk levels provide guidance, some units also find it useful to create more granularity within these categories to guide local work. For example, in the context of student-facing analytics, there may be gradations of Risk Level 2 that assign additional levels depending on what specific data elements are exposed and their potential for misuse or harm to students. Such factors are highly contextual,

---

[2] https://security.psu.edu/

and one must consider when it's appropriate to go beyond institutionally defined risk categories.

The higher the classification of data, the more defined security protocols need to be in place to work with these data. An additional challenge is the nature of learning analytics work as it relates to data science. Many data science tools are cloud based and require data to leave local, secured storage solutions and networks and travel to cloud platforms such as Amazon Web Services® (AWS), Microsoft® Azure, or the Google® Cloud Platform. For example, if a goal of a project is to create a machine learning model that can leverage past data to predict current student performance in each course, this may require access to specialized computational hardware, particularly if the model needs to run on a frequent cadence, such as daily. Purchasing this hardware locally is one solution, while leveraging cloud resources is another way to enable this work. When engaging in learning analytics projects, the Office of Information Security, or similar unit at your institution, is a valuable collaborator to ensure the data associated with a learning analytics project are appropriately secured.

Privacy

While security is certainly a challenge with learning analytics projects, privacy often presents a larger challenge. This is due to several reasons:

- Different regulations directly impact how a university handles individual data, and the legal counsels at institutions can sometimes differ in their interpretation of the finer points of these regulations.
- The concept of privacy is complex and challenging, particularly in the context of student learning data.
- Not every institution has a dedicated office or individual spending significant time defining privacy from an institutional perspective that is easily applicable to learning data.

A good starting point when considering privacy as it relates to a learning analytics project is to consult with the individual(s) at your institution responsible for ensuring adherence to federal regulations. In the United States, this is the Family Educational Rights and Privacy Act (FERPA). FERPA plays an important role in how student educational records can be leveraged at an institution. A challenge is how an institution, often through a legal counsel, interprets FERPA. Conservative interpretations may make it difficult for learning analytics projects to access and leverage student educational data records. More liberal interpretations point to FERPA as a catalyst for things like learning analytics, where institutions desire to leverage student educational data records to improve student learning and outcomes. Another regulation is the European Union's (EU) General Data Protection

Regulation (GDPR), which applies to any school, regardless of geographic location, where EU citizens are enrolled. Depending on the data required for a learning analytics project, the Health Insurance Portability and Accountability Act (HIPAA) might also come into play, dictating if and how health data can be leveraged.

An important distinction to be made early in a learning analytics project relates to the project's context. Specifically, is the project a research project as defined by an institution's research office, or is the project an administrative project to support administrative goals, such as accelerating time to graduation? If a project falls into the research category, engaging your institution's research protections office is vital to ensure all the necessary steps are in place to ensure an individual's privacy with relation to data. If the project is an administrative project, it is important to try and find an office or individual at your institution who can review your learning analytics project from a privacy perspective. An asset at Penn State is the Privacy Impact Assessment (PIA),[3] a tool provided by the Privacy Office that helps determine potential privacy challenges that need to be addressed when we initiate a learning analytics project.

Another challenge with privacy is that it feels like a moving target: with social media, online entertainment platforms, and e-commerce, our data are being captured and leveraged in a plethora of unexpected and sometimes hidden ways (Prinsloo & Slade, 2015). The field of learning analytics is still nascent, with a small (yet growing) body of research around student perceptions of privacy, which often differ across cultures (Arnold & Sclater, 2017). While the field of learning analytics wrestles with these complex questions around privacy, at the same time we must continue to experiment with how we use data to support student success in all its forms (Slade & Prinsloo, 2013). In addition to examining the literature around privacy as it relates to your learning analytics project, another important resource is a Chief Privacy Officer, or someone in a similar role, who focuses on examining the usage of data at an institution as they pertain to matters of privacy.

Ethics

Ethics is arguably the most challenging of the triumvirate of security, privacy, and ethics. Like privacy, ethics can be shaped by a multitude of factors, including age, race, socio-economic status, culture, education, and gender. Not only do we need to consider holistic ethical challenges when using data, we also need to apply an ethical design lens, making sure ethics plays a role in how we design learning analytics tools, particularly the aspects of the tools that end users engage (Shilton, 2018). When exploring ethical considerations related to learning analytics projects, some units to consider engaging include:

---

[3] https://security.psu.edu/services/privacy-impact-assessment

- Researchers and research centers that specialize in ethics
- Units focused on education equity
- Units focused on diversity and inclusivity

Many individuals today are uncomfortable with the amount of data different entities collect about them, as well as how they use those data. This is particularly true of members of marginalized groups. When examining recent trends in artificial intelligence, there are issues of AI-driven job screening applications being biased against women (Dastin, 2018) as well as facial recognition software used for things like prison sentencing, security, and exam proctoring that show a bias against individuals of color (Raji et al., 2020). As these stories continue to appear in our popular media outlets, people are rightfully skeptical about the uses, or more aptly misuses, of data. Members of a core learning analytics project team are unlikely to have expertise in ethics, which makes it vital to engage a diverse group of individuals at your institution that do have the appropriate ethical expertise to help guide decisions.

Finding Balance

As you traverse learning analytics projects, you will undoubtedly confront important decision points that directly relate to privacy and ethics. The gold standard in terms of privacy is opt-in. This is very challenging for learning analytics in general, as many projects involve the use of secondary data from platforms such as a SIS or LMS. If students first need to be invited to participate, then opt in to have their data used in a project, there's a real risk of not having enough data to discover meaningful trends or insights around teaching and learning. If students are automatically opted in with regards to their data, should they have the ability to opt out, having their specific data removed from the project's dataset? While this is a good practice, it is sometimes difficult technically to put into place a mechanism whereby a student can opt out of their data being part of a learning analytics project. When it comes to using AI in learning analytics projects, the line is less clear. What does opt-out mean, exactly? Is it opting out of having a student's data appear in an interface, thus hiding them from anyone using a learning analytics tool? Or does it also mean removing their data altogether from the dataset being used to create different types of machine learning algorithms?

In our work to date, we find engaging the right individuals on our campus at these decision points helps us feel comfortable and confident in the way we're using data, as well as builds trust with our end users and the individuals whose data we use. In addition to questions around opt-in and opt-out, a good practice is to always be as transparent as possible with individuals regarding how their data are being used and for what purpose. Even if a student can't opt out, they at least have access to information explaining how their data are being used and to what end. This again creates challenges for the learning analytics project team, as there aren't always good mechanisms to message to the entire student body about how data are being used on a per-project basis. Some institutions, such as Wisconsin, are using the news features of their learning management systems to alert students of new learning analytics projects and pointing students to a web presence designed to catalog each project, the data being used, and the goals.[4]

Advancing Analytics Initiatives at Your Institution

An uncoordinated and piecemeal approach to building analytics capacity can lead to inconsistent results, misalignment with policy that will undermine trust, and inefficient use of resources. The following recommendations represent best practices from over a decade of work in this field at Penn State.

Iterating Toward Success

A strategy many institutions may want to adopt early on is to build their analytics capacity gradually, through highly intentional risk-managed iterations. This can be particularly useful where there is not an established data-informed decision-making culture in place. Overcoming a reticence for widespread use of data and analytics borne out of traditionally conservative data policies and procedures should happen over time, with an explicit goal of building trust and confidence. Rather than large-scale enterprise analytics initiatives, Penn State pursued small departmental projects focused on discrete problems for specific audiences. The limited scope of these projects allowed us to precisely articulate their parameters to data stewards and privacy officers and provide unambiguous responses to their questions. While early successes had relatively small impact, we evangelized these successes with stakeholders and credited our constructive relationships with our institutional partners. As problems with infrastructure or confusions about policy arose, we had frank conversations and made what progress we reasonably could. This slow development of trust and evolution of process benefited us greatly as we tackled successively larger initiatives.

We often say analytics is a team sport, meaning it takes a wide variety of individuals with diverse perspectives and skillsets to all come together and work harmoniously towards a common goal. Universities often have catalysts for these

---

[4] https://at.doit.wisc.edu/evaluation-design-analysis/learning-analytics-projects

sorts of collaborations, such as internal grant or award programs. Some of our earliest work was catalyzed by seed grants from an internal innovation center that ran annual calls for proposals focused on enhancing teaching and learning via technology. These calls often brought together diverse individuals and provided us a venue to bring together faculty from our College of Education and Math department, along with institutional researchers, developers, and instructional designers to explore how analytics might play a role in supporting student success in a large calculus course. While our prototype and associated results showed some promise, the project wound down at the end of the grant funding. We still viewed this as a success, as it began to lay the foundation in terms of the different people and stakeholders who we would go on to work with on future, larger learning analytics projects.

Consortium, Research Partnerships, and Standards

Another effective strategy for bootstrapping your institution's capacity for learning analytics is by looking to external partnerships. The Society for Learning Analytics (SoLAR) held the first Learning Analytics and Knowledge (LAK) Conference in 2012, and attendees are often credited with helping to shape the first definition for the field of learning analytics. SoLAR continues to host the LAK conference, as well as smaller events such as the Learning Analytics Summer Institutes, that present a great venue and network to engage as you think about growing learning analytics initiatives locally. You can also find a great deal of research on the SoLAR website,[5] both originating from SoLAR events as well as through other outlets.

Another consideration as you begin to grow learning analytics efforts are consortiums. Even without joining a consortium, which at times can be costly, most consortiums make publicly available different resources on their websites. One example is Unizin, a consortium that strives to "meet the moment of digital transformation by developing and delivering solutions that address the pressing and complex challenges of data, analytics and digital content.[6]" Of specific note is a platform developed by the Consortium called the Unizin Data Platform (UDP), a cloud-based platform that allows universities to capture and leverage, in a single platform, a diverse set of learning data that is all standards driven. Even if a university is not a member of Unizin, the UDP recently launched as a product in the Google Cloud Platform storefront, allowing non-members to leverage this infrastructure. Another example is the IMS Global Learning Consortium®. Part

---

[5] https://www.solaresearch.org/
[6] https://unizin.org/about

of this consortium's work encompasses K–12 and higher education to support the adoption and growth of learning analytics through standards.

Technical standards can also help save time, pave the way for future interoperability, and generally accelerate project development. Both IMS's Caliper®[7] and xAPI[8] are examples of data-formatting standards that streamline data analysis by establishing consistent vocabularies in your data definitions. When the concept of a grade or a page view is the same regardless of the data source, that consistency can help otherwise disparate systems speak the same language. This facilitates data federation, or combining of datasets, which in turn leads to a more comprehensive description of student behaviors and performance and greater statistical power.

Beyond technical standards, organizations such as IEEE have worked to define new job profiles with competencies critical to supporting learning analytics efforts such as "learning engineers" (Goodell, 2018). Such job profiles can help organizations hire people with the right skillsets and create new capabilities that may be necessary to solve novel problems. If institutions don't have the funding or existing buy-in to create new positions, conducting a broad skills inventory across the organization may surface existing positions that could help move early analytics efforts forward.

Some institutions may choose to avoid this internal capacity building and simply license a learning analytics platform from a vendor. While this is a valid strategy and may suit your needs, especially if you have significant time constraints, it has been our experience at Penn State that the competencies described above are equally important when establishing a productive working relationship with such vendors. Entirely outsourcing your learning analytics capabilities may lead to avoidable implementation problems and an inability to appropriately challenge a vendor's methodologies. Given the highly contextual nature of the problems that learning analytics attempt to address, institutions should never settle for one-size-fits-all, "black box" solutions, nor should they enter into agreements with vendors who are not willing to at least discuss, at a high level, proprietary algorithms. Having the competencies in-house to facilitate those conversations is an important prerequisite.

Penn State Projects

The following projects represent a range of approaches to learning analytics that we've explored at Penn State. While each project originated in different organizations within the university, collaboration within formal governing bodies as well as informal sharing amongst like-minded peers has established a common

---

[7] http://www.imsglobal.org/activity/caliper
[8] https://xapi.com

philosophy and shared understanding of university priorities, policies, technology infrastructure, and individual unit roadmaps that together keep us on a similar orientation. We've categorized each project using our project dimensions to help you situate these individual efforts in the larger landscape of learning analytics.

Penn State Projects: Analytical Design Model

Table 7.5 Project Dimensions: Analytical Design Model

Project Dimensions: Analytical Design Model	
Purpose	Utilize empirical evidence of student performance and behavior to inform course revisions.
Audience	Instructor(s)-of-record and instructional designers.
Data sources	Learning management system, content management system, third-party student learning environments, surveys.
Risk factors	Moderate risk. Student grades and pseudoanonymized PII are used during analysis. All reporting is of aggregate trends. The intended audience has pre-existing approval to view this data. Analysis is facilitated by instructional designers to minimize erroneous interpretation and use of data.

Penn State World Campus Learning Design (WCLD) is a large, online course development unit with over 50 instructional designers, production specialists, multimedia specialists, editors, and programmers who support an average of approximately 1,200 course sections each semester. The unit was established in 1998, and in that time has supported the creation and ongoing offering of 45 academic programs. The traditional revision cycle within WCLD has been calendar based, relying on revisiting each course on a three- to four-year basis to refresh the content and assessments, create novel multimedia assets, and integrate new technologies based on course author and instructional designer insights, preferences, expertise, and best practices.

As our access to detailed course data from a variety of sources improves, WCLD has turned to developing a more refined revision process that supports targeted course improvements through identifying high-impact needs and supporting continuous, iterative, and data-informed updates. By more precisely identifying barriers to student success, we are better equipped with the information necessary to make course improvements that serve our learners, while simultaneously enhancing our use of resources and addressing institutional and unit goals related to student retention and program optimization.

We've based our new strategy for improving courses on the Analytical Design Model (ADM) (Millet & Resig, 2021), a five-phase, holistic approach to course revision that places an increased emphasis on the "analysis" stage of the instructional design process. The five phases are outlined below, along with examples in practice.

The five phases of the ADM are planning, analysis, validation, design and development, and evaluation (Millet & Resig, 2021). During the planning phase, the course author, instructional designer, and other relevant stakeholders meet both to discuss the course and the motivations for revision and to establish a set of guiding questions that serve as hypotheses to be explored during the analysis. The analysis phase involves compiling and triangulating the data to advance insights that address the guiding questions. Those insights are then validated by stakeholders to surface well-supported revision prioritizations. As IDs and authors move into the design and development phase, they utilize the priorities and analyses alongside their expertise in the content and learning sciences to revise the course. Lastly, the evaluation phase calls for ongoing data collection and analyses to monitor the efficacy of changes and to support continuous improvement.

The design of each analytical visualization or dashboard is deliberated on by a core analytics team who together represent the relevant pedagogical and technical competencies to ensure it is grounded in sound learning theory, intuitive to use, secure, and scalable. Over time, a designer toolkit has developed composed of reusable dashboards that address the most common instructional questions, and each includes inline scaffolding to guide designers and instructors in the appropriate use of the analytic (see Figures 7.1 and 7.2 on following pages). This iterative cycle drives the continued evolution of our datasets, refinement of our data sensors, more precise questions, and better procedures that embed data insights into course improvement practice.

Penn State Projects: Elevate

Table 7.6 Project Dimensions: Elevate

Project Dimensions: Elevate	
Purpose	To provide academic advisers access to Canvas activity data in order to help identify students as early as possible in a semester who may need proactive support.
Audience	Academic advisers.
Data sources	Student Information System (SIS) and Learning Management System (LMS).
Risk factors	Moderate risk. Advisers misinterpreting data may lead to unintended consequences in student communication strategies. Small number of instructors voiced concern this could be used to compare Canvas activity across courses for evaluation purposes.

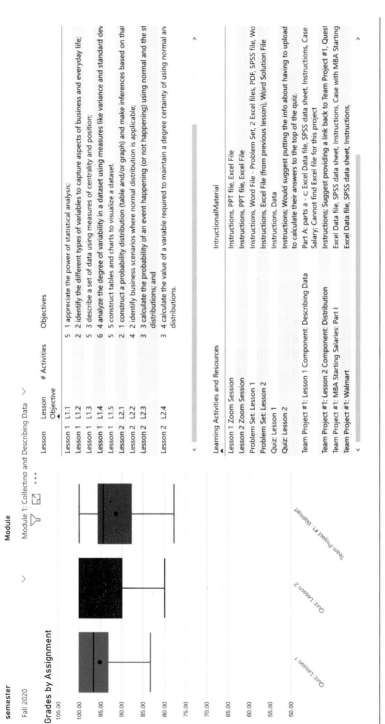

Figure 7.1   Dashboard of Lesson Learning Objectives, Activities, and Instructional Materials Alongside Student Performance Data

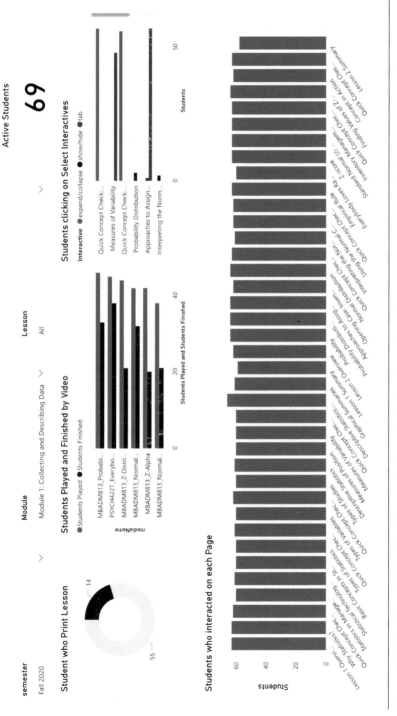

Figure 7.2 Dashboard of Student Interaction Data, Including Page Views, Printing Frequency, Media Consumption, and Engagement with Selected Course Elements

Elevate is an application that visualizes a combination of SIS and Canvas® activity data. The core functionality of Elevate involves taking every undergraduate course section across the University and calculating each student's interaction within Canvas for that specific course. This includes all the various actions a student might take, such as posting to a discussion forum, viewing a file, or submitting a homework assignment. All student activity from within a single course is then averaged together to create a fictitious, average student, as defined by Canvas activity. Once the fictitious average student is created, each student is then compared to the fictitious average student. Based on this comparison, one of three things happen within the interface of Elevate:

- If the student being explored has similar activity to the fictitious average student, or exhibits significantly more activity, no alerts are displayed in Elevate.
- If the student being explored is active in Canvas, but at a significantly lower rate of activity compared to the fictitious average student, Elevate assigns a yellow icon next to the student.
- If the student being explored has been inactive in Canvas for seven consecutive days or more, Elevate assigns an orange icon next to the student to indicate inactivity.

Recognizing that not every instructor uses Canvas, Elevate includes logic to make sure we are only comparing students within Canvas course sections where engaging Canvas is a consistent part of the course experience. For example, if a faculty member is not using Canvas at all, Elevate would only show a roster view with no icons.

Elevate renders the Canvas activity data in three different visualizations:

- **Rolling seven-day average.** This visualization considers the different habits of students with how they engage courses. Some students might engage heavily during the week, some students might wait until Sunday to do most of their coursework. By having a rolling seven-day average Canvas activity metric, we can account for differences in when a student engages Canvas, providing a standard way to compare student activity to the course average. (See Figure 7.3.)
- **Cumulative activity.** This visualization shows the fictitious average student activity from day one of the semester to the present, compared to the specific student we are exploring.
- **Daily activity.** A visualization that shows the number of Canvas actions taken by a student each day in a course.

The onset of the COVID-19 pandemic presented a catalyst for engaging our Canvas data, which led to Elevate. The original concept for Elevate was to provide instructors a web-based application that included a few different Canvas data visualizations, in order to help identify students who might be falling behind as

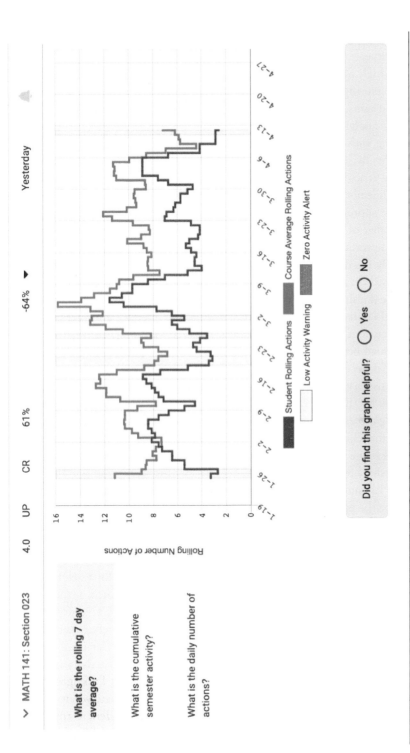

Figure 7.3 The rolling seven-day average graph. The blue line represents the fictitious average student's Canvas activity, while the red line represents the student we are interested in exploring.

the entire University braced for courses being delivered online for an unknown amount of time.

The first high-fidelity mockups for Elevate emerged in the summer of 2020, as well as exploring different methods to visualize Canvas data that can lead to actionable insights. While working on Elevate, we continued to support an earlier learning analytics application that is a collaboration between our Teaching and Learning with Technology (TLT) unit and our advising community. When meeting with advising leadership, we showed them our early work on Elevate, and they quickly articulated how valuable something like this can be in the hands of advisers. While not our original audience, Elevate was pivoted to an adviser-facing tool with the appropriate design changes. By the start of the Fall semester of 2020, a small number of advisers were piloting Elevate. Throughout the Fall semester, Elevate was introduced to more advisers via training sessions in specific colleges or campuses. By the middle of the Spring 2021 semester, over 400 advisers from 15 campuses used Elevate to explore Canvas data related to 2,800 students.

While the dominant data source for Elevate is Canvas data, the tool also relies heavily on SIS data. Advisers can see in the same user interface information about a student's current and past performance, semester standing, cumulative GPA, and course load beside information on how active the student is in their courses compared to other students in those same courses. These two data sources are fairly common to use in efforts around learning analytics. A new data source that proved to be relevant for this project was data from Starfish™, a tool that is in place to support advising across the University and a critical part of most advisers' workflows. In order to make sure Elevate was not an application outside of existing adviser workflows, Elevate was designed to push data, specifically alerts for students with low or no activity in Canvas, directly into Starfish. This was very important to the adoption of Elevate, as it didn't require a change in workflow and still allows for Starfish to be the primary tool used for advising.

Throughout the last year, advisers are sharing interesting use cases regarding how Elevate provides new insights in specific situations and helps to frame how an adviser might engage a student in varying situations. A common example are students impacted by COVID, whether sick themselves, caring for a sick friend or family member, or facing challenges in quarantine. In one instance, a student fell ill to COVID and was diagnosed by a family physician, so the University had no way of knowing the student's status. All the various COVID safety nets designed to assist students never sprang into action. This student's adviser is an Elevate user and noticed that the student went from lower-than-normal activity in all his Canvas courses one week, to no Canvas activity the following week, prompting the adviser to reach out to the student. The adviser discovered the student was sick and was able to alert the appropriate instructors and help the student re-engage his coursework after missing nearly two weeks of classes in the middle of a semester.

Another anecdote from an adviser illustrates the value of having access to near real-time data, something advisers never had in the past. Like many universities, Penn State has points in time during semester in which instructors provide feedback to students as part of a progress reporting effort. This takes place within the Starfish application, so if an instructor flags a student for poor performance a third of the way through a course, the adviser sees that and can follow up with the student. In one instance, an instructor recognized a student was disengaging from her course and emailed the student multiple times, encouraging a visit to office hours. The instructor then alerted an adviser via Starfish that the student was showing signs of disengagement, prompting the adviser to reach out to the student. Unfortunately, the adviser also did not receive a response. The instructor and adviser got together over Zoom® to discuss next steps, when the adviser decided to examine the student in Elevate. Upon reviewing the Canvas activity data, it was apparent that the student was disengaged in the course based on very limited Canvas activity when compared to others in the class. Elevate also revealed, after receiving the most recent instructor email and email from the adviser, a large burst of Canvas activity from the student. This alleviated some of the anxiety that originated from no student response, as they could now visibly see the student was trying to re-engage the course and ended up doing so successfully.

When leveraging data such as Canvas and SIS data, training end users on how to interpret the data is of critical importance. Introducing and consistently reinforcing the notion of being data-informed in contrast to data-driven helps contextualize how advisers can leverage the data. For example, just because someone shows low activity in Canvas does not mean they require a proactive message. Different scenarios, such as a high-performing student working ahead in a course, can lead to Elevate triggering alerts. The adviser should consider all the other factors known about the student, such as historical performance, the personal relationship with the student, and most importantly, the adviser's professional experience and intuition when deciding to reach out to the student. When Elevate data do contribute to an adviser's engaging a student, we advocate the adviser use information from Elevate (and all the other information sources used in advising) to ask the student probing questions, compared to bluntly stating something akin to, "I see you're not very active in Canvas in your calculus class." Advisers do not need to be sneaky about using Elevate, while at the same time relying too heavily on the data can result in misinterpretation or confusing messaging to the student.

Ensuring that you can communicate a clear goal with your stakeholders is also vital to a project's success. For example, as Elevate began to take shape, we did a "socialization tour" for three months, talking to specific administrators about Elevate, as well as various committees and task forces, such as our Faculty Senate and Strategic Planning committees. Engaging these audiences early, and with a clear message, helped them field questions about Elevate they received locally.

Penn State Projects: Spectrum

Table 7.7 Project Dimensions: Spectrum

Project Dimensions: Spectrum	
Purpose	Encourage reflective teaching practices by providing a method for instructors to explore aspects of their course that unfold across an entire semester.
Audience	Instructors, instructional designers.
Data sources	Class recordings, BERT (Google's Natural Language Processing model).
Risk factors	Low risk. A small number of faculty voiced concern that a tool like this might be used to compare how faculty that teach the same course differ from one another, both in pedagogy as well as content.

A colleague often refers to learning management systems as "learner" management systems, commenting that the systems themselves do not provide much support for learning, though they do help a great deal in managing students through things like assignment dropboxes and gradebooks. Others make a similar observation about learning analytics: current work rarely measures learning and is more a proxy to a learner's activity, as evidenced by clicks or records in a student information system (Kitto et al., 2020).

The first two examples in this chapter represent more common uses of learning analytics, at least from a data source perspective, and are primarily proxies for learning and engagement. These projects are still incredibly valuable to our institution, though we have engaged a parallel path of learning analytics prototypes designed to help faculty design, deliver, and reflect on courses. These include recommendation engines designed to help faculty create Open Educational Resources (OER) such as textbooks (Pursel et al., 2019), recommendation engines to help instructors identify plausible distractors when writing assessments (Liang et al., 2018), and tools to help instructors brainstorm in order to find new, relevant content for inclusion in assignments, case studies, activities, and lectures (Pursel, 2018; Hellar et al., 2019).

Our Spectrum prototype is designed to support student learning through catalyzing instructor reflective teaching practices. If we can incrementally help instructors improve pedagogy through learning analytics, the end results are better learning experiences for students. The primary data used by Spectrum are recorded class sessions. Spectrum takes a semester's worth of class recordings, then sends them to the cloud for transcription. Once voice is transcoded to text, Spectrum leverages Google's BERT natural language processing model to put meaning to the words and phrases uttered in each class session. At this point, a topic modeling approach is employed across the entire dataset that represents a semester, identifying clusters of topics. Once the topic modeling is complete, Spectrum provides an instructor a visualization depicting the entire semester, illustrating the various collections of topics discussed in the semester, and how those topics are distributed within classes as well as across the entire semester. (See Figure 7.4 on following page.)

This visualization is designed to support reflective teaching practices, helping to uncover patterns across the semester. When visualizing one instructor's course, he found Spectrum useful in comparing his identified learning objectives covered in the course to the topic areas identified by Spectrum. He was specifically looking to see if each primary learning objective was receiving equal attention in the course. Through Spectrum, it was clear that some of the broader objectives were receiving much less time from a lecture and discussion perspective compared to others. Another faculty member was interested in exploring the notion of interleaving, which deals with how an instructor makes connections between seemingly different topics, which is a valid method to help students learn and retain complex information. In both cases, Spectrum provided insights that led to minor revisions to the courses.

In addition to topic modeling, Spectrum has similar visualizations for modeling certain types of language such as questions. Figure 7.5 illustrates a visualization where each blue line represents a point in a class where a question was asked. Spectrum can't differentiate between who asked the question or if it was rhetorical, just a high likelihood of a question being asked.

As we worked with a faculty member tasked with redesigning his course, this visualization led to several decisions to redesign specific parts of the course. First, one class session had a rather large number of questions in comparison to the other class sessions. The instructional designer observed that students must have been highly engaged that day. The instructor thought for a moment, then indicated those questions represented confusion. He was able to reflect that the weekly quiz grades were below average for this content and that students found this content to be some of the most challenging in the course. This led to splitting that content area over two course periods, with new activities to help the students better understand the material. Later in the same course, one class session had almost no questions, which again was abnormal to the pattern of questions through most class sessions. When prompted why, the faculty member chuckled, indicating this is his personal area of research, and he's so excited to talk about it he doesn't give the students time to ask questions! This led to more intentional breaks in the content during that section, to solicit student questions and encourage engagement.

One of the last visualizations in Spectrum is a speaker analysis, shown in Figure 7.6. When put in front of a small number of faculty, this visualization appears to help with reflecting on pacing. For example, one instructor observed getting off to a good start in the semester in terms of student engagement during

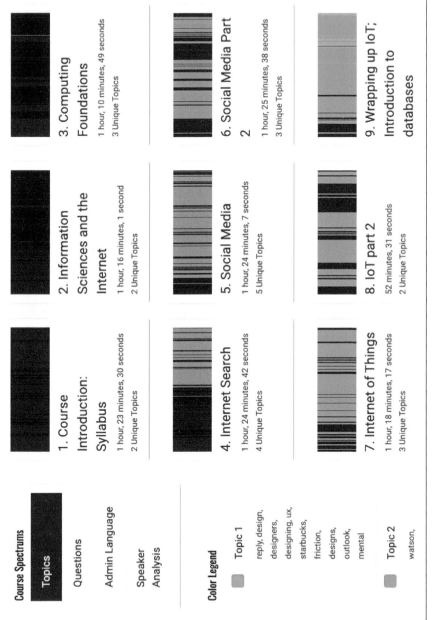

Figure 7.4   A Visualization of Topics Across Several Class Sessions of a Course

Figure 7.5   A Visualization of Questions Being Asked Across Several Class Sessions of a Course

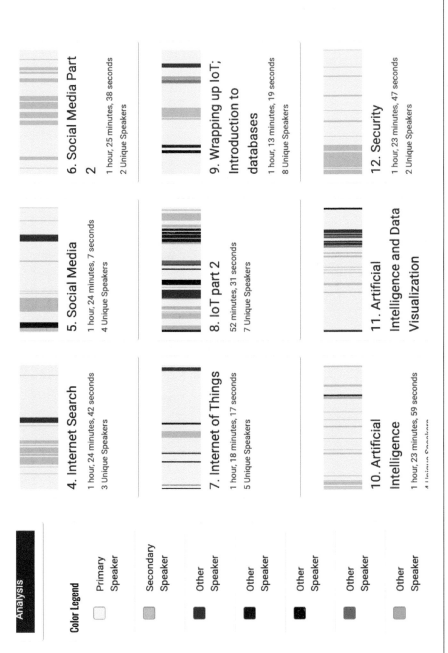

Figure 7.6   A Visualization Showing the Number of Unique Speakers Across Class Sessions

class, seeing that his in-class activities were driving great discussion. Then, as the semester progressed, class sessions with more than a primary and secondary speaker diminished. This led to the faculty member's more intentionally creating in-class activities specific to content later in the course to try and maintain a high level of student engagement via the activities throughout the semester.

While a project like Spectrum may not come with as many privacy and ethical challenges as Elevate, some faculty are concerned it could be used to compare their teaching to their peers, particularly those that may teach the same class. Depending on your university's culture, this could be viewed as an infringement on academic freedom and faculty autonomy. For example, if a department head could use Spectrum to compare three instructors teaching the same course, they may use the data to dictate to one faculty member to conform more closely to how the other two faculty members are teaching. On the other hand, we do have groups of faculty members who, on their own accord, plan to use Spectrum for a similar purpose: to compare how each teaches their version of the course, identify similarities and differences, and collectively come together to make iterative improvements based on the experiences of each individual teacher.

Conclusion

For institutions that are struggling to establish a data-informed decision-making culture or are in the early phases of launching learning analytics initiatives, we hope that this chapter offers some practical recommendations. First and foremost among these recommendations is to establish institutional values or guiding principles related to learning analytics as early as possible. These high-level principles will help to orient all subsequent efforts and create logical opportunities for collaboration, even at large and complex universities. Be prepared to engage individuals and offices at your institution that might be foreign to you. When we began, our privacy office, education equity office, and ethics research center represented units we hadn't engaged in the past. Individuals from these offices are now vital collaborators on nearly all our projects. Additionally, we strongly recommend institutions mature mindfully. Penn State has benefited from a very measured and reflective approach, using limited-scope, low-risk projects as a starting point and deliberately translating early lessons into the basis of more complex initiatives. Consider reviewing outdated policies and procedures that govern data use that don't align with modern challenges in higher education. But do so in a way that prioritizes privacy assurance and security and promotes ethical behavior. Learning analytics does not need to rely on expensive technology platforms or massive efforts to solve enterprise-wide problems. Making better decisions with data is achievable by all institutions.

References

Arnold, K. E., and Sclater, N. (2017, March). Student perceptions of their privacy in learning analytics applications. *Proceedings of the Seventh International Learning Analytics & Knowledge Conference,* 66–69.

Clagett, C. A. (1991). *Institutional Research: The Key to Successful Enrollment Management.* Office of Institutional Research and Analysis, Prince George's Community College, Largo, MD.

Dastin, J. (2018, October 10). Amazon scraps secret AI recruiting tool that showed bias against women. *Reuters.* Retrieved from: https://www.reuters.com/article/us-amazon-com-jobs-automation-insight/amazon-scraps-secret-ai-recruiting-tool-that-showed-bias-against-women-idUSKCN1MK08G

Goodell, J. (2018). *Learning Engineering.* IEEE. https://sagroups.ieee.org/icicle/learning-engineering-key-elements/

Hellar, D. B., Pursel, B., and Wham, D. (2019). Leveraging AI to support data-empowered learning. *Educause annual meeting,* Chicago, IL, United States. https://events.educause.edu/annual-conference/2019/agenda/leveraging-ai-to-support-dataempowered-learning

Jones, K. M. L., and McCoy, C. (2019) Reconsidering data in learning analytics: Opportunities for critical research using a documentation studies framework. *Learning, Media and Technology, 44*(1), 52–63. doi: 10.1080/17439884.2018.1556216

Kitto, K., Whitmer, J., Silvers, A., and Webb, M. (2020, September). *Creating Data for Learning Analytics Ecosystem* [position paper]. https://www.solaresearch.org/wp-content/uploads/2020/09/SoLAR_Position-Paper_2020_09.pdf

Liang, C., Yang, X., Dave, N., Wham, D., Pursel, B., and Giles, C. L. (2018). Distractor generation for multiple choice questions using learning to rank. *Proceedings of the Thirteenth Workshop on Innovative Use of NLP for Building Educational Applications,* 284–290.

Means, B., Padilla, C., DeBarger, A., and Bakia, M. (2009). *Implementing Data-Informed Decision Making in Schools: Teacher Access, Supports, and Use.* US Department of Education.

Millet, C., and Resig, J. (2021). Data-informed design for online course improvement. In: J. Stefaniak et al. (Eds.), *A Practitioner's Guide to Instructional Design in Higher Education.* EdTech Books.

Murray, J. (2014). Critical issues facing school leaders concerning data-informed decision-making. *Professional Educator, 38*(1), 1–8.

Prinsloo, P., and Slade, S. (2015, March). Student privacy self-management: Implications for learning analytics. *Proceedings of the Fifth International Conference on Learning Analytics and Knowledge,* 83–92.

Pursel, B. K. (2018). Building an Initiative Around Data Science and Learning. Educause learning initiatives annual meeting, New Orleans, LA, US. https://events

.educause.edu/eli/annual-meeting/2018/agenda/building-an-initiative-around-data
-science-and-learning

Pursel, B. K., Ramsay, C., Dave, N., Liang, C., and Giles, C. L. (2019). BBookX: Creating semi-automated textbooks to support student learning and decrease student costs. *Proceedings of the First Workshop on Intelligent Textbooks* (iTextbooks 2019), collocated with *AIED* 2019, Chicago, IL, USA, June 25, 2019.

Raji, I. D., Gebru, T., Mitchell, M., Buolamwini, J., Lee, J., and Denton, E. (2020, February). Saving face: Investigating the ethical concerns of facial recognition auditing. *Proceedings of the AAAI/ACM Conference on AI, Ethics, and Society,* 145–151.

Shen, J., Cooley, V. E., Ma, X., Reeves, P. L., Burt, W. L., Rainey, J. M., and Yuan, W. (2012). Data-informed decision making on high-impact strategies: Developing and validating an instrument for principals. *The Journal of Experimental Education, 80*(1), 1–25.

Shilton, K. (2018). Values and ethics in human-computer interaction. *Foundations and Trends in Human–Computer Interaction, 12*(2).

Slade, S., and Prinsloo, P. (2013). Learning analytics: Ethical issues and dilemmas. *American Behavioral Scientist, 57*(10), 1510–1529.

Chapter 8

The Benefits of the 'New Normal'

Data Insights for Improving Curriculum Design, Teaching Practice, and Learning

Deborah West and Pablo Munguia[1]

Abstract

The Covid-19 pandemic has accelerated and significantly changed the learning and teaching environment to create a 'new normal'. In this chapter, we discuss how pedagogical frameworks and theories need to shift and incorporate online-only modalities and how we can measure and evaluate teaching effectiveness and student progression, engagement, and belonging. Using the Community of Inquiry learning framework and learning analytics, we describe how we can construct questions, hypotheses, and testable variables to understand learning and teaching in this new space. We propose that a new framework may be needed to expand from the Community of Inquiry to provide a more holistic view of the student experience—which includes program curriculum design, a different sense of belonging for students—and recognize the learning challenges caused by distractions.

---

[1] Flinders University, Bedford Park, SA, Australia, 5042

Keywords: Learning analytics, community of inquiry, COI, online learning, teaching framework

Introduction

Online learning has made significant progress in the last 20 years, providing increased flexibility and accessibility for larger and more diverse cohorts of students. However, the outcomes have not been equal to campus-based experiences. Various studies have shown that student retention is lower and the student experience is generally poorer for students studying online (Sorensen & Donovan, 2017; Bawa, 2016). However, the reasons for this have been heavily debated, with possible factors including a higher percentage of equity students being enrolled online, less academic preparedness, time constraints, limited effective use of technologies, and the idea that students online can feel isolated and unsupported by their teachers and/or peers (Dekker, Pechenizkiy & Vleeshouwers, 2009; Frankola, 2002; Rivera & Rice, 2002; Diaz, 2000). While much has moved on since that time, there continues to be some discrepancy in the student experience.

Students often provide feedback about their university experience, which helps shape strategic institutional improvements. For example, the Student Experience Survey, funded by the Australian government, seeks responses from all higher education students in Australia to gauge their experience of study (see Quality Indicators for Learning and Teaching, 2020). It is structured into five scales made up of various items which gather students' views on skills development, learner engagement, teaching quality, student support, and learning resources. These data show over time that while there is little difference between internal/mixed study mode and external (online) study mode in relation to quality of the entire educational experience, some metrics are quite different—in particular, learner engagement, which is made up of items related to feeling a sense of belonging, being able to participate in discussion, interaction, or collaboration with other students—shows a significant difference, generally in the range of 40% less agreement for external students compared to on-campus students in the years from 2016 to 2019.

However, in 2020, the percentage of agreement dropped considerably for students who were enrolled in an on-campus course, which coincided with the Covid-19 pandemic, further reinforcing the idea that the online experience is less positive in relation to these items. Understanding and unpacking the reasons for this online experience are critical to making improvements. This chapter provides a framework for how we can measure and evaluate teaching effectiveness and student progression, engagement, and belonging, utilising a robust and theoretically grounded approach. This requires attention to various aspects or levels (i.e., teaching practice, assessment, curriculum design) of the experience, drawing on key theoretical bodies of knowledge. This will both leverage and inform the move to the 'new normal'.

While most universities have harnessed the benefits of educational technology, this has predominantly been to enhance face-to-face teaching or provide a 'blended' model. Up until early 2020, a relatively small number of institutions globally actively pursued the fully online model, including developing the full range of institutional capabilities necessary to deliver fully online courses for students. Where this has occurred and been done well, consideration is given to instructional design for online learning as well as transition of all student support services into an online and broadly accessible format, including library, academic language, literacy and numeracy support, tutoring, IT and platform helpdesks, and health and counselling services. However, the knowledge, skills, and expertise required to provide high-quality, fully online delivery and service has typically been scarce in most institutions in both faculty and professional support staff (Bawa, 2016). Additionally, while some good work has occurred over the years related to curriculum design and pedagogy for fully online education, it has remained limited, with a small audience. However, the Covid-19 pandemic has disrupted the 'normal' paradigm.

In the last 18 months, universities globally have made an emergency transition at scale to online teaching, providing study continuity for students and to remain financially viable. Due to the global pandemic, this was done in a very short space of time, and in the vast majority of cases, courses were transitioned in a way which reflected the urgent need, resulting in emergency remote teaching rather than intentional design for online learning (Hodges et al., 2020). While not optimal in design, the forced move to online learning has resulted in a rapid upskilling of staff and an increased amenability to online learning. Additionally, a transition took place in relation to student support services. With this upskilling of staff and broader societal disruption to work and life, tertiary institutions are now considering how some of the benefits of online learning might be incorporated into the 'new normal'.

This shift to emergency remote teaching and the new view of what is possible has also created an opportunity to harness the potential of learning analytics. Learning analytics can be defined as, ". . . the measurement, collection, analysis and reporting of data about learners and their contexts, for purposes of understanding and optimising learning and the environments in which it occurs" (Long & Siemens, 2011, p. 34). This is a relatively new field, which draws together a range of disciplines which come from three different philosophical paradigms: science, cognition, and learning (Munguia & Gibson, *in review*). The bringing together of these three fields is critical with the application of data science to educational design and learning. The development of this transdisciplinary field has been somewhat limited, both due to being a new field, but also because complex insights require a range of appropriate data which is reliant on the use of educational technology.

In higher education, particularly in relation to online education, there is considerable work to be done to understand effective curriculum design and teaching to optimise learning. Much of the teaching that occurs continues to be based on traditional understandings of education or, in fact, tradition itself. While the last 20 years has seen a trend to educators as facilitators or guides, this has been slow to occur. The traditional lecture/tutorial model is still firmly in place in most institutions and was largely replicated during the emergency remote teaching period. Yet, the advent of educational technology, along with shifts in society, suggests a need to move to a new model of education (West & Thompson, 2015). While instructional design expertise has evolved, models for online education based on educational theory, and subsequently robustly tested, has been lacking.

A significant exception to this has been the Community of Inquiry (COI) model, which has been developed for online education (Garrison, Anderson & Archer, 1999; Anderson et al. 2001; Garrison & Anderson 2003; Garrison & Arbaugh 2007; Garrison et al. 2010). Explicitly based on a social constructivist approach, it has three domains—social presence, teacher presence, and cognitive presence—each with a set of empirically tested items. In essence, this brings together two key paradigms: cognition and learning. Some work has also been done with this in relation to learning analytics. For example, Moodle® (2021) has done some work on identifying a range of indicators based on the COI model; however, this does not yet appear to have been tested. However, both the COI and the testing focuses on teaching practice within a subject/course rather than at the degree/program level. The learning design elements also remain implicit in items rather than explicitly being called out even at the subject/course level, meaning that there is no explicit connection to curriculum design or teaching practice at the degree/program level.

Similarly, assessment practices have remained largely static and traditional, despite the affordances of technology (Sweeny et al., 2017). This international study, which reviewed published journal articles on the use of technology in and for assessment practice, found that the use of technology in a way that could be seen as 'transformative' was limited. Rather, the majority of cases reported transferring traditional assessment practices into a technological environment. While these did enhance functionality or efficiency, it did not show a substantive shift from traditional approaches of assessment. Yet, these traditional approaches are not necessarily seen as the most effective way to assess learning outcomes in a way which can translate to the workplace (JISC, 2016). Additionally, it is noted that assessment transformation needs to be based on a research-informed approach and critical evaluation (Elkington & Evans, 2017).

Both educators and students are interested in what learning analytics can bring to education (Luzeckyj, A., 2020; West et al. 2019; West, Luzeckyj et al., 2018; West, Tasir et al., 2018; West et al., 2015; Corrin et al. 2016; Ifenthaler & Schumacher, 2016) in relation to both curriculum design, teaching practice and assessment.

Studies have identified that teaching academics are interested in the insights that might be provided to improve curriculum design, teaching practice, student retention (Colvin et al., 2016; Lawson, Beer, Rossi, Moore & Fleming, 2016; Liu, Rogers, & Pardo, 2015; Marbouti, Diefes-Dux, & Madhavan, 2016; Sclater & Mullan, 2017), student success (Fritz & Whitmer, 2017; Li & Tsai, 2017), assessment (Fidalgo-Blanco et al., 2017; Knight, Shibani & Buckingham-Shum, 2018). Studies undertaken by West et al. (2015), West, Luzeckyj et al. (2018), and West, Tasir et al. (2018) analysed responses from 353 Australian teaching academics in relation to how they thought learning analytics could help improve the educational experience. The highest response rates were related to evaluating teaching practice, improving student retention, students monitoring their progress and taking action, and understanding how learning could occur (West, Luzeckyj et al., 2018).

The data from these projects (West, Luzeckyj et al., 2018; West, Tasir et al., 2018) was subsequently mapped to the COI and showed that teaching academics in Australia were particularly interested in items that mapped to cognitive and social presence, while Malaysian academics were more interested in teaching presence items. There were no responses from academics that could not be mapped to the COI, suggesting that is it a useful framework for learning analytics work related to curriculum and teaching improvements.

Students are also interested, although cautious, in relation to how learning analytics can support their learning (West, 2019; Brooker et al., 2017; Khan, 2017; Ifenthaler & Schumacher, 2016; Roberts et al., 2016; Fisher et al., 2014). Students thought that learning analytics could be useful to help them improve their learning (West et al., 2019). They were particularly interested in having reports or information provided to them which would provide prompts about additional learning materials, progression through learning materials, and additional services. They were also generally positive (over 90% agreement based on a sample of 2017) about this being based on assessment grades (West, 2019).

Of course, the use of data in any context raises ethical considerations related to privacy (Tsai et al., 2019; Jones & VanScoy, 2019; Reidenberg & Schaub, 2018; Pardo & Siemens, 2014), informed consent (Howell et al., 2018; West et al., 2018; Ifenthaler & Schumacher, 2016; Lawson et al., 2016; Prinsloo & Slade, 2016), transparency (Klein et al., 2019; Jones & VanScoy, 2019; Ifenthaler & Schumacher, 2016; West et al., 2016; Slade & Prinsloo, 2014) and ethical application (Tsai et al., 2019; West, Huijser & Heath, 2016; Drachsler & Greller, 2016; Slade & Prinsloo, 2013). Studies have shown that both academic staff (West et al., 2015) and students (West et al., 2019; Arnold & Sclater, 2017) are concerned about the ethical use of data. However, the Australian study (West et al., 2019) indicated that students were reasonably comfortable with data collected in relation to their studies being used to improve their educational experience and outcomes. Key elements to consider include providing information and reminders about the data collected and how they will be used, providing data security, and not sharing data with third parties. Additionally, students were more comfortable with data directly related to their educational experience being used to improve the learning and teaching experience.

The 'new normal' provides an opportunity to apply learning analytics to significantly improve online learning. While many students will likely go back to an on-campus experience, there is also evidence to suggest that a blended model and fully online model will be part of the new landscape. This will mean that more complete data sets will be available to apply data science techniques to improve the experience, quality, and outcomes for students. With more students studying in these modes, the impetus to improve the outcomes is also likely to be stronger.

The key themes that emerge, however, are the need to look at multiple levels of practice from the subject/course to the degree/program and up to the university experience level. Additionally, consideration needs to be given to both the teaching practice and the curriculum design, which is based on educational theory and paradigms. With this framework, one can then turn one's attention to the use of data science to provide key insights into both learning (cognition) and education. These insights and a research-informed approach can inform a 'new normal', which has improved outcomes and flexibility for all.

Testing the Benefits of the New Normal

Learning and teaching activities in the new normal still require an empirical understanding of the relationships between teacher, learner, and the curriculum driving the learning ecosystem. While the new normal requires a robust pedagogical framework to describe learning and teaching practice in an online-dependent world, as discussed above, there is also a need to measure and evaluate the three points of the COI and the interactions between them (see Figure 8.1).

We assume that, because of the 2020 disruption, only two modes of curriculum ecosystems will be in existence in the near future: online only and a blended modality with online and F2F components. Therefore, whenever we rely on creating or modifying curricula using evidence, we need to compare these two ecosystems, as this provides a powerful contrast. Comparisons at this level test the null hypothesis that online modality does not differ from the blended modality, forcing assessors to unpack alternative explanations to understand deviations from this null hypothesis. Deviations arising from this initial comparison require clear articulation of the question being addressed and a good understanding of the variables used to address the question.

The next two sections will focus on variables and testing methods, and here we will discuss the types of questions that can drive our reflection surrounding the

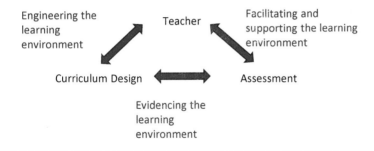

Figure 8.1   Heuristic Model Emerging from the Community of Inquiry Framework. Showing the relationship between the curriculum design, teaching practice, and tools for assessment and engagement. In (gold) are the domains of the engineering phase, facilitating phase, and evidencing phase in the process.

new pedagogical framework and theory. These sample questions are not meant to be prescriptive, rather stimulating.

Questions that interrogate and help evaluate teaching practice can be organized systematically to include the broad aspects of online learning and teaching (Table 8.1). At the highest level, we can articulate questions about the learning ecosystem. In the new normal, where things are online, the ecosystem can refer to the Learning Management System (LMS) (or any other platform that is for student-teacher-subject content engagement). We suggest that questions about the ecosystem are structural in nature and are useful to inform the teaching landscape for comparative purposes, establish testable hypotheses, and help reflect on best ways to organise the ecosystem (Munguia et al., 2020a). For example, Canvas LMS courses have a series of pages (or modules) to organise course content (Munguia et al., 2020b). By knowing how individual courses present their content and how they integrate learning resources within disciplines and across disciplines, academics can share their insights without judgement and help ask the question, for example, "Why do I need to structure my course this way in the LMS?"

Questions surrounding the teaching material are discipline specific and should focus on the best way to present information for students to learn. Teaching material can include the usage of educational tools. These questions need to address whether teaching is synchronous or asynchronous, as the time between a student's interrogating the material and asking questions about it may have a delayed response from the instructor, potentially affecting learning. Further, material should be easily digestible online. Therefore, questions are strongly linked to the discipline and the teaching theories associated with the discipline. Using the COI could stimulate greater student–student interaction.

Teacher engagement is the next level that should be considered once an understanding of the learning ecosystem and the content structured has been reflected

Table 8.1 Evidence Levels, Questions, and Evaluating Approaches Needed to Test the Pedagogical Framework in the New Normal*

Question Level	Question Type	Evaluating Structure
Learning ecosystem	Structural, associated with LMS design	The evaluation endpoint is hypothesis creation—e.g., highly structured content should be more accessible than unstructured information.
Teaching material (content structure)	Content accessibility and ease of absorption, relative to synchronous and asynchronous teaching	Are there content bottlenecks affecting curriculum delivery? Evaluation of student progress through content and ability of students to synthesize across content.
Teacher engagement	Is the teacher engaging with their students, acknowledging learner diversity?	What is the teacher response time to student inquiries? Does teacher engagement stimulate learner engagement?
Student engagement	Dynamic questions: How are students progressing through content?	What is the student trajectory through content, and what are the sizes of the pauses?
Academic support (correlations and assumptions)	Relational questions: from which learning activity students engage with academic support?	Understanding the added value of support within a course, and when. For example, are students more likely to engage with support after the first assessment or with a resubmission?

* We are constraining each level to a single example.

upon. How are teachers engaging with learners and facilitating the course? In passive teaching, such as lecturing, engaging teachers were usually those that were good orators and could spin stories into the content (Novak, 2011; Davies et al., 2013). In an online world, where material is often digested in isolation by students, teachers need to incorporate other engagement approaches, and these in turn can be measured and evaluated.

Student engagement was measured by early learning analytics practitioners as time on task (Kovanović et al., 2015), with one hypothesis being that the greater time on a task, the greater the engagement by the student. However, this has proven problematic for several reasons (Kovanović et al., 2015; Ferguson & Clow 2017). Student engagement can be more easily seen either as single events at different times in a semester, where different patterns are explored (Munguia et al.,

2020a), or how students navigate across material and the latency patterns they exhibit. For example, when accessing a particular LMS page, where do students go next? In the past, students used to physically enter a learning environment, whether it was enter a classroom, arrive at a campus, or open a book. Engaging with an online environment is quite different—opening a file, playing a video, navigating an LMS—which may require a different way to understand engagement with academic information (Brennan et al., 2019).

Universities often offer academic support and resources to complement and enhance academic skills, such as writing and critical thinking. The creation, delivery, and engagement with these resources and services needs to be addressed in conjunction with the learning activities within a learning ecosystem, if possible. These services may be generic in nature (e.g., writing support across faculties) or bespoke (e.g., high level mathematics), yet interrogating its value can be beneficial if questions are associated with the learning ecosystem.

Variables and Proxies

With the emergence of learning analytics and online platforms that capture very granular activity patterns, the data available to evaluate pedagogy is exponentially increasing, and the challenge has been to identify variables and proxies that are meaningful with expected levels of accuracy and precision (Taylor & Munguia, 2018; Munguia & Brennan, 2020). Variables need to be clearly identified when formulating questions, as this allows for a clear construction of a hypothesis to be tested. Here we will focus on differentiating between variables that describe a specific activity and proxies that help us understand activities that cannot be directly measured.

Variables can either be static events or represent dynamic activities. For example, attrition is a static metric that identifies the endpoint of an event (leave or continue with studies) and are often transactional in nature (e.g., activities completed by a student). Comparisons of such metrics are useful to identify initial patterns (e.g., course X has greater attrition than course Y). In contrast, dynamic variables are reflecting changes in activities within a defined amount of time or space, and these events may be associated with performance and acquisition of learning skills (e.g., difference in performance between first and last assignment is measuring a rate of change). For example, consider these two variables: submission time relative to deadline (measured in hours) and change in submission times between first and last assignment. Submission times can be negative or positive depending on whether submissions were before or after the deadline. The first variable measures a level of time management regarding assignments and the second whether time management has improved.

Proxies are often necessary when there is no clear measurement of an activity, and proxies often rely on assumptions that need to be tested to be validated. For example, 'student engagement' is hard to measure as such, as engaging in the online space can vary depending on how the variable is measured, and it may not be reflecting actual engagement (Kovanović et al., 2015). Therefore, proxies become suitable approximations that describe a mechanism, and often proxies can be a synthesis of different variables.

Synthesising variables can inform us about change in student perception, about studying, and about their actual studying patterns. For example, Brennan et al. (2019) combined a series of static variables associated with LMS information material (e.g., watching videos, downloading PDFs, engaging in discussion boards). The synthetic variable helps describe the behavioural trends when accessing LMS information and allows us to understand the common and rare patterns of engagement across the student body.

When comparing these synthetic patterns of engagement between the early and late moments in a semester, we can ask questions about changes in behavioural patterns and start exploring mechanisms driving these changes (Brennan et al., 2019). These data can be shared with students to work on reflection of student skills in class, helping them prepare for university studies. Another example would be relying on the total number of posts greater than x words within the course discussion board as a proxy for the level of engagement with peers and content (e.g., Ezen-Can et al., 2015; Chen et al., 2018).

Finally, variables can complement each other when measuring patterns at different scales. The combination of within-classroom events and among-classroom events allows for understanding of curriculum design and effectiveness from first-year studies to graduation (Raji et al., 2017; Munguia & Brennan, 2020). Program-level approaches and variables often focus on demographic variables and performance to predict students' finishing programs (Golding and Donaldson, 2006; Jeffreys, 2007).

However, variables measuring progression, repetition, dropouts, and graduation can be coupled with variables measuring activities within a classroom, and when mapped against the curricula, we can better understand the quality of teaching and the student experience. The metrics that commonly provide us insights into the university experience include direct student feedback via surveys deployed at the start and end of any program, and these can be treated as a dynamic variable. For example, sentiment statements describing greatest perceived challenge in a university at the start and end of the program can be a proxy for the level of preparedness to undertake a degree at the start and end of the program. These two variables are analysed using a frequency histogram to understand sentiment at the cohort level.

Digging Deeper: How to Separate Curriculum, Assessment, and Teacher Effects on Learning

Online learning and teaching are often informed by a large number of events and variables, and it is often easier to understand a single variable in isolation than the broader picture. For this reason, transactional variables (e.g., number of students attritting or number of students graduating), and questions surrounding these variables (e.g., which programs have the greatest attrition or graduation rates) are often the most common ones (e.g., Massy, 2016; Munguia, 2020). Therefore, if tests have a hierarchical nature, we can test the effects of events in isolation and how these effects change when combined with other parameters.

Using two dimensions of the COI, we can create an example of how these tests can be set up. We may be interested in the intersection between the teaching presence and the cognitive presence from the student (Garrison et al., 1999) in the online environment; therefore, we need to understand the variables associated with each presence in isolation and then test the interaction between the two.

Questions surrounding the teachers' dimension could be (a) how the curriculum is structured in the LMS, measured in information items (videos, references, and LMS pages, and a composite variable can be used to describe the combination of these); (b) when and how discussion opportunities are created, measured in number of discussion prompts, and time allotted for each discussion (assuming synchronous teaching); and (c) how many content elements are used in an assessment piece, measured as a proportion of ideas/elements relative to the content material until the assessment date. Questions surrounding the students' cognitive presence could be (1) how students engage with information (*sensu* Brennan et al., 2019) using synthetic variables describing the diversity of engagement patterns; (2) distance from submission to assignment due date measured in hours; and (3) number of academic learning support resources accessed before the assessment due date.

Next, each of these elements would require a hypothesis that describes potential mechanisms driving each pattern. Recognizing that there are six different questions, a systematic list of all possible outcomes is needed—for example, if teaching presence is strong (i.e., a–c reflect strong teacher agency), should we expect strong student cognitive presence (1–3)? If not, why not? Clearly stating the questions and the measured variables will therefore allow us to understand the teacher–learner dynamic in the online space.

This process may take several iterations and can be compared with overall student outcome in terms of continuing engagement with the course and performance in the subject and the student sentiment. And most importantly, the ultimate comparison is with a blended teaching environment to understand how the new normal operates relative to the current state.

The hierarchical approach to asking questions and seeking answers with data may allow practitioners to build the new normal learning and teaching framework, test it, and refine it (see Figure 8.2). This new framework can easily build upon the within-classroom COI and connect it with associated courses, expanding to elements of student progression, student belonging, and the learning headspace in

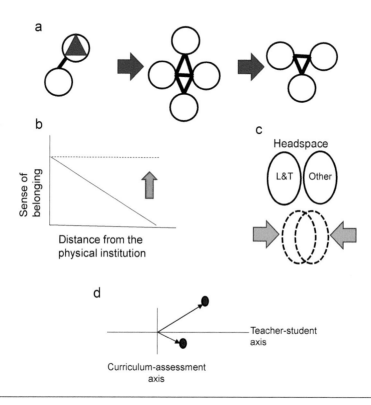

Figure 8.2   The New Normal Theoretical Framework for Online-Only Learning and Teaching. (a) Each circle represents an online subject/course, and connecting lines represent co-enrollments. The triangle inside a course represents the COI framework and L&T frameworks, which often focus at the within-course level. The new normal framework incorporates three key elements and identifies their challenges: (b) Sense of belonging in an online space. Belonging tends to decrease as the distance from a physical institution decreases, and the challenge is to uplift in an online environment. (c) Incorporating everyday life. In a physical L&T space, there are distinct boundaries that help students maintain focus: get to campus, walk into a classroom, walk into a library, open a book with your hands. A virtual space lacks these physical actions, and the challenge is to incorporate outside distractions to improve focus (rather than forcing isolation). (d) Learning analytics to help reflect and improve teacher and student agency, interactions, and curriculum design and delivery. Where each circle represents a course in this landscape.

the online academic world. We argue that this approach will facilitate the identification of stronger connections between curriculum design and assessment and between teacher and student agency through learning analytics.

Conclusion

Do we need a new theoretical framework for this pedagogy? As discussed above, most existing theoretical frameworks and teaching practices reflect a more traditional model of learning and teaching, which does not translate well or leverage the online environment, which is the 'new normal'. The COI is a robust model that guides and informs teaching practice within an online classroom setting, which provides a strong structure to utilise data to explore teaching practice at the level of a subject/course. However, in an online world, a new theoretical teaching framework is required, or existing ones need to be enhanced to accommodate new challenges (refer again to Figure 8.2).

First, how students develop a sense of belonging to an institution, degree, and subject unit, given that there is no face-to-face interaction in the virtual university (LaPointe & Reisettter, 2008; Delahunty et al., 2014) and how this impacts their overall experience.

Second, there is a need to incorporate program/degree-level curriculum structures to explore relationships between how teaching and learning in a single subject/course relates to others in the program and how these build to program/degree learning outcomes (Munguia & Brennan, 2020). Without the face-to-face component online, it is paramount that we strengthen the relationship between subjects from a student perspective to support learning and outcomes.

Additionally, the theories themselves need to be tested in this new environment. We would argue that data science approaches, together with theory from learning sciences and education, provide the framework to do this. However, it requires clarity in relation to theoretically informed questions at the various levels. This can both support the improvement of the 'new normal' experience and also inform pedagogical frameworks which both reflect and inform this environment.

References

Anderson, T., Rourke, L., Garrison, D. R., and Archer, W. (2001). Assessing teaching presence in a computer conferencing context. *Journal of Asynchronous Learning Networks, 5*(2), 1–17.

Arnold, K. E., and Sclater, N. (2017). Student perceptions of their privacy in learning analytics applications. *Proceedings of the 7th International Conference on Learning*

Analytics and Knowledge (LAK '17), 66–69. 13–17 March 2017, Vancouver, Canada. New York, NY: ACM. https://doi.org/10.1145/3027385.3027392

Bawa, P. (2016). Retention in online courses: Exploring issues and solutions—A literature review. *Sage Open*, January–March, 1–11. https://doi.org/10.1177/2158244015621777

Brennan, A., Sharma, A., and Munguia, P. (2019). Diversity of online behaviours associated with physical attendance in lectures. *Journal of Learning Analytics, 6*, 34–53. https://doi.org/10.18608/jla.2019.61.3

Brooker, A., Corrin, L., Fisher, J., and Mirriahi, N. (2017). Defining 'data' in conversations with students about the ethical use of learning analytics. In: H. Partridge, K. Davis, and J. Thomas. (Eds.), Me, Us, It! *Proceedings ASCILITE2017: 34th International Conference on Innovation, Practice and Research in the Use of Educational Technologies in Tertiary Education.* Toowoomba, Queensland (pp. 27–31).

Chen, B., Chang, Y-H., Ouyang, F., and Zhou, W. (2018). Fostering student engagement in online discussion through social learning analytics. *The Internet and Higher Education, 37*, 21–30. https://doi.org/10.1016/j.iheduc.2017.12.002

Chen, S.-J. (2007). Instructional design strategies for intensive online courses: An objectivist-constructivist blended approach. *Journal of Interactive Online Learning, 6*(1), 72–86.

Colvin, C., Rogers, T., Wade, A., Dawson, S., Gasevic, D., Buckingham Shum, S., Nelson, K., Alexander, S., Lockyer, L., Kennedy, G., Corrin, L., and Fisher, J. (2016). *Student Retention and Learning Analytics: A Snapshot of Australian Practices and a Framework for Advancement.* Canberra, ACT: Australian Government Office for Learning and Teaching. http://www.olt.gov.au/project-student-retention-and-learning-analytics-snapshot-currentaustralianpractices-and-framework

Corrin, L., Kennedy, G., de Barba, P. G., Lockyer, L., Gašević, D., Williams, D., Dawson, S., Mulder, R., Copeland, S., and Bakharia, A. (2016). *Completing the Loop: Returning Meaningful Learning Analytic Data to Teachers.* Sydney: Office for Learning and Teaching. http://melbourne-cshe.unimelb.edu.au/__data/assets/pdf_file/0006/2083938/Loop_Handbook.pdf

Davies, R. S., Dean, D. L., and Ball, N. (2013). Flipping the classroom and instructional technology integration in a college-level information systems spreadsheet course. *Education Tech Research Dev, 61*, 563–580. https://doi.org/10.1007/s11423-013-9305-6

Dekker, G., Pechenizkiy, M., and Vleeshouwers, J. (2009). Predicting students' drop out: A case study. *Proceedings of the 2nd International Conference on Educational Data Mining (EDM '09)*, 41–50. Cordoba, Spain. http://www.educationaldatamining.org/EDM2009/uploads/proceedings/dekker.pdf

Delahunty, J., Verenikina, I., and Jones, P. (2014). Socio-emotional connections: Identity, belonging and learning in online interactions. A literature review. *Technology, Pedagogy and Education, 23*, 243–265, doi: http://10.1080/1475939X.2013.813405

Diaz, D. (2000). *Comparison of Student Characteristics, and Evaluation of Student Success, in an Online Health Education Course.* Unpublished doctoral dissertation, Nova Southeastern University. http://home.earthlink.net/~davidpdiaz/LTS/pdf_docs /dissertn.pdf

Drachsler, H., and Greller, W. (2016). Privacy and analytics—It's a DELICATE issue. A checklist for trusted learning analytics. *Proceedings of the 6th International Conference on Learning Analytics and Knowledge (LAK '16),* 89–98. 25–29 April 2016, Edinburgh, UK. New York, NY: ACM. https://doi.org/10.1145/2883851.2883893

Elkington, S., and Evans, C. (2017). *Transforming Assessment in Higher Education.* UK: Advance HE.

Ezen-Can, A., Boyer, K. E., Kellogg, S., and Booth, S. (2015). Unsupervised modeling for understanding MOOC discussion forums: A learning analytics approach. *Proceedings of the Fifth International Conference on Learning Analytics and Knowledge,* 146–150. https://doi.org/10.1145/2723576.2723589

Ferguson, R., and Clow, D. (2017). Where is the evidence? A call to action for learning analytics. *Proceedings of the Seventh International Learning Analytics & Knowledge Conference,* 56–65.

Fidalgo-Blanco, A., Sein-Echaluce, M. L., Garcia-Penalvo, F., and Conde, M. A. (2017). Using learning analytics to improve teamwork assessment. *Computers in Human Behaviour, 47,* 149–156. https://doi.org/10.1016/j.chb.2014.11.050

Fisher, J., Valenzuela, F.-R., and Whale, S. (2014). *Learning Analytics: A Bottom-Up Approach to Enhancing and Evaluating Students' Online Learning.* http://www.olt.gov .au/system/files/resources/SD12_2567_Fisher_Report_2014.pdf

Frankola, K. (2001). *Why Online Learners Drop Out.* Workforce.com. http://www.work force.com/articles/why-online-learners-drop-out

Fritz, J., and Whitmer, J. (2017). Learning analytics research for LMS course design: Two studies. *EDUCAUSE Review.* https://er.educause.edu/articles/2017/2/learning -analytics-research-for-lms-course-design-two-studies

Garrison, D. R., and Anderson, T. (2003). *E-Learning in the 21st Century.* Routledge Falmer.

Garrison, D. R., Anderson, T., and Archer, W. (1999). Critical inquiry in a text-based environment: Computer conferencing in higher education. *The Internet and Higher Education, 2*(2–3), 87–105. https://doi.org/10.1016/S1096-7516(00)00016-6

Garrison, D. R., and Arbaugh, J. B. (2007). Researching the community of inquiry framework: Review, issues and future directions. *The Internet and Higher Education, 10*(3), 157–172. http://doi.org/10.1016/j.

Golding, P., and Donaldson, O. (2006). Predicting academic performance. *Proceedings of the 36th Annual Frontiers in Education Conference (FIE 2006),* 21–26. 27 October–1 November 2006, San Diego, CA. Washington, DC: IEEE Computer Society.

Hodges, C., Moore, S., Lockee, B., Trust, T., and Bond, A. (2020). The difference between emergency remote teaching and online learning. *EDUCAUSE Review.* https://er.educause.edu/articles/2020/3/the-difference-between-emergency-remote -teaching-and-online-learning

Howell, J. A., Roberts, L. D., Seaman, K., and Gibson, D. C. (2018). Are we on our way to becoming a 'helicopter university'? Academics' views on learning analytics. *Technology, Knowledge and Learning, 23*(1). https://doi.org/10.1007/s10758-017-9329-9

Ifenthaler, D., and Schumacher, C. (2016). Student perceptions of privacy principles for learning analytics. *Educational Technology Research and Development, 64*(5, SI), 923–938. https://doi.org/10.1007/s11423-016-9477-y

Jeffreys, M. R. (2007). Tracking students through program entry, progression, graduation, and licensure: Assessing undergraduate nursing student retention and success. *Nurse Education Today, 27*(5), 406–419. https://dx.doi.org/10.1016/j.nedt.2006.07.003

JISC. (2016). *Enhancing Student Employability Through Technology-Supported Assessment and Feedback*. UK: JISC. https://www.jisc.ac.uk/guides/enhancing-student-employability-through-technology-supported-assessment-and-feedback#

Jones, K. M., and VanScoy, A. (2019). The syllabus as a student privacy document in an age of learning analytics. *Journal of Documentation, 75*(6), 1333–1355. https://doi.org/10.1108/JD-12-2018-0202

Khan, O. (2017). *Learners' and Teachers' Perceptions of Learning Analytics (LA): A Case Study of Southampton Solent University (SSU)*. Paper Presented at the 14th International Association for 43 Development of the Information Society (IADIS) International Conference on Cognition and Exploratory Learning in Digital Age (CELDA), Algarve, Portugal.

Klein, C., Lester, J., Rangwala, H., and Johri, A. (2019). Technological barriers and incentives to learning analytics adoption in higher education: Insights from users. *Journal of Computing in Higher Education, 31*(3), 604–625. https://doi.org/10.1007/s12528-019-09210-5

Knight, S., Shibani, A., and Buckingham-Shum, S. (2018) Augmenting formative writing assessment with learning analytics: A design abstraction approach. In: J. Kay and R. Luckin (Eds.) *Rethinking Learning in the Digital Age: Making the Learning Sciences Count*. 13th International Conference of the Learning Sciences (ICLS) 2018, 3. London, UK: International Society of the Learning Sciences. https://doi.dx.org/10.22318/cscl2018.1783

Kovanović, V., Gašević, D., Dawson, S., Joksimović, S., Baker, R. S., and Hatala, M. (2015). Does time-on-task matter? Implications for the validity of learning analytics findings. *Journal of Learning Analytics, 2*(3), 81–110. http://dx.doi.org/10.18608/jla.2015.23.6

LaPointe, L., and Reisetter, M. (2008). Belonging online: Students' perceptions of the value and efficacy of an online learning community. *International Journal on E-Learning. 7*(4), 641–665. Waynesville, NC, USA: Association for the Advancement of Computing in Education (AACE).

Lawson, C., Beer, C., Rossi, D., Moore, T., and Fleming, J. (2016). Identification of 'at risk' students using learning analytics: The ethical dilemmas of intervention strategies in a higher education institution. *Educational Technology Research and Development, 64,* 957–968. https://doi.org/10.1007/s11423-016-9459-0

Li, L. Y., and Tsai, C. C. (2017). Accessing online learning material: Quantitative behavior patterns and their effects on motivation and learning performance. *Computers and Education, 114,* 286–297. https://doi.org/10.1016/j.compedu.2017.07.007

Liu, D. Y., Rogers, T., and Pardo, A. (2015). Learning analytics: Are we at risk of missing the point. In *Proceedings of the Australasian Society for Computers in Learning and Tertiary Education Conference (ASCILITE2015).* 29 November–2 December 2015, Perth, Australia.

Long, P., and Siemens, G. (2011). Penetrating the fog: Analytics in learning and education. *EDUCAUSE Review,* 46(5), 31–40. https://er.educause.edu/articles/2011/9/penetrating-the-fog-analytics-in-learningand-education

Luzeckyj, A., West, D., Searle, B., Toohey, D., Vanderlelie, J., and Bell, K. (2020). Stakeholder perspectives (staff and students) on institution-wide use of learning analytics to improve learning and teaching outcomes, pp. 177–200. In: D. Ifenthaler and D. Gibson (Eds.), *Adoption of Data Analytics in Higher Education Learning and Teaching.* Springer.

Marbouti, F., Diefes-Dux, H. A., and Madhavan, K. (2016). Models for early prediction of at-risk students in a course using standards-based grading. *Computers & Education, 103,* 1–15. https://dx.doi.org/10.1016/j.compedu.2016.09.005

Moodle. (2021). *Learning Analytics Indicators.* Moodle. https://docs.moodle.org/310/en/Learning_analytics_indicators

Massy, W. F. (2016). *Reengineering the University.* Johns Hopkins University Press.

Munguia, P. (2020). Preventing student and faculty attrition in times of change. In: D. Burgos (Ed.), *Radical Solutions in Higher Education,* 115–129. Springer. https://dx.doi.org/10.1007/978-981-15-4526-9_8

Munguia, P., and Brennan, A. (2020). Scaling the student journey from course-level information to program level progression and graduation: A model. *Journal of Learning Analytics, 7*(2), 84–94. https://doi.org/10.18608/jla.2020.72.5

Munguia, P., Brennan, A., Taylor, S., and Lee, D. (2020a). A learning analytics journey: Bridging the gap between technology services and the academic need. *The Internet and Higher Education, 46.* https://doi.org/10.1016/j.iheduc.2020.100744

Munguia P., Cheong C., Cheong F., and Gharaie E. (2020b). Exploratory variations in course structure consistency within the learning management system. In T. McLaughlin, A. Chester, B. Kennedy, and S. Young (Eds.), *Tertiary Education in a Time of Change,* 99–111. Springer. https://doi.org/10.1007/978-981-15-5883-2_8

Munguia, P., and Gibson, A. (*in review*) Strengthening the foundations: Towards a philosophical framework for learning analytics. *Journal of Learning Analytics.*

Novak, G. M. (2011). Just-in-time teaching. *New Directions for Teaching and Learning, 2011*(128), 63–73. http://doi:10.1002/tl.469

Pardo, A., and Siemens, G. (2014). Ethical and privacy principles for learning analytics. *British Journal of Educational Technology, 45*(3), 438–450. https://doi.org/10.1111/bjet.12152

Prinsloo, P., and Slade, S. (2016). Student vulnerability, agency, and learning analytics: An exploration. *Journal of Learning Analytics, 3*(1), 159–182. https://doi.org/10.18608/jla.2016.31.10

Quality Indicators for Learning and Teaching. (2021). *Student Experience.* Canberra: Australian Government. https://www.qilt.edu.au/qilt-surveys/student-experience

Raji, M., Duggan, J., DeCotes, B., Huang, J., and Vander Zanden, B. (2017). Modelling and visualizing student flow. *IEEE Transactions on Big Data.* https://doi.org/10.1109/TBDATA.2018.2840986.

Reidenberg, J. R., and Schaub, F. (2018). Achieving big data privacy in education. *Theory and Research in Education, 16*(3), 263–279. https://doi.org/10.1177/1477878518805308

Rivera, J., and Rice, M. (2002). A comparison of student outcomes & satisfaction between traditional & web based course offerings. *Online Journal of Distance Learning Administration, 5*(3).

Roberts, L. D., Howell, J. A., Seaman, K., and Gibson, D. C. (2016). Student attitudes toward learning analytics in higher education: The Fitbit version of the learning world. *Frontiers in Psychology, 7,* 1959. https://doi.org/10.3389/fpsyg.2016.01959

Sclater, N., and Mullen, J. (2017). *Jisc briefing: Learning Analytics and Student Success—Assessing the Evidence, JISC.* http://repository.jisc.ac.uk/6560/1/learninganalytics_and_student_success.pdf

Slade, S., and Prinsloo, P. (2013). Learning analytics: Ethical issues and dilemmas. *American Behavioral Scientist, 57*(10), 1510–1529. https://doi.org/10.1177/0002764213479366

Slade, S., and Prinsloo, P. (2014). Student perspectives on the use of their data: Between intrusion, surveillance and care. *Proceedings of the European Distance and E-Learning Network 2014 Research Workshop (EDEN 2014)*, 291–300. 27–28 October 2014, Oxford, UK.

Sorensen, C., and Donovan, J. (2017). An examination of factors that impact the retention of online students at a for-profit university. *Online Learning, 21*(3), 206–221. https://doi:10.24059/olj.v21i3.935

Sweeney, T., West, D., Groessler, A., Haynie, A., Higgs, B., Macaulay, J., Mercer-Mapstone, L., and Yeo, M. (2017) Where's the transformation? Unlocking the potential of technology-enhanced assessment. *Teaching and Learning Inquiry, 5*(1), 41–57. http://dx.doi.org/10.20343/teachlearninqu.5.1.5

Taylor, S., and Munguia, P. (2018). Towards a data archiving solution for learning analytics. *Proceedings of the 8th International Learning Analytics & Knowledge Conference,* 260–264.

Tsai, Y. S., Poquet, O., Gašević, D., Dawson, S., and Pardo, A. (2019). Complexity leadership in learning analytics: Drivers, challenges and opportunities. *British Journal of Educational Technology, 50*(6), 2839–2854. https://doi.org/10.1111/bjet.12846

West, D. (2019). Making the connections between academic work and learning analytics: A framework for driving learning analytics take-up. *Higher Education Research and Development Journal, 6,* 65–89. http://www.herdsa.org.au/herdsa-review-higher-education-vol-6/65-89

West, D., Huijser, H., and Heath, D. (2016) Putting an ethical lens on learning analytics. *Educational Technology Research and Development, 64,* 903–922. https://doi.org/10.1007/s11423-016-9464-3

West, D., Huijser, H., Heath, D., Lizzio, A., Miles, C., Toohey, D., Searle, B., and Bronni-mann, J. (2015). *Learning Analytics: Assisting Universities with Student Retention*. Australian Office for Learning and Teaching. https://ltr.edu.au/resources/SP13_3268_West_Report_2015.pdf

West, D., Luzeckyj, A., Searle, B., Toohey, D., and Price, R. (2018). *The Use of Learning Analytics to Support Improvements in Teaching Practice*. Innovative Research Universities. https://www.iru.edu.au/action/international/

West, D., Searle, B., Vanderlelie, J., Toohey, D., Luzeckyj, A., and Bell, K. (2019). *Learner Facing Analytics: Analysis of Student Perspectives*. Innovative Research Universities. https://www.iru.edu.au/news/learner-facing-analytics-report/

West, D., Tasir, Z., Luzeckyj, A., Si Na, K., Toohey, D., Abdullah, Z., Searle, B., Farhana Jumaat, N., and Price, R. (2018). Learning analytics experience among academics in Australia and Malaysia: A comparison. *Australasian Journal of Educational Technology, 34*(3), 122–139. https://doi.org/10.14742/ajet.3836

West, D., and Thompson, S. (2015). Mobile knowledge: Driving a paradigm shift. *Journal of Applied Research in Higher Education, 7*(1), 43–54. http://dx.doi.org/10.1108/JARHE-02-2014-0021

Chapter 9

Learning Information, Knowledge, and Data Analysis in Israel

A Case Study

Moria Levy[1] and Ronit Nehemia[2]

Abstract

Adapting to the 21st century requires new skills and capabilities. Any state willing to make a thorough change to its system should begin with education, preparing the students to be better future citizens by leveraging themselves and the organizations and businesses they will eventually work in. Israel, as similar to other countries, has technology and knowledge as her main economic drivers. Not without reason, Israel has been named many times as "a startup nation." The Israeli Ministry of Education, research institutes, and educational core suppliers continuously invest in research, strategy teams, and entrepreneurship-nurturing initiatives, enabling both top-down and bottom-up updates of educational programs. Thus, 18-year-old students entering adult life would be prepared with the skills and tools to adapt their learning and thinking to what's required of

---

[1] Bar Ilan University
[2] Ministry of Education, Israel

them. This chapter discusses a case study in Israel that addresses key skill sets that students need to possess to be successful in their adult life.

Keywords: Data analysis, knowledge management, K12, 21st-century skills, digital information, ICT, data integration, data management, visualization, knowledge nation, knowledge engineering, the future worker

Introduction: The 21st-Century Skills

Many researchers are challenged with exposing the skills required of future workers. The ingredients of such a formula are of interest to all those who seek academic or business competency and want to prepare and excel as a society, nation, or organization. Bell (2010) analyzed the Project-Based-Learning (PBL) idea. Implementing PBL in schools can help students develop questions and guide them, under the teacher's supervision, to create and share projects related to their research. Through this approach, they can develop the required 21st-century skills such as using technology as a means of increasing information fluency via computers, communication, and social interactions leading to collaboration and high-order thinking that is key to problem solving.

Rotherham and Willingham (2010) claimed that the required skills for the 21st century are not anything new and refer to the same list of required skills found in other studies: critical thinking, problem solving, and mastery of different kinds of knowledge. They argued that knowledge and skills are intertwined and should be taught in combination (Rotherham & Willingham, 2010).

Voogt and Roblin (2010) conducted an in-depth analysis of 32 research works investigating 21st-century skills. The major findings can be summarized as follows: "First, it is encouraging to see that—ultimately—the frameworks seem to converge on a common set of 21st century skills (namely: collaboration, communication, ICT literacy, and social and/or cultural competencies (including citizenship). Most frameworks also mention creativity, critical thinking and problem solving)" (p. 1).

In his work, Wagner (2008) defined the seven survival skills as follows:

1. Critical thinking and problem solving
2. Collaboration across networks and leading by influence
3. Agility and adaptability
4. Initiative and entrepreneurialism
5. Effective oral and written communication
6. Accessing and analyzing information
7. Curiosity and imagination

Van Laar et al. (2017) referred to digital competence as a required skill in the knowledge society, which includes "information management, collaboration, communication and sharing, creation of content and knowledge" (p. 578).

Ananiadou and Claro (2009) reported the findings as learned from 18 OECD countries and suggested a framework conceptualizing the learned 21st-century skills and competencies, which are as follows:

1. Information dimension
   a. Information as a source: searching, selecting, evaluating, and organizing information
   b. Information as a product: restructuring and modeling information; development of own ideas and knowledge
2. Communication dimension
   a. Effective communication: sharing and transmitting information and knowledge, including processing, transforming, formatting, and presenting
   b. Collaboration and virtual interaction: both within and among schools.
3. Ethics and social impact dimension
   a. Social responsibility
   b. Social impact

To conclude, 21st-century skills, as determined from the literature review, include information management skills (searching, analyzing, processing, and presenting); knowledge management skills (sharing, communicating, collaborating); cognitive skills (critical thinking, problem solving, and creativity); social responsibility skills; and ICT literacy.

Developing the Digital Information Discovery and Detection Programs

Planning for future needs is key in all educational systems worldwide. To set the infrastructure for future studies in Israel, the Ministry of Education initiated several new programs in 2014. Naturally, some were hardware and software oriented; however, the Ministry decided to also design programs to answer the need for 21st-century skills in additional dimensions, understanding that the required skills go beyond merely computers and robotics. This gave birth to the pioneering Digital Information Discovery and Detection Program, which aimed to address creative and high-order thinking students. The three-year program included theoretical studies, laboratory work, and a final one-year project, covering five of the following clusters:

a.   Internet and social media
b.   Coping with foreign languages
c.   Information studies and informatics
d.   Knowledge sharing, knowledge retention, and knowledge development
e.   ICT and cyber basics

The program was designed in conjunction with leading experts in the information, knowledge, and cyber industries, providing a holistic and integrated approach to information and knowledge. Its planning took into consideration the new disciplines that were important for preparing the students for the future content, skills, and ways of education while adjusting the materials to the context of 15- to 18-year-old students. The program was initiated in 2016 with eight schools and classes.

Upgrading the Program: Data and Information

As with new programs, the digital information discovery and detection program had its share of issues. In the first year, the cyber component was overrated and over-branded, misleading the audience of the program and driving away some dissatisfied students and parents interested in cyber programs. Other problems had to do with the education of teachers with regard to the new disciplines. Even though the knowledge management community volunteered to help and mentor the teachers, educating the teachers in knowledge management topics turned to be a challenge, ending with non-uniform teaching and subpar results. The new program didn't catch on; several hundreds of students took part in the program, but a critical number of schools decided against implementing it.

Studying information, knowledge, and data analysis has been gaining interest in recent years due to the unimaginable amount of data that is being collected each second. On the educational level, these disciplines are gaining popularity, with several reports emphasizing the importance of data sciences in pre-university education. Therefore, in 2018, the Ministry of Education decided to upgrade the program to studying information, and the subsequent actions were taken.

A new team was assigned, and the "why" of the program remained the same: Israel wishes to prepare students for 21st-century skills by establishing the best infrastructure for young people entering organizations and serving as wise citizens. The "who" was updated: The audience is talented, top-class students (math, English, and literacy), and the "how" and "what" (Sinek, 2009) were re-thought thoroughly. A new enlarged committee was established, including over 30 experts from academia, government, education, and business communities. All members were experts in disciplines of data sciences, knowledge management, social media, and/or informatica.

The redesigned "how" included the following guiding principles:

1. **A leading holistic approach.** No more of the five connected clusters (listed above), as opposed to the one leading model of data sciences, where all clusters and modules are embedded as part of the leading data sciences model.
2. **Working committee.** The committee was (and still is) active in decision making as well as preparing lessons, outlining requirements for the final project, etc. For each specific need, sub-teams are to be produced and assigned with clear tasks to accomplish.
3. **Wisdom of the team.** No one knows all the answers. Most decisions are taken after considering both the committee and representative teachers, providing perspective of both the academic and business needs as well as ensuring these are suited to the young students' abilities.
4. **Trust and collaboration.** Trust is built among the committee members through physical meetings, changing sub-teams, and an active WhatsApp group where ideas, trends, and news regarding the discipline and the program are shared.
5. **Rebranding.** The program was rebranded and a new name chosen—Data and Information (limited by the Ministry of Education to two words). A slogan was chosen by teachers and students: "Knowledge Is Power." Subsequently, marketing campaigns were prepared.
6. The "what" was based, as described above, on a leading model, developed by Professor Ahituv (2019), the program chair (see Figure 9.1).

The list of topics included in the program are outlined in Table 9.1.

The program, for both teachers and students, is based on new education methods. Further, short video chunks are prepared, enabling the teachers and students to learn in a new, experiential, and fun way. Each lesson is divided into five- to seven-minute components, and these lessons typically end with a dilemma, leaving

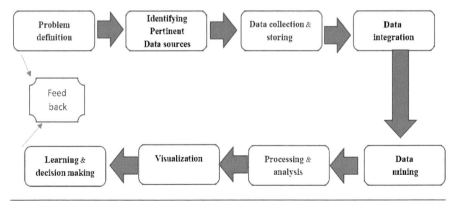

Figure 9.1   The Data Analysis Model (*Source:* Ahituv, 2019; used with permission.)

Table 9.1 Program Syllabus

Component	Topics Taught
Problem definition	• Formulation tools • Quantitative models • Qualitative approaches • Mathematical tools
Identifying pertinent data sources	• Browsers • Indices • Search engines • International organizations • Governmental departments, public institutes • Statistics bureaus
Data collection and storing	• Data transfer technology—communications • Clouds • Database management software • Data validation tools
Data integration	• Conversion programs • Indices • Metadata tools
Data mining	• Filters • Data retrieval techniques • Identification tools • AI tools • Heuristics
Processing and analysis	• AI tools • Machine learning • Data processing programs • Heuristics
Visualization	• Dashboard tools • Graphical tools • Reporting system software tools • Interactive systems • UI/UX • Visualization tools
Learning and decision making	• Decision-support tools • What-if software • Simulation tools
Knowledge management	• Lessons learned • Knowledge sharing • Knowledge retention and continuity • Personal knowledge management • Knowledge development • Feedbacking

the student both curious and with a homework task to implement the learned materials in analyzing real-life situations. The concept of the program is based on independent learning—the teacher directly instructs and mentors the students. The students also learn through storytelling, gamification, and escape room riddles.

All study materials were recorded for the program by professional experts in the academy, industry, and government offices, such as Dr. Moria Levy and Dr. Boris Gorelik. The materials are all shared on the program's website and are open to the general public for free learning and usage.

Assessments are held as formative evaluations through the application of the material via research papers of various types: academic research, government research, and business research, as well as an applied matriculation test on solving applied problems. Exams all take place as open study material; all of these techniques are worth appreciating in the 21st century.

Several academic programs were approved, expanding the certification for teachers in universities in Israel with a teaching certificate for this program, as certification is necessary. As of writing this article, no specific full academic program yet exists for the discipline of information, knowledge, and data analysis in Israel. What is in place is a system of teaching certificate studies and converting academics from the high-tech industries to serving as teachers—all this in addition to applied courses for teachers.

The first two years take place in class, at the end of which the students have to pass a final exam verifying that they have understood and internalized the information taught. The exam is mainly based on analysis and understanding rather than memorizing; however, in order to prepare the students for the future, more effort is required.

Thus, the third year is designed to deal with this need. The students must choose and implement a final project on which they are to work all year. The teachers are trained in order to mentor such studying. There are four main clusters for the final project, enabling the students to specialize, just like in life, in different ways, suiting their personality and attitude. The main project clusters and project types based on them are outlined in Table 9.2 and will be implemented gradually in the coming years.

Moreover, additional elements involve mentoring students, exposing students to industry experts through lectures, and holding tours to companies and factories. Thus, the students are exposed to the industrial applications of studied topics, and their employment prospects begin while they are still in school. Connecting the program, teachers, and students with field experts also promises a program that adapts itself dynamically to the changing needs and trends of the industry.

The Israeli Ministry of Education is currently preparing a curriculum for information practical engineers. The additional program will be an applied curriculum for two years after high school and will teach practical software for analyzing, processing, and managing knowledge, thus providing a continual education path towards data, information, and knowledge.

Table 9.2 Final Projects

Cluster	Project types
Quantitative research project	Performing a research serving a specific existing business or governmental need. Working with the customers of the need.
	Collaborative research—interdisciplinary project. Working with students of other projects, specializing, for example, in industrial engineering or product design. Performing a research that will serve the other students' work and the project they are performing.
	Social cultural research. Defining, designing, and performing research, producing enlightening new understandings on an actual social or cultural dilemma.
	Scientific research—writing a research using the format, structure, and guidelines of academic scientific research: abstract, literature review, thesis, research approach and methodology, findings, discussion, and conclusion.
Qualitative research project	Developing a limited business model for running a website, a small business, marketing, etc. Demonstrating the implementation in an organization and building a method of copying it to additional organizations.
	Knowledge capturing—documenting of a defined body of knowledge related to a culture, discipline, or specific topic. Integration of the information learned into a unified significant body of knowledge.
	Digital platform. Planning, designing, and bringing up a digital platform environment including a website, a Facebook® page, and a communication and collaboration channel, for a specific audience.
	Lessons learned—running a series of debriefings dealing with a complicated significant event or project. Analyzing the related processes and decisions taking and learning from them.
Experience in the business/ social environment	Internship in an organization, implementing either data analysis or knowledge management tasks.
	Working in and for the community—working with a nonprofit organization, helping with tasks of data analysis and/or knowledge management. The final project is a reflection report describing the work.
	Entrepreneurship/product development—following stages of a startup and planning, designing, and prototyping a MVP (minimum viable product).
Learning and implementing a new tool	Self-learning, during the year, a software tool, such as Python, Tableau, or Power BI. Implementing data processing, analysis, and learning, as taught in the past two years on a defined set of data using the tool learned.

In addition, new initiatives are being examined to enable the better integration between schools and the industry. Industry professionals will work one day a week at the school and guide students in preparing industry-relevant projects in the field. This will be a win–win situation: the students will get to know the business world, and the teachers from the industry will contribute to preparing suitable graduates—that is, potential good workers for developing dynamic business needs.

COVID-19

COVID-19 has had a tremendous influence on the new program. Students had to learn from home all year long, and educational programs for teachers were stalled. Everything had to be re-thought to fit the new situation. Following the pandemic, it was necessary to redesign the conventional learning methods that still took place and to immediately develop techniques for distance teaching, making learning as independent as possible. The ideas of new learning were in place, yet to be implemented. Academy and field experts were called in to help turn the full syllabus into recorded lessons. The Ministry of Education hired a studio, enabling high-standard video recording, and access was granted for the purpose of self-study to all students. So far, as of now, about 500 videos have been recorded and uploaded to the program's open and free-to-use website. The program website includes the syllabus, videos, written materials, and supplementing tools.[3]

This website has over 700 items, some of them being teaching materials, presentations, videos, and related articles.[4] Materials on information management, knowledge management, professional knowledge management, personal knowledge management, organization and knowledge management in a smart way, knowledge retention, knowledge sharing, and personal information management are added to each area on an ongoing basis. Materials are written in Hebrew, with some content also in English. The materials are currently being translated into Arabic for the relevant population in Israel. COVID-19 resulted in a great boost for the new educational approaches, enabling the information, data, and knowledge program students to profit from not only new content but also new learning concepts.

---

[3] The website can be accessed at https://pop.education.gov.il/tchumey_daat/data-analysis /high-school/

[4] An example of a page in the curriculum that deals with the field of knowledge management can be found at https://pop.education.gov.il/tchumey_daat/data-analysis/high -school/study-topics/data-management/

Current Situation

When the program opened six years ago, about 150 students in eight schools studied there. Today, about 850 students from 25 schools are currently part of the new information, data, and knowledge program. After the change, and despite the COVID-19 pandemic, next year, 25 additional classrooms with 400 new students are expected to open all over the country, and more are on the way; hence, the number of students is slated to double. The goal is to have an exponential increase in the number of schools, and the trend will be studied each year.

Today, about 30 teachers have undergone short-term training processes, and 20 new teachers are in the pipeline to join them to train for a teaching certificate specific to the program next year. We expect the number of teachers to double and even triple in the coming five years.

Summary

Data and information around the world are doubling every few years. The need for new skills enabling us to handle this large mass of content, understand it, and turn it into value is undoubtedly essential. The Israel Academy of Sciences and Humanities (2020) and the Planning and Budgeting Committee of the Israel Council for Higher Education (2020) stated in their reports that learning data sciences is important and should be considered a national program. This understanding is what formed the base that led the new educational program of data, information, and knowledge. Learning how to process, communicate, and share the data and information and collaborate using critical thinking and smart decision making, based on the given data and information, are the key to success, and new studies are focused on obtaining these skills and knowledge.

The new program also applies new teaching and assessment methods as part of technology education studies; however, the vision is that the essence of these bodies of knowledge and taught skills will be taught to all age groups and students in schools in the future. Israel hopes that this and similar educational programs will help us leverage the society to be a "knowledge nation" that is innovative, successful, and best prepared for the challenges of tomorrow.

References

Ahituv, N. (2019, September). What should be taught in an academic program of data sciences? *Conference Proceedings of the The Ninth Digital Presentation and Preservation of Cultural and Scientific Heritage (DiPP2019)*. Sofia, Bulgaria: Institute of Mathematics and Informatics, BAS.

Ananiadou, K., and Claro, M. (2009). 21st century skills and competences for new millennium learners in OECD countries. *OECD Education Working Papers, 41.* https://doi.org/10.1787/19939019

Bell, S. (2010). Project-based learning for the 21st century: Skills for the future. *Clearing House, 83*(2), 39–43. https://doi.org/10.1080/00098650903505415

Bukhari, D. (2020). Data science curriculum: Current scenario. *International Journal of Data Mining and Knowledge Management Process, 10*(3). https://doi.org/10.5121/ijdkp.2020.10301

Rotherham, A. J., and Willingham, D. T. (2010). 21st-century skills. *American Educator, 17*(1), 17–20.

Sinek, S. (2009). *Start With Why: How Great Leaders Inspire Everyone to Take Action.* Penguin.

The Israel Academy of Sciences and Humanities (2020). *Data Science Instruction for All Disciplines: Expanded Summary of the Committee Report.* https://www.academy.ac.il/System Files2015/2-1-21-English.pdf

The Israel Council for Higher Education, Planning and Budgeting Committee (2020). *Data Sciences Report.* http://online.anyflip.com/cdkp/bdmr/mobile/index.html

Van Laar, E., Van Deursen, A. J., Van Dijk, J. A., and De Haan, J. (2017). The relation between 21st-century skills and digital skills: A systematic literature review. *Computers in Human Behavior, 72,* 577–588. https://doi.org/10.1016/j.chb.2017.03.010

Voogt, J., and Roblin, N. P. (2010). 21st-century skills. *Discussienota. Zoetermeer: The Netherlands: Kennisnet, 23*(3), 2000.

Wagner, T. (2008). *Rigor Redefined: The Seven Survival Skills for Careers, College, and Citizenship.* Advisors corner. www.hosa.org/.../advisors_corner_oct08_pg2

Chapter 10

Scaling Up Learning Analytics in an Evidence-Informed Way

Justian Knobbout[1] and Esther van der Stappen[2]

Abstract

Worldwide, the interest in learning analytics is rising, and higher educational institutions seek ways to benefit from the digital traces left behind by learners. The successful adoption of learning analytics comprises different phases, ranging from initialization to scaling. However, institutions with no or limited experience with learning analytics face many challenges when going through these phases. This chapter explores how institutions can proceed to implement learning analytics on a large scale. For this purpose, institutions need the right organizational capabilities as well as measures to assess the effect on learning. Based on literature and empirical data, we distinguish five critical learning analytics categories of organizational learning analytics capabilities: *Data, Management, People, Technology,* and *Privacy & Ethics.* The ability to develop these categories benefits the impact of learning analytics on learning. Furthermore, this chapter also provides operational definitions of affected learning. This enables institutions to assess the impact of learning analytics continuously. Based on learning

[1] HU University of Applied Sciences Utrecht, The Netherlands
[2] Avans University of Applied Sciences, The Netherlands

theories, we identify three categories of learning that learning analytics can affect: learning process, learning outcome, and learning environment. The operational definitions we found during our research are classified accordingly. This allows educational institutions to measure, compare, and improve the effects of learning analytics on learning.

Keywords: Learning analytics, capabilities, adoption, implementation, resource-based view, information systems, impact measures

Introduction

In this age of big data, the Internet of Things, and artificial intelligence, it is not surprising we start to look differently at education. Due to modern technologies, it is possible to observe, monitor, and analyze learning as never before. We can see how much time students interacted with learning materials, whether they practiced and with what result, who is collaborating with whom, and so on. Learning data play a key role here. Using data to enhance learning is not a new phenomenon, as a genealogy by Joksimović et al. (2019) shows that this already goes back to the 1920s. However, with the possibilities nowadays, the interest in using data to enhance education exponentially grew. This led to the emergence of different communities that wish to exploit educational data (Romero & Ventura, 2020).

One of these communities is learning analytics. Learning analytics can be defined as, "the measurement, collection, analysis, and reporting of data about learners and their contexts, for purposes of understanding and optimizing learning and the environments in which it occurs" (LAK, 2011). One of its main drivers is the digitalization of learning (Ferguson, 2012)—that is, the use of the Internet, virtual learning environments, and digital resources in education. While this was already a trend, the rapid shift towards online education due to the COVID-19 pandemic boosted it even further.

As a result, large volumes of data can be sourced from, among others, learning management systems, questionnaires, student information systems, video systems, and MOOC platforms (Samuelsen et al., 2019). After collection, the digital traces that learners leave behind can be analyzed, visualized, and used for pedagogical interventions (Clow, 2012). Intervention strategies include posting signals, contacting learners via email or telephone, proving guidelines and advice, or modifying learning materials (Na & Tasir, 2017).

The learning analytics implementation process comprises multiple phases: initialization, prototyping, piloting, and scaling (Broos et al., 2020). However, the complexity grows exponentially while going though these phases, and higher educational institutions face many challenges when implementing learning analytics

(Tsai & Gašević, 2017). As a result, examples of institutions that apply learning analytics at scale are scarce (Gasevic et al., 2019; Viberg et al., 2018). To successfully scale up the use of learning analytics, higher educational institutions need to carefully plan its adoption and measure whether the intended improvements to learning are achieved.

To support higher educational institutions in this task, we developed a capability model for learning analytics (Knobbout et al., 2020; Knobbout & van der Stappen, 2020a). The model helps us to understand what organizational capability must be developed by educational institutions for the successful adoption of learning analytics. The model is the result of multiple studies, including literature reviews, case studies, and pluralistic walkthroughs.

Our research is grounded in the resource-based view, where *capabilities* refer to an institution's ability to use various resources to perform tasks or activities (Grant, 1991). Resources can be tangible (data, technology, investments), human (managerial skills, technical skills), or intangible (culture, organizational learning) (Gupta & George, 2016). Our Learning Analytics Capability Model supports practitioners—senior managers, policy makers, educational experts, IT staff, etc.— in their task to adopt learning analytics at scale at their institution.

However, just implementing learning analytics is not enough. One must also evaluate the effect learning analytics have on learning processes, learning environments, and learning outcomes to improve the learning analytics function. Therefore, this chapter describes the capability model and its design process and also provides insight into what measures to use to assess the impact of learning analytics on learning. This helps to identify change caused by learning analytics and fuel its further development.

A Capability Model for Learning Analytics

In this section, we first describe the Learning Analytics Capability Model. This model elaborates on what capabilities are important for learning analytics adoption. Next, we explain in what way we developed the model.

Capabilities for Learning Analytics

Resource-based capabilities can variate in level and thus be structured in a hierarchical order (Ambrosini et al., 2009). The Learning Analytics Capability Model comprises four orders (see Figure 10.1). We positioned the core concept (i.e., learning analytics capabilities) at the top of the model. Next, the learning analytics capabilities are divided into five categories—that is, critical dimensions

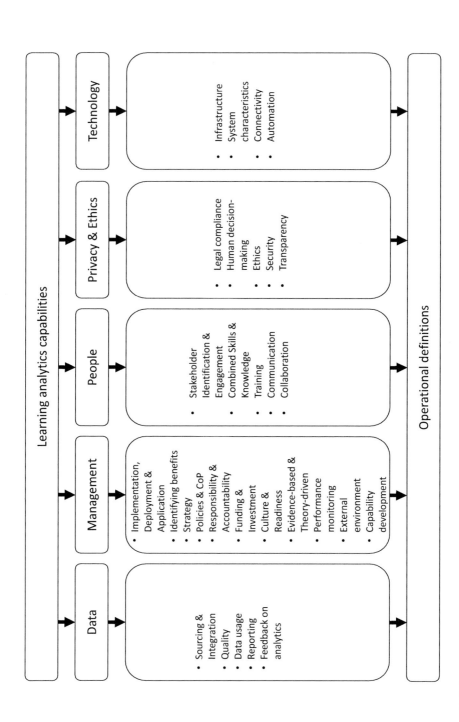

Figure 10.1   Learning Analytics Capability Model

that need to be present at an institution. They are critical in the sense that when one or more are missing, institutions cannot successfully adopt learning analytics. Each category comprises the actual capabilities that are important to successful learning analytics adoption.

Furthermore, to help practitioners to build the right capabilities at their institution, we provide operational definitions that help to operationalize the model. For example, the capability *Quality* provides recommendations about data cleaning, data formatting, and documentation to ensure the quality of the data used for analytical processes. The provision of operational definitions distinguished the Learning Analytics Capability Model from other implementation models in the learning analytics domain, as the latter often lack practical guidelines on how to operationalize them (Broos et al., 2020). To understand the Learning Analytics Capability Model better, we will now elaborate on each capability.

Data

The category *Data* describes in what way data institutions should handle data. By definition, data lay at the root of learning analytics, and the learning analytics function's effectiveness highly depends on the way the data are processed into information and action. As the capability *Sourcing & Integration* shows, data for learning analytics can be sources from different systems and often need central storage in a single repository.

Collected data need to be linked and cleaned. As described earlier, the capability *Quality* provides recommendations on how to do so. The capability *Data usage* presents multiple use cases—that is, for what purposes learning analytics can be applied. For example, learning analytics can help to identify early students who might get delayed, to analyze student success, and to make study plans and predict their realizability. As the required data and analyses differ per application, it is important to formulate the learning analytics functions' goals well in advance.

After the analyses, the outcomes are reported to users (*Reporting*). This is often done via dashboards but also reports, presentations, and learning summaries. It is important that outcomes are clearly presented, that they are actionable, and that justifications are provided. Only then can the users effectively use and trust the results. The last capability in this category—*Feedback on analytics*—prescribes the need to ask for feedback from users so the learning analytics function can be improved.

Management

The category *Management* describes the (governance) processes around the use of data. With 11 capabilities, this is by far the model's largest category. The capability *Implementation, Deployment, & Application* describes the project management regarding the entire adoption process—for example, planning, risk evaluation, and connection with existing organizational functions. Before starting with learning analytics, institutions need to know what benefits they want to achieve with it.

The capability *Identifying benefits* provides generic goals such as curricula improvement, improved student care, and addressing problems and requirements experienced during learning and teaching. *Strategy* describes the need to align learning analytics with the organizational strategic goals and policies. These aims and benefits, along with clear descriptions of what is done with learning analytics and who the stakeholders are, need formal formulation in learning analytics policies and codes-of-practice (*Policy & CoP*).

It is necessary to identify different stakeholder groups, as responsibilities and accountabilities need to be assigned (*Responsibility & Accountability*). Moreover, institutes need to invest in resources and secure proper funding for learning analytics projects. The capability *Funding & Investment* highlights the need for financial budgets and how to get it—for example, via management buy-in, senior managers and executives who advocate the use of learning analytics, and by developing a human and fiscal resource investment plan.

Institutes also need to invest in *Culture & Readiness* capabilities so the use of learning analytics is accepted. This includes cultural aspects, where people accept learning analytics as a standard of practice, and stakeholders possess a data-informed mindset. Top management can promote the use of learning analytics in the organization, and enthusiastic pioneers can act as learning analytics ambassadors within the institution. The use of existing evidence could convince others about the need for change. This aligns with the capability *Evidence-based & Theory-driven,* which states that learning analytics need support from pedagogical theory and best practices.

When learning analytics are used, their performances need monitoring. Ways to operationalize the capability of *Performance monitoring* are described in depth later in this chapter. The capability *External environment* shows how knowledge from outside the institution can help learning analytics' adoption within the institution itself. Finally, it is important to note that capabilities are not static, but that they develop over time. This aligns with the idea of dynamic capabilities (Ambrosini et al., 2009). Therefore, the last capability in this category is *Capability development,* which describes how existing capabilities can develop and mature.

People

The category *People* describes the human aspects necessary for learning analytics. Learning analytics knows different stakeholder groups. For example, Greller and Drachsler (2012) distinguish between data subjects and data clients. The former are the data suppliers, where the latter refer to those who act upon the analytics. We can add stakeholders such as learning analytics personnel, managers and executives, and educational experts. The capability of *Stakeholder Identification & Engagement* prescribes the need to identify and engage these stakeholders. That is, they need both to be involved in learning analytics policymaking and the design and validation of learning analytics tools and to contribute their professional knowledge to the design and implementation of learning analytics. Each stakeholder group needs relevant skills and knowledge, which is elaborated on by the capability *Combined skills & Knowledge*.

Training plays a major role in the acquisition of the right skills and knowledge. Learning analytics staff must be well trained, but the same is true for actors such as tutors, teachers, and students. The capability *Communication* describes in what way stakeholder groups can communicate with each other—for example, by organizing workshops and intake interviews for learning analytics projects. In contrast, the capability *Collaboration* describes how the various groups could collaborate—for example, by having experts check used methods and letting learning analytics staff think along with the users about their needs.

Privacy & Ethics

Finally, the category *Privacy & Ethics* describes the use of learning analytics from privacy and ethical points of view. Privacy and ethics are sensitive issues in the learning analytics domain (Drachsler & Greller, 2016), and they are often connected with aspects such as trust, accountability, and transparency (Pardo & Siemens, 2014). The capability of *Legal compliance* describes in what way to comply with privacy laws such as the General Data Protection Regulation (GDPR). This involves fostering the rights students have (to be forgotten, to get insights into what data are collected) and ways to use data in a privacy-sensitive way, such as asking consent or by making personal data unrecognizable.

Related to this capability is *Human decision making*, as learning analytics systems cannot and should not make all decisions. One must also realize that, even when the law allows certain things, they may go against what is considered as correct behavior. The capability *Ethics* helps to handle ethical considerations—for example, by establishing an ethics committee and a learning analytics policy. The capability *Security* highlights the need for sound security of data and information security policies and practices. This limits the chances of a data breach, which in turn might lead to less trust in learning analytics. Another way to increase trust is by creating transparency about what is done with data, by whom, and why. Therefore, the capability of *Transparency* is included in this category.

Technology

The Learning Analytics Capability Model's fifth and last category, *Technology*, describes the technical side of learning analytics. The capability *Infrastructure* explains the different technology resources that are necessary for successful learning analytics. This mainly includes data storage, such as data warehouses and ERP systems, but also software to perform analyses (e.g., RStudio®), to visualize data (e.g., Tableau® or Power BI®), and to manage learning analytics projects (e.g., Git® and Slack®). Possible setups for systems are described by the capability *System characteristics*. For example, platform agnostic and cloud-based systems can provide flexibility that helps to adopt learning analytics at different departments of an institution. The capability *Connectivity* provides help in cases where data must be exchanged between (external) systems. Finally, the capability *Automation* describes in what way automation can help to speed up the process and increase data quality. Especially when institutions adopt learning analytics at scale, automation is crucial to providing analytical outcomes to the end users on time and in a cost-efficient way.

Design Process

For the readers interested in the Learning Analytics Capability Model's design process, we now provide a brief overview of its development. Information Systems play an important role in learning analytics. Therefore, to design a capability model for learning analytics, we applied Design Science Research principles for Information Systems research (Hevner et al., 2004). At the start, a systematic literature review was conducted to research what capabilities for successful learning analytics are already present in the knowledge base (Knobbout & van der Stappen, 2020a). As learning analytics is a relatively young research field, literature from more mature, adjacent fields such as business analytics and big data analytics were included in the review.

The starting point for the search process was to review studies that provide implementation models for business analytics and big data analytics (Adrian et al., 2018) and implementation models for learning analytics (Colvin et al., 2017). We sourced additional papers via Google® Scholar, the Education Resources Information Center (ERIC) database, and the Association for Computing Machinery (ACM) database. Applying inclusion and exclusion criteria, 10 key studies for business analytics and big data analytics and six key studies for learning analytics remained. Based on open coding principles, we grouped capabilities for business analytics and big data analytics based on the underlying operational definitions. This resulted in 23 distinct capabilities that, in turn, were categorized into four categories: *Data, Management, People,* and *Technology*.

Next, we coded the models for learning analytics based on axial coding. Codes were derived from the capabilities found in the previous step. As not all capabilities found in learning analytics literature fitted the codes, the remainders were coded based on open coding. As a result, 11 additional capabilities were distinguished. Moreover, one additional category emerged from the data: *Privacy & Ethics*. It is surprising that this category is absent from business analytics and big data analytics, as these domains often also involve personal data. In total, our theoretical capability model for learning analytics now comprised 34 capabilities divided over five categories.

To refine the model, we conducted a single case study to collect additional, empirical data. This way, we extended the theoretical model into an empirical model. Data were collected during four interviews with stakeholders—that is, members of the analytics team and end users. By coding the interview transcriptions along with the theoretical capability model, we got some new insights. Most importantly, no capabilities seemed to be missing from the theoretical model. Nonetheless, some improvements could be made. In theory, some capabilities can exist alongside each other. In practice, they overlap or cannot exist without each other. For example, the theoretical model comprises the capabilities of *Knowledge, Skills,* and *Combined knowledge & skills.*

However, the interviews showed that in practice, these capabilities go hand in hand and are highly interconnected. Therefore, in the empirical model, these three capabilities were merged. The same goes for the capabilities of *Stakeholder identification* and *Stakeholder engagement* (now *Stakeholder Identification & Engagement*) and the capabilities of *Planning* and *Implementation & Deployment* (now *Implementation, Deployment, & Application*).

Next to merging some capabilities, we renamed three others. For example, the name '*Market*' makes sense in a highly commercial environment but less in the context of educational institutions. For that reason, we renamed it to *External environment*. Finally, based on the interview data, the capability definitions were improved. The case study resulted in a refined, empirical model with 30 capabilities. To validate it in practice, the model is used to plan the learning analytics scaling process of five educational institutions. This is described in the next section of this chapter.

Using the Learning Analytics Capability Model in Practice

In this section, we will elaborate on the use of the Learning Analytics Capability Model in practice. First, we describe in what way the model is empirically evaluated. Next, we will discuss the phases of learning analytics implementation and what capabilities need development during what phase.

Evaluation of the Learning Analytics Capability Model

As part of the model's evaluation process, we organized sessions with practitioners from five different educational institutions (Knobbout et al., 2021). Most institutions had gained some experience with learning analytics and now wish to use it in a more systematic and broader way. In each session, participants aimed to design a learning analytics scaling plan (roadmap). To support this task, the Learning Analytics Capability Model was instantiated via a digital tool. The tool measures the current presence of the different capabilities and shows what capabilities are yet missing and need development (see the tool's dashboard in Figure 10.2).

First, the practitioners made a roadmap without help from the Learning Analytics Capability Model. Next, the model and the tool were introduced and used to enhance the roadmap. This way, we could compare the roadmaps and see what capabilities the participants overlooked. Although the outcomes differ per institution, the results showed that the participants often initially did not include capabilities from the categories *Data, People,* and *Privacy & Ethics*. With the model's support, the participants were able to add specific capabilities to their enhanced plan.

Furthermore, it was noticeable that during the session, participants discussed many aspects, but not all of them appeared in the roadmap. The Learning Analytics Capability Model tool helped to spot these deficiencies. Overall, the participants highly appreciated the model and tool, as it helped them to check whether they included all necessary capabilities in their plans. They perceived the model as useful and wished to use it further in their task towards learning analytics adoption in their respective institution.

Developing capabilities for learning analytics are time and budget consuming. Therefore, the question is how to prioritize what capabilities to develop first. Based on the outcomes from the practitioner sessions, we can provide some insights into what capabilities to develop at what moment in the adoption process.

Phases of Learning Analytics Implementation

Viewing the implementation process as a timeline, Broos et al. (2020) distinguish among four phases. In the *Initialization phase,* the basic needs for learning analytics are determined, and a common understanding of the problems that learning analytics will target is created. During the *Prototyping phase,* learning analytics instruments are built to feed design activities and foster discussion. These instruments will be iteratively improved. Next, in the *Piloting phase,* the instruments are used in a real setting—that is, with real users and real data. Finally, during

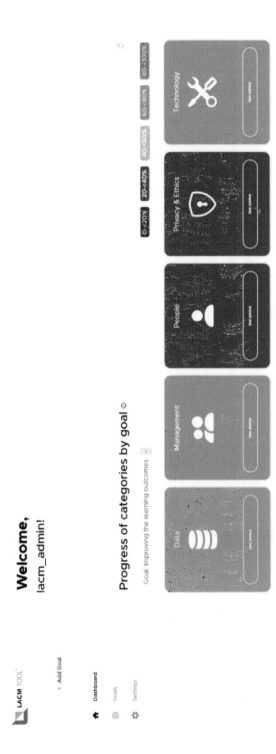

Figure 10.2 LACM Tool Dashboard

the *Scaling phase,* the institution deploys the designed solutions at scale—that is, make it available for the full population of courses, programs, and faculties. During the evaluation of the model, we let participants use it to make roadmaps. Although the sessions' participants were not learning analytics experts, they have experience with the first phases of learning analytics implementation within their respective institution. The constructed roadmaps showed that a certain sequence of capability development is present in the plans. In practice, this means that not all capabilities are needed at the start of learning analytics implementation, but that they can be developed over time.

We now discuss what capabilities require development in what phase. This is preliminary work as yet, and the sequence of capability development might differ given particular contexts. It is important to note that this is not a 'one-time exercise' but that capabilities need continuous adjustment and re-development over time. Figure 10.3 shows our current insights on what capabilities need particular attention in what phase of learning analytics implementation.

In the *Initialisation phase,* a lot of preparation and planning is done. A learning analytics policy and/or Code-of-practice must be formulated. This must explicitly state what stakeholders are involved, what benefits learning analytics must achieve, how learning analytics align with the institution's strategy, how ethical and legal requirements will be met, and who is responsible for what. Moreover, funding must be secured to finance this and consecutive stages.

Many technical details are worked out during the second phase, *Prototyping.* This involves building the right infrastructure, sourcing and integrating the right data, thinking about solutions to guarantee data quality, getting data security in order, and establishing system characteristics. Moreover, learning analytics must be coupled with pedagogical theory and best practices.

In the *Piloting phase,* real users start to use the instruments. They need to develop a data-informed mindset and must be willing to apply learning analytics in their educational activities. Being transparent about what learning analytics does and with what goal helps to foster this mindset and creates trust. To investigate whether learning analytics are beneficial, the performance of the learning analytics function must be thoroughly measured and demonstrated. Moreover, users should provide feedback on learning analytics so it can be improved. With larger numbers of stakeholders in play, aspects such as communication and collaboration become more important at this point in the implementation process.

In the final stage of *Scaling,* learning analytics will be launched at full scale. Due to the massive amounts of data that need processing at this moment, automation comes into play. Automated processes can help to quickly turn data into insights but also to check data quality. Another aspect at this stage is training. Especially users such as students and teachers need training to understand how to interpret visualizations and dashboards and learn what to do with the provided information.

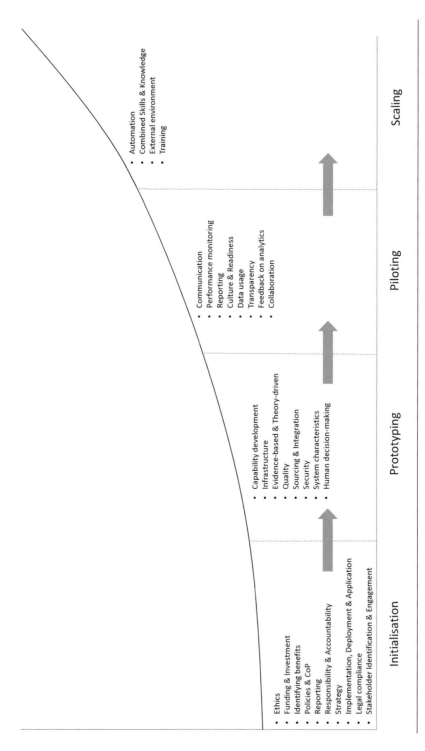

Figure 10.3   Capabilities Required per Implementation Phase

Learning analytics manuals, courses, and training videos can help to efficiently educate large groups of users. Now that learning analytics is applied at scale, collaboration with external parties becomes more important. For example, data from their previous schools can be sourced to create a completer picture of students' study career. Also, data between institutions can be shared for scientific purposes. Connectivity between the focal institution and other institutions helps to support this data exchange.

Measuring Impact on Learning

During the implementation process, institutions need to assess the quality of the learning analytics function. The Learning Analytics Capability Model prescribes the development of the capability of *Performance monitoring*. This capability is instantiated by establishing performance indicators and by constantly monitoring these indicators' fulfillment. Different quality indicators for learning analytics exist (Scheffel et al., 2014). As the definition of learning analytics states that learning analytics should optimize learning and the learning environment (LAK, 2011), we focus on this quality aspect in particular.

However, to establish whether learning analytics are indeed beneficial, institutions need to measure the impact on learning. This is not a trivial task, as learning analytics can affect different parts of learning, and a variety of measures can be used to assess the effect. Often, learning analytics researchers use grades as a dependent variable. For example, there is much research that tries to predict end-of-course grades based on learning activities.

However, grades are only a proxy of learning and do not reflect what is learned during a course. Therefore, we suggest using other metrics when researching the impact of learning analytics. To help educational institutions to measure and compare the effects of learning analytics, we performed a systematic literature review to identify operational definitions of affected learning (Knobbout & van der Stappen, 2020b). In this section, we show what learning categories learning analytics can enhance and how to measure the effects in practice.

What 'learning' really is depends on one's perspective. Different learning theories exist. While some describe learning as a *process* (e.g., Kolb, 1984), others argue that is it actually about the *outcomes* of this process (see, for example, Cooper, 1993). A third element is the learning context (Biggs & Telfer, 1987; Joksimović et al., 2018), which we call learning *environment*. During our research, we analyzed 62 key studies and synthesized operational definitions of affected learning as used in learning analytics research. We classified the definitions into one of the three categories: learning process, learning outcome, and learning environment (see Figure 10.4). We understand that the concept of learning is complex and that the

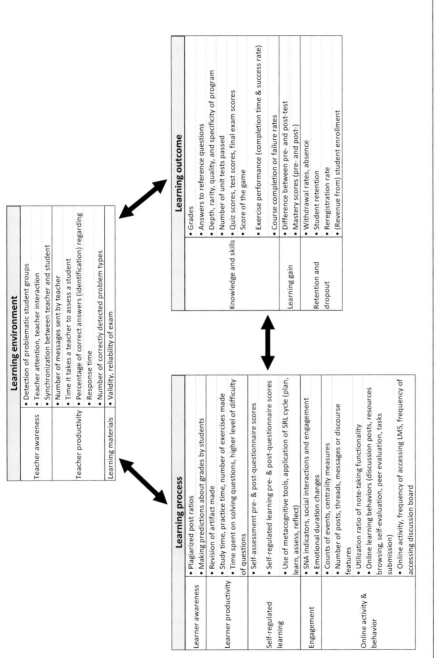

Figure 10.4   Operational Definitions of Learning

categories interact with each other. Inspired by the work of Biggs and Telfer (1987), in Figure 10.4 we indicated this interaction with arrows). For example, by improving materials used in a course based on an analysis (learning environment), future students may gain more knowledge during the same course next year (learning outcome).

Nonetheless, when analyzing the key studies, it became apparent that most studies—53 out of 62—used definitions that fit within a single category. This means that while learning analytics might affect multiple aspects, only one is measured. In the previous example, an institution perhaps regards the impact that learning analytics has on knowledge gain but not on the improved learning materials. This provides a too-shallow view of the true effect that learning analytics have on learning. We recommend that educational institutions use cross-categorical measures of learning analytics, as these provide a better, multi-perspective view of its impact. Next, we briefly explain each category. Figure 10.4 displays the operational definitions that relate to the three categories and various subgroups.

The *learning environment* considers the context in which learning takes place. The learning analytics definition explicitly mentions its optimization: "[. . .] optimizing learning and *the environments* in which it occurs" (LAK, 2011). Within this category, we distinguish three subgroups. In two of these groups—*Teacher awareness* and *Teacher productivity*—teachers are the focal units of the learning analytics. The third group focuses on *learning materials*. In the literature we studied, this aspect is rarely considered. In line with the earlier explanation, the effects that learning materials have on outcomes—for instance, student grades—are often researched, but there are almost no indicators for the quality of the learning materials themselves.

The category with the most subgroups and diverse operational definitions is the *learning process*. Similar to teachers in the previous category, learning analytics can measure *learner awareness and learner productivity*—for example, by assessing the time students spent practicing and the number of revisions they made to a learning product. Learning analytics can also gauge the degree of *self-regulated learning* by students via, for example, pre- and post-scoring self-assessments. Two groups that relate to each other are *engagement* and *online activity & behavior*. While the latter is often measured via counting clicks, posts, and login frequency, the former is more complex and also involves emotional state and more diverse interaction measures.

The last group of operational definitions regards *learning outcomes*. In our research, this was the category that contained the most key studies. Not surprisingly, many researchers try to measure the impact learning analytics have on students' *knowledge and skills* and their *learning gain*. After all, education is about transferring knowledge and skills from one person to the other. Often, grades and test scores are used for this purpose. They are widely available, they must be archived to establish students' achievements, and their export from grade systems or LMS is often an easy task. However, many factors influence grades and scores. For example, the time of the day a test was made, the test items' quality, any distractions in the test location's surroundings, the assessor's skills and experience, and so on. None of these factors has to do with the actual knowledge of students, but they can significantly affect grades and scores. Therefore, use them with the utmost caution, and consider including other measures as well. The group *retention and dropout* relates to larger groups of students and focuses more on a macro level. Here, learning analytics measure variables such as retention, reregistration rates, and withdrawal rates. They provide an indicator of learning outcomes for the program, faculty, department, or even entire educational institution.

Conclusion and Recommendations

In this chapter, we elaborate on the Learning Analytics Capability Model—a resource-based capability model for learning analytics. The model comprises 30 capabilities divided into five categories. By developing these capabilities, educational institutions work towards the successful adoption of learning analytics. Not all capabilities need development at the same time, but this depends on what implementation phase an institution is in. By progressively building capabilities for learning analytics, institutions can mature and eventually deploy learning analytics at scale.

It is important to view learning analytics success in terms of learning. To measure the effects learning analytics have on education, we provided several operational definitions. We conclude this chapter with several recommendations for practitioners who want to (further) implement learning analytics at their institution:

- Start small and scale up later on. Small-scale learning analytics initiatives lead to hands-on experience, show what is possible, and help to grow a data-informed mindset by stakeholders. Educational institutions can easily initiate small projects by providing a group of 'learning analytics pioneers' with access to some data and funding. On the other hand, the large-scale adoption of learning analytics requires significant planning. Develop an institutional vision on learning analytics that includes for what purpose learning analytics will be used, what data are needed for this task, and what stakeholders will be involved and when. Clearly describe this in learning analytics policy or a Code-of-Practice. To support the policymaking process, tools such as SHEILA[3] can be used.

---

[3] https://sheilaproject.eu/

- Learning analytics is a multi-disciplinary field and thus requires the involvement of different stakeholder groups. In the past, learning analytics was often viewed as a technical endeavor, and pedagogy came in second place. However, this is not the road to impactful learning analytics. From the start, it is important to engage students, teachers, educational experts, IT staff, senior management, and many others. During the design process, user demands need particular attention and consideration. That is the only way that learning analytics can truly influence the primary process.
- Plan what learning analytics capabilities must be developed and in what order. Evidence shows that without central coordination in the form of learning analytics policies and Codes-of-Practice, it is hard to scale learning analytics initiatives. Align learning with the institution's strategy and vision on education and address ethical and privacy issues early on. Realize that capabilities from all categories of the Learning Analytics Capability Model need to be present for successful learning analytics. As elaborated on in this chapter, not all capabilities need development at the same time. Nonetheless, it is important to plan and formulate future steps well in advance.
- Continuously measure the impact learning analytics have on learning. This supports learning analytics adoption in multiple ways. It helps to show the benefits and foster a culture towards data-informed decision making. Moreover, it allows improvement of learning analytics–driven interventions—for example, by collecting evidence on what interventions yield the best results in terms of learning. To measure the effects, we provided several operational definitions of affected learning. We distinguish three categories: learning process, learning outcome, and learning environment. We recommend using learning analytics to affect multiple categories. Especially since grades are only a proxy of learning, educational institutions should be very carefully measuring the impact of learning analytics based on grades (alone).

References

Adrian, C., Abdullah, R., Atan, R., and Jusoh, Y. Y. (2018). Conceptual model development of big data analytics implementation assessment effect on decision-making. *International Journal of Interactive Multimedia and Artificial Intelligence, 5*(1), 101–106.

Ambrosini, V., Bowman, C., and Collier, N. (2009). Dynamic capabilities: An exploration of how firms renew their resource base. *British Journal of Management, 20,* S9–S24.

Biggs, J. B., and Telfer, R. (1987). *The Process of Learning.* McGraw-Hill/Appleton & Lange.

Broos, T., Hilliger, I., Pérez-Sanagustín, M., Htun, N., Millecamp, M., Pesántez-Cabrera, P., Solano-Quinde, L., Siguenza-Guzman, L., Zuñiga-Prieto, M., Verbert, K., and De Laet, T. (2020). Coordinating learning analytics policymaking and implementation at scale. *British Journal of Educational Technology, 51*(4), 938–954. https://doi.org/10.1111/bjet.12934

Clow, D. (2012). The learning analytics cycle: Closing the loop effectively. *Proceedings of the 2nd International Conference on Learning Analytics and Knowledge,* 134–138.

Colvin, C., Dawson, S., Wade, A., and Gašević, D. (2017). Addressing the challenges of institutional adoption. In C. Lang, G. Siemens, A. Wise, and D. Gasevic (Eds.), *Handbook of Learning Analytics* (1st ed., 281–289). https://doi.org/10.18608/hla17

Cooper, P. A. (1993). Paradigm shifts in designed instruction—From behaviorism to cognitivism to constructivism. *Educational Technology, 35*(3), 12–19. https://www.learntechlib.org/p/170882/share/

Drachsler, H., and Greller, W. (2016). Privacy and analytics: It's a DELICATE issue: A checklist for trusted learning analytics. *Proceedings of the Sixth International Conference on Learning Analytics & Knowledge,* 89–98.

Ferguson, R. (2012). Learning analytics: Drivers, developments and challenges. *International Journal of Technology Enhanced Learning, 4*(5–6), 304–317.

Gasevic, D., Tsai, Y.-S., Dawson, S., and Pardo, A. (2019). How do we start? An approach to learning analytics adoption in higher education. *The International Journal of Information and Learning Technology, 36*(4), 342–353.

Grant, R. M. (1991). The resource-based theory of competitive advantage: Implications for strategy formulation. *California Management Review, 33*(3), 114–135.

Greller, W., and Drachsler, H. (2012). Translating learning into numbers: A generic framework for learning analytics. *Educational Technology & Society, 15*(3), 42–57.

Gupta, M., and George, J. F. (2016). Toward the development of a big data analytics capability. *Information & Management, 53*(8), 1049–1064.

Hevner, A. R., March, S. T., Park, J., and Ram, S. (2004). Design science in information systems research. *MIS Quarterly, 28*(1), 75–105.

Joksimović, S., Kovanović, V., and Dawson, S. (2019). The journey of learning analytics. *HERDSA Review of Higher Education, 6,* 37–63.

Joksimović, S., Poquet, O., Kovanović, V., Dowell, N., Mills, C., Gašević, D., Dawson, S., Graesser, A. C., and Brooks, C. (2018). How do we model learning at scale? A systematic review of research on MOOCS. *Review of Educational Research, 88*(1), 43–86. https://doi.org/10.3102/0034654317740335

Knobbout, J., and van der Stappen, E. (2020a). A capability model for learning analytics adoption: Identifying organizational capabilities from literature on big data analytics, business analytics, and learning analytics. *International Journal of Learning Analytics and Artificial Intelligence for Education (IJAI), 2*(1), 47–66.

Knobbout, J., and van der Stappen, E. (2020b). Where is the learning in learning analytics? A systematic literature review on the operationalization of learning-related constructs in the evaluation of learning analytics interventions. *IEEE Transactions on Learning Technologies.* https://doi.org/10.1109/TLT.2020.2999970

Knobbout, J., van der Stappen, E., and Versendaal, J. (2020). Refining the learning analytics capability model. *Proceedings of the 26th Americas Conference on Information Systems (AMCIS)*.

Knobbout, J., van der Stappen, E., Versendaal, J., and van de Wetering, R. (2021). A comprehensive model to support the adoption of learning analytics: A mixed-method approach. Manuscript submitted for publication.

Kolb, D. A. (1984). Experiential learning: Experience as the source of learning and development. In *Prentice Hall, Inc.* (Issue 1984). Prentice Hall. https://doi.org/10.1016/B978-0-7506-7223-8.50017-4

LAK. (2011). *1st International Conference on Learning Analytics and Knowledge 2011*. https://tekri.athabascau.ca/analytics/

Na, K. S., and Tasir, Z. (2017). A systematic review of learning analytics intervention contributing to student success in online learning. *2017 International Conference on Learning and Teaching in Computing and Engineering (LaTICE)*, 62–68.

Pardo, A., and Siemens, G. (2014). Ethical and privacy principles for learning analytics. *British Journal of Educational Technology, 45*(3), 438–450.

Romero, C., and Ventura, S. (2020). Educational data mining and learning analytics: An updated survey. *Wiley Interdisciplinary Reviews: Data Mining and Knowledge Discovery, 10*(3). https://doi.org/10.1002/widm.1355

Samuelsen, J., Chen, W., and Wasson, B. (2019). Integrating multiple data sources for learning analytics—Review of literature. *Research and Practice in Technology Enhanced Learning, 14*(1), 11. https://doi.org/10.1186/s41039-019-0105-4

Scheffel, M., Drachsler, H., Stoyanov, S., and Specht, M. (2014). Quality indicators for learning analytics. *Journal of Educational Technology & Society, 17*(4), 117–132.

Tsai, Y.-S., and Gašević, D. (2017). Learning analytics in higher education—Challenges and policies: A review of eight learning analytics policies. *Proceedings of the Seventh International Learning Analytics & Knowledge Conference*, 233–242.

Viberg, O., Hatakka, M., Bälter, O., and Mavroudi, A. (2018). The current landscape of learning analytics in higher education. *Computers in Human Behavior, 89*, 98–110. https://doi.org/10.1016/J.CHB.2018.07.027

Chapter 11

The Role of Trust in Online Learning

Joanna Paliszkiewicz and Edyta Skarzyńska[1]

Abstract

As a result of the health crisis (COVID-19), higher education has moved to deliver courses online. Many students worldwide had to transfer from face-to-face instruction to an online learning environment in the middle of the semester. It has benefits and also adverse effects. The more successful transitions to online learning are influenced by the user's intention and the usefulness of the technology, as well as the trust. The chapter aims to present the role of trust in online learning and present research results conducted among the students from Warsaw University of Life Sciences in Poland. A review of the literature about trust and online learning is presented in the chapter, followed by the research methodology. Next, the research results are discussed. In the end, the discussion, conclusion, and limitations are described. Recommendations for future research are provided.

Keywords: Trust, online learning, University, active learning, trust building, online education

Introduction

The COVID-19 pandemic has raised significant challenges for higher education (Almaiah et al., 2020; Daniel, 2020; Rapanta et al., 2020). Many countries have decided to close educational institutions. According to specialists, social distancing is a critical factor in breaking the virus transmission chain. As a result, schools and colleges have been looking for methods to deliver the curriculum within specific time frames based on the academic calendar. The teaching staff has had to prepare and deliver their classes from home, with all the practical and technical challenges (Hodges et al., 2020).

The limitations caused some degree of inconvenience and allowed for educational innovations using digital technology and increased digital competencies among teachers and students. In a short time, most universities have switched to online learning using dedicated online platforms. For the purposes of this chapter, online learning refers to learning that is mediated by the technology and design of online learning that influences learning outcomes (Wang et al., 2013; Bower, 2019; Rapanta et al., 2020). Online education means that students are physically distant from the instructors and require a delivery method (Wilde & Hsu, 2019).

Educational institutions, guided by the appropriate level of quality of the offered education, built an online learning environment. This solution differs from traditional teaching in many aspects, such as motivation, student satisfaction, and interaction (Bignoux & Sund, 2018).

To have an effective learning environment, the instructor needs to develop and maintain trust between and among the students and the teacher through good course design and appropriate interactions and communication. The trust has to be established immediately. Nowadays, we do not have enough information about how COVID-19 measures (stay-at-home) and online learning have affected the learning process from the students' point of view (Aguilera-Hermida, 2020). Further research is needed in this area.

The aim of the chapter is to present the role and importance of trust in online learning and to present research results conducted among the students from Warsaw University of Life Sciences in Poland. In the chapter, a review of the literature about trust and online learning is presented, followed by the research methodology. Next, the research results are discussed. In the end, the discussion, conclusion, limitations, and future directions are described.

Trust and Online Learning—Literature Review

Trust plays an important role in our lives (Liebowitz et al., 2018; Liebowitz et al., 2019; Koohang et al., 2020). Building trust is primarily based on relationships between people and the history of a given group, so traditional trust is believed to be built over the years. Technological changes of globalization significantly affect different perceptions of trust. This view is becoming problematic with the increase in globalization and change in technologies and an increased reliance on temporary groups—for example, in education during COVID-19.

Paliszkiewicz (2010) described trust as the belief that another party (a) will not act in a way that is harmful to the trusting firm, (b) will act in such a way that it is beneficial to the trusting firm, (c) will act reliably, and (d) will behave or respond in a predictable and mutually acceptable manner. Digital trust is related to the environments where physical and direct contacts do not occur, where moral and social pressures can be differently perceived, and where digital devices mediate interactions. According to Wang and Jeong (2018, p. 163), digital trust "means general beliefs in online service providers that result in behavioral intentions." Digital trust can be successful when the communication is honest and transparent (Demolombe, 2004). Shin (2017) confirmed a significant impact of trust on behavioral outcomes. Meyerson et al. (1996) developed the concept of swift trust. Swift trust is a form of trust occurring in temporary organizational structures, including quick starting groups. According to swift trust theory, a group assumes trust initially and later verifies and adjusts trust beliefs accordingly.

The key to this concept is juxtaposing it with such social features as uncertainty, risk, the expectation of benefits, and the hope that others will care and act according to the indicated norms and principles. The set of these features is essential for students and lecturers who have been obliged to learn online due to the pandemic. Comparing the traditional way of learning with the virtual learning mode, one can observe more significant uncertainty and the presence of risk. Indeed, the level of these features is higher when starting online learning—having no experience in this type of learning, the participant is unsure how to proceed or what to expect. This can arouse fear but also be motivated because the interest in a new way of learning and effective cooperation in an unknown and ambiguous environment allows one to broaden knowledge and acquire new skills. However, it is an environment with a limited transmission of social signals and constant risk. When using training in online learning software, students and teachers cannot be sure that the software will be interoperable and there will be no complications when learning online.

Trust is a crucial factor in the functioning of social relations. However, in a virtual environment, the importance of swift trust is growing. The dynamics of this phenomenon allow for the leveling or alleviation of the feeling of isolation among students. Students and teachers have a limited amount of time to get to know each other during online classes, so they assign observations based on their experiences and professional stereotypes (Oppola et al., 2004). Through the performance of tasks, activity, and joint analysis of a given issue, these teams maintain and strengthen trust quickly. According to Meyerson et al. (1996, p. 180), "The *more* forceful the *action*, the *greater* the *willingness* to *trust*, and the *more* rapidly does *trust develop*."

Iacono and Weisband (1997) also dealt with the issue of swift trust. They researched to understand how temporary and distributed student teams build and maintain trust. The result of this study was the discovery of a high level of trust in groups characterized by high interaction and commitment. The authors of this study define it as "doing trust work" (p. 413). When analyzing the given example, it can be observed that the critical factors in building trust, both in a fast and traditional way, are communication and commitment by performing duties honestly.

Research on the concept of swift trust at the global virtual team was conducted by Jarvenpaa and Leidner (1998). They extended this concept to definitions of a global virtual team, characterizing it as a temporary, geographically dispersed, culturally diverse, electronic communication workgroup. The conducted research analyzed the behavior and actions at the early and later stages of group work. The result of the considerations is the indication of activities and behaviors that facilitate building trust in a virtual group.

At an early stage, the actions to foster trust will be (Jarvenpaa and Leidner, 1998):

- **Communication.** Focus on conveying emotions, enthusiasm, social exchanges, social communication.
- **Team activities.** Individual initiative, suggestions, opinions, solving problems with technical uncertainty, proposing topics, presenting areas of interest.

At a later stage, the behaviors and activities to facilitate trust will be (Jarvenpaa and Leidner, 1998):

- **Communication.** A systematic course, timely and substantive answers, feedback on getting acquainted with a given issue, explanations and answers to the questions asked.
- **Team activities.** Active participation in the activities of all team members, transition from lecture to task mode, the ability to react and concentrate in unforeseen situations.

Analysis by Jarvenpaa and Leidner (1998) identifies unique communication and trust-building behaviors in global virtual teams. Appropriate task communication allows maintaining the trust and showing commitment allows strengthening trust in the online environment.

Coppola et al. (2004), based on their studies, proposed the following trust-building strategies in the online environment: establish early communication, develop a positive social atmosphere, reinforce predictable patterns of communication and action (students need structured activity, repetition, and feedback), and involve team members in tasks.

In the literature, different behaviors which support trust-building (which can be implemented in online education) are described—for example, by Bracey, 2002; Galford & Seibold Drapeau, 2002; Bibb & Kourdi, 2004; Six, 2005; Paliszkiewicz et al., 2015; and Paliszkiewicz & Koohang, 2016: be transparent; be open; show that you understand the needs of the person; establish the guiding principles of how you will operate; explain the resources you will use in this work; keep to the principles you have elaborated; manage mutual expectations; engage in constant, honest, two-way communication; reinforce through consistent behaviors; be responsive; use caring; be sincere; be trustworthy; create authentic communication; be competent; have positive intent; be able to forgive.

Research Method

Characteristics of the Research Sample

The survey was conducted among students at the Warsaw University of Life Sciences in Poland. The respondents were students of economics and construction, as well as doctoral students representing various scientific disciplines. The study was conducted online using a Google® form. Two hundred twenty-seven people participated in the study.

The Instrument and Data Analysis

The instrument was created based on the previous work of Booth (2012), Wang (2014), and Muthuprasad et al. (2021). It consisted of the questions concerning technological availability and software used, benefits, bottlenecks, and factors affecting online learning. In the study, the Likert scale was used: 5, strongly agree; 4, agree; 3, I do not know; 2, disagree; 1, strongly disagree. The frequency of the ratings given was calculated for questions.

Research Results

Demographic Characteristics of Respondents

The average age of the respondents is 22 years. There were 78.41% women and 21.59% men. Among them were 60.35% of bachelor's degree students, 33.04% of master's degree students, and 6.61% of participants of the doctoral school (see Table 11.1).

Table 11.1 Demographic Data

Demographic data Number of respondents = 227		
Gender	Female	78.4%
	Male	21.6%
Degree of studies	Bachelor's degree	60.4%
	Master's degree	33%
	Doctoral School	6.6%

Source: Own elaboration based on the conducted research.

Technological Availability and Software Used

The variety of devices used by students to participate in online classes influences the perception of it. When choosing an online learning platform, a university should pay attention to its compatibility with various tools. Most students prefer laptops as the most used tool (60.4%). Next, they like smartphones (34.8%), computers (16.4%), and tablets (8.8%). The respondents could choose from several tools. The prospect of participating in virtual classes with the help of the available tools reduces the likelihood of technological difficulties.

When analyzing the software used during online learning at the university, most students indicated the Microsoft® Teams® program (91.2%). A small group of respondents also mentioned the communication using e-mail, Moodle®, and the publication of information on university websites. By using different applications, the instructor can maintain constant contact with students. The possibility of asking questions in written and oral form allows them to communicate and build trust.

Benefits of Learning Online

The answers to the questions concerning the benefits of online learning are presented in Table 11.2.

The survey results indicate that the respondents recognized comfort during classes as important benefit of online education. The answers, 4 (agree) and 5 (strongly agree), were chosen by 68.28% of respondents. Also, flexible classes and easier access to the presented materials were underlined as an essential benefit by 59.91%. Development and acquisition of new technological skills were indicated as a very important benefit only by 16.30% of respondents; for 26.43%, it was neutral. Most of the students (answers 1 and 2) assess negatively that greater ability to concentrate (63%) and more possibilities of contact (online) with the lecturer (64.31%) were benefits of online education. Learning self-discipline and greater responsibility got 47.57% negative answers and 38.76% positive; 13.66% was neutral.

Table 11.2 Benefits of Learning Online

Questions	Strongly disagree 1	Disagree 2	Neutral 3	Agree 4	Strongly agree 5
More comfort during classes	0.88	17.18	13.66	22.91	45.37
Flexible schedule of classes and easier access to the presented materials	1.32	12.33	26.43	22.47	37.44
Development and acquisition of new technological skills	18.94	23.35	26.43	14.98	16.30
Greater ability to concentrate	39.65	23.35	3.52	17.18	16.30
More possibilities of contact (online) with the lecturer	43.61	20.70	13.22	8.37	14.1
Learning self-discipline and greater responsibility	26.87	20.70	13.66	27.75	11.01

(Likert scale: 5 = most important and 1 = least important) *(Source:* Own elaboration based on the conducted research.)

Bottlenecks in Online Learning

The answers to the questions concerning the bottlenecks in online learning are presented in Table 11.3.

The analysis of the results shows that the most significant problem in online learning is the self-discipline of the respondents (56.83% strongly agree or agree with this statement). The respondents also indicated the lack of interpersonal contacts as important factors lowering online learning effectiveness (57.26% strongly agree or agree with this statement). Data problems resulting from the inability to actively participate in the implementation of the curriculum significantly affect the evaluation of the quality of teaching (46.7% of respondents agree or strongly agree with the statement that poor quality of teaching is the bottleneck in online learning; for 16.3% it is neutral, and 37% disagree or strongly disagree). In many cases, issues with the Internet infrastructure are also problematic, which negatively affects the perception and trust in this type of learning. In the research, the following aspects were taken under consideration:

- Data speed (39.65% agree or strongly agree, 30.40% neutral, 29.95% disagree or strongly disagree)
- Problem with Internet connection (41.85% agree or strongly agree, 24.23% neutral, 33.92% disagree or strongly disagree)

Table 11.3 Bottlenecks in Online Learning

Questions	Strongly disagree	Disagree	Neutral	Agree	Strongly agree
	1	2	3	4	5
Self-discipline	7.49	11.45	24.23	23.35	33.48
Little or no face-to-face contact and interaction	23.35	11.45	7.93	28.63	28.63
Poor quality of teaching	3.08	33.92	16.30	23.35	23.35
Data speed	9.25	20.70	30.40	22.91	16.74
Problem with Internet connection	15.42	18.5	24.23	23.79	18.06
Lack of proper equipment	23.35	25.55	20.70	22.47	7.93
Data limit	31.28	28.19	14.54	18.06	7.93

(Likert scale: 5 = most important and 1 = least important) (*Source*: Own elaboration based on the conducted research.)

- Lack of proper equipment (48.9% agree or strongly agree, 20.70% neutral, 48.90% disagree or strongly disagree)
- Data limit (25.99% agree or strongly agree, 14.54% neutral, 59.47% disagree or strongly disagree)

Technological infrastructure is a critical factor in fostering trust in online learning. The constantly arising problems contribute to the emergence of fears, or at the crucial moment, there will be no problems that cannot be quickly resolved. The quality of the presented multimedia material is an essential factor when learning online. The occurring disruptions and problems with showing the content affect the audience negatively. To a lesser extent, there is a problem with access to appropriate devices. The compatibility of programs with various devices allows everyone to participate in such activities. However, in many fields of study, specialized programs are used to develop skills and implement the curriculum. Therefore, there may be a problem with access to such software, which has a negative impact on the perception of this learning mode.

Factors Affecting Online Learning

Factors affecting online learning are presented in Table 11.4.

The key factors that positively influence the achievement of effective online learning are ranked from 1 to 10, taking under consideration the number of answers. In the first place is the ability to concentrate (70.48% positive answers, 21.15% neutral, and 8.37% negative). Ability to concentrate is related to focusing

Table 11.4 Factors Affecting Online Learning

Questions	Total number of grades	Strongly disagree 1	Disagree 2	Neutral 3	Agree 4	Strongly agree 5	Rank
Ability to concentrate	936	0.44	7.93	21.15	18.50	51.98	1
Amount of content uploaded	926	0.44	7.93	17.62	31.28	42.73	2
Motivation of the students	922	0.44	0.00	32.16	27.75	39.65	3
Communication skills of the instructor	905	7.49	1.32	21.15	25.11	44.93	4
Classes conducted with the use of presentations	884	7.49	0.88	24.23	29.52	37.89	5
The level of knowledge of the lecturer in the field of the content provided	849	14.10	0.44	15.86	36.56	33.04	6
Technical skills of the instructor	844	13.22	2.64	21.15	25.11	37.89	7
Classes conducted with the use of prepared film material	792	1.32	9.25	43.61	30.84	14.98	8
Systematized structure of classes	778	13.66	9.25	24.23	26.43	26.43	9
Technical skills of the students	774	7.93	14.10	32.16	20.70	25.11	10

Source: Own elaboration based on the conducted research.

attention on the presented content and avoiding discrepancies. The amount of content is also crucial (74.01% positive answers, 17.62% neutral, and 8.37% negative).

When arranging a plan for the lecture, the teacher should consider such elements as discussion or student activity. Although the instructor is the most critical player in establishing trust in online teaching, course design can have an impact as well. Appropriately designed content and presentation are crucial factors in achieving an effective teaching experience in online classes and can help trust building. The course needs to be designed with the most opportunities for communication between and among the students and the instructor and the opportunity for students to give feedback to one another. Motivation is essential to achieve the set goals and increase efficiency in learning (67.4% of respondents agree or strongly agree with this statement, 32.16% were neutral, and 0.44% disagree). Also, respondents indicated communication as a critical factor in online learning, so the lecturers should skillfully convey new content to interest the audience and create engaging conversations (70.04% of respondents agree or strongly agree with this statement, 21.15% were neutral, and 8.81% disagree or strongly disagree).

The respondents prefer multimedia presentation as the primary tool for providing information (67.41% of respondents agree or strongly agree with this statement, 24.2% were neutral, and 8.37% disagree or strongly disagree). By possessing a high level of knowledge in a given field, the lecturer builds the image of a trustworthy person, which also helps create an effective online learning environment (69.06% of respondents agree or strongly agree with this statement, 15.86% were neutral, and 14.54% disagree or strongly disagree).

Respondents also mentioned the technical skills of the instructors as a factor influencing learning (63% of respondents agree or strongly agree with this statement, 21.15% were neutral, and 15.86% disagree or strongly disagree). Students also like the video materials prepared by teachers and used during classes (45.82% of respondents agree or strongly agree with this statement, 43.61% were neutral, and 10.57% disagree or strongly disagree). A high average of answers also got the systematized structure of classes. This facilitates learning and allows returning to the presented content (52.86% of respondents agree or strongly agree with this statement, 24.23% were neutral, and 22.91% disagree or strongly disagree).

Technical skills of students also influence the level of online education (45.81% of respondents agree or strongly agree with this statement, 32.16% were neutral, and 22.03% disagree or strongly disagree).

Additionally, the respondents were asked to assess students' ways of verification of participation and knowledge level. The results are presented in Table 11.5.

When analyzing the respondents' activity, which is crucial in building swift trust, the highest score was given to assigning specific tasks and conducting online tests for assessment (48.45% of respondents agree or strongly agree with this statement, 17.18% were neutral, and 34.36% disagree). Involving students to prepare projects

Table 11.5 The Ways of Verification of Participation and Knowledge Level

Questions	Total number of grades	Strongly disagree 1	Disagree 2	Neutral 3	Agree 4	Strongly agree 5	Rank
Assigning assignments and conducting online tests for assessment	741	15.42	18.94	17.18	20.70	27.75	1
Encourage discussion and asking questions	667	14.54	20.26	27.31	32.60	5.29	2
Monitoring students during classes (calling selected people to answer)	640	24.23	24.23	17.62	13.22	20.70	3

Source: Own elaboration based on the conducted research.

in a given area consists of building a committed team and increasing interactions between students. It requires students to rely on each other to complete them. To get students to participate fully during online lectures, active participation should be required, and the instructor should maintain a presence and motivate the students. Respondents also indicated encouragement in discussion and asking questions (37.89% of respondents agree or strongly agree with this statement, 27.31% were neutral, and 34.80% disagree). Monitoring students during classes (calling selected people to answer) was ranked lower (33.92% of respondents agree or strongly agree with this statement, 17.62% were neutral, and 48.46% disagree).

Discussion

Studies are showing that properly designed online classes are an excellent substitute for traditional teaching. However, when analyzing the current situation and the lack of thorough preparation for introducing online learning, several problems can be observed. One of them is the quality of teaching—that is, designing and presenting a given issue. Effectiveness depends to a large extent on the appropriate adaptation of the content to the online environment. A significant factor causing anxiety concerning virtual learning is the lack of trust resulting from introducing the new learning mode. Many students have not had contact with such a mode of teaching because it was not raised on such a scale, so it can be concluded that it is a social experiment.

Proper building of the schedule of classes allows avoiding the cognitive and physical burden resulting from the use of electronic equipment. To have a productive learning environment, the instructor needs to develop and maintain a sense of trust between and among the students and the instructor through good course design and facilitation (Coppola, 2004). Access to the materials presented during classes and engaging students to actively create their structure contribute to the increase in the level of trust. Technological development allows carrying out both theoretical and practical online classes. Introducing innovative solutions increases the effectiveness of online learning. A perfectly developed topic, connectivity, and the use of appropriate multimedia tools can influence the perception of online learning on a par with traditional teaching. The ability to use such tools and the communication skills of the lecturers are important factors in building trust. Continuous interaction with students is essential to maximize the satisfaction of working in a virtual environment. Research by Jonhson et al. (2008) confirms the existence of a dependency in this area. Students' frequent involvement influences their concentration, and the importance of interaction frequency was also presented by Huggett (2014). In the current situation, online learning makes it possible to reach all students and continue the curriculum.

Conclusion

This paper contributes to the debate concerning the role of trust in online learning. The transition to online learning was sudden, so universities did not have time to properly design their online curriculum. The student experience can be incorporated to improve the productivity and efficiency of this learning mode. Another aspect of improving remote learning and building trust is that it is unknown how long the COVID-19 pandemic will last. Even after restrictions are withdrawn, there is a high probability that different institutions will combine these two forms of learning. The results of the research can contribute to the teaching process as well as to the choice of the type of research method. Increasing confidence in online learning can contribute to increasing interest in this form of education.

Adapting education to the current pandemic situation has contributed to establishing online learning as the primary learning mode. The consequences of implementing this teaching mode depend on two factors. The first is the correct approach leading to this learning mode. Appropriate design of the presented content and constant stimulation of social communication will build trust among students. With the technological development of that time, this type of teaching could be perceived as on equal footing with traditional methods in the future. Another factor is the involvement of students in the design of the course. The ability to formulate opinions, provide content, and perform specific tasks allows one to actively participate in meetings (Muthuprasad et al., 2021).

The results of the survey showed a positive attitude of respondents to online learning. Learning through commitment allows optimizing the learning process. The benefits contribute to increasing trust in online learning. From the research analysis, it can be concluded that the main benefits are more comfort during classes, flexible schedule of classes, and easier access to the presented materials. The main bottlenecks concerning online courses are self-discipline and little or no face-to-face contact and interactions. Respondents also underlined factors affecting online learning. The main are the ability to concentrate, the amount of content uploaded, and the students' motivation.

These factors should be considered when designing an online course to eliminate anxiety and fear of possible failure. In the future, academic units may use online platforms, combining them with traditional classes. Therefore, the conducted research is a valuable element in constructing courses to increase students' trust and engagement in this teaching type.

This study was limited to a sample of convenience from one higher education institution in Poland. Future studies should focus on a larger sample population from diverse institutions and/or organizations to enhance the generalizability of the findings. Further research should also consider the inclusion of possible emerging users' privacy concerns and cybersecurity issues. More research is needed to understand how the lack of physical contact and the limitations in social interaction influenced students' performance if they could develop self-discipline.

References

Aguilera-Hermida, P. (2020). College students' use and acceptance of emergency online learning due to COVID-19. *International Journal of Educational Research Open, 1*, 100011.

Almaiah, M. A., Al-Khasawneh, A., and Althunibat, A. (2020). Exploring the critical challenges and factors influencing the e-learning system usage during COVID-19 pandemic. *Education and Information Technology, 25*, 5261–5280.

Bibb, S., and Kourdi, J. (2004). *Trust Matters for Organizational and Personal Success.* New York, NY: Palgrave Macmillan.

Bignoux, S., and Sund, K. J. (2018). Tutoring executives online: What drives perceived quality? *Behaviour & Information Technology, 37*(7), 703–713.

Booth, S. E. (2012). Cultivating knowledge sharing and trust in online communities for educators. *Journal of Educational Computing Research, 47*(1) 1–31.

Bower, M. (2019). Technology-mediated learning theory. *British Journal of Education Technology, 50*, 1035–1048,

Bracey, H. (2002). *Building Trust. How to Get It! How to Keep It!* Taylorsville, GA: Hyler Bracey.

Coppola, N. W., Hiltz, S. R., and Rotter, N. G. (2004). Building trust in virtual teams. *IEEE Transactions on Professional Communication*, (June), 95–104.

Daniel, S. J. (2020). Education and the COVID-19 pandemic. *Prospects, 49*, 91–96.

Demolombe, R. (2004). *Reasoning About Trust: A Formal Logic Framework.* Berlin: Springer.

Galford, R., and Drapeau, A. S. (2002). *The Trusted Leader. Bringing Out the Best in Your People and Your Company.* New York, NY: Free Press.

Hodges, C., Moore, S., Lockee, B., Trust, T., and Bond, A. (2020). The difference between emergency remote teaching and online learning. *EDUCAUSE Review, 27* (March). https://er.educause.edu/articles/2020/3/the-difference-between-emergency -remote-teaching-and-online-learning

Huggett, C. (2014). The virtual training guidebook: How to design, deliver, and implement live online learning. *American Society for Training and Development.* https://d22bbllm j4tvv8.cloudfront.net/01/24/636c0c59d7a8cd834581467c1614/111306-ch2.pdf

Iacono, C. S., and Weisband, S. (1997). Developing trust in virtual teams. In *Proceedings of Hawaii International Conference Systems Science, 2*, 412–420.

Jarvenpaa, S. L., and Leidner, D. E. (1998). Communication and trust in global virtual teams. *Organization Science, 10*(6), 791–815.

Johnson, R. D., Hornik, S., and Salas, E. (2008). An empirical examination of factors contributing to the creation of successful e-learning environments. *International Journal of Human-Computer Studies, 66*(5), 356–369.

Koohang, A., Nowak, A., Paliszkiewicz, J., and Nord, J. (2020). Information security policy compliance: Leadership, trust, role values, and awareness. *Journal of Computer Information Systems, 60*(1), 1–8.

Liebowitz, J., Y. Chan, T. Jenkin, D. Spicker, J. Paliszkiewicz, and F. Babiloni, F. (Eds.), (2019). *How Well Do Executives Trust Their Intuition*, Boca Raton, FL, USA: CRC Press, Taylor & Francis Group.

Liebowitz, J., J. Paliszkiewicz, and J. Gołuchowski, J. (Eds), (2018). *Intuition, Trust, and Analytics*. Boca Raton, FL, USA: CRC Press, Taylor & Francis Group.

Meyerson, D., Weick, K. E., and Kramer, R. M. (1996). Swift trust and temporary groups. In M. Kramer and T. R. Tyler (Eds.), *Trust in Organizations: Frontiers of Theory and Research*, 166–195. Thousand Oaks, CA: Sage Publications.

Muthuprasad, T., Aiswarya, S., Aditya, K. S., and Jha, G. K. (2021). Students' perception and preference for online education in India during COVID -19 pandemic. *Social Sciences & Humanities Open, 3,* 100101.

Oppola W. C, Hiltz R., and Otter N. (2004). Building trust in virtual teams. *IEEE Transactions on Professional Communication, 47*(2).

Paliszkiewicz, J. (2010). Organizational trust—A critical review of the empirical research. In *Proceedings of 2010 International Conference on Technology Innovation and Industrial Management,* 16–18 June 2010 Pattaya, Thailand.

Paliszkiewicz, J., Gołuchowski, J., and Koohang, A. (2015). Leadership, trust, and knowledge management in relation to organizational performance: Developing an instrument. *Online Journal of Applied Knowledge Management, 3*(2), 19–35.

Paliszkiewicz, J., and Koohang, A. (2016). *Social Media and Trust: A Multinational Study of University Students*. Santa California, CA: Informing Science Press.

Rapanta, C., Botturi, L., Goodyear, P., Guàrdia, L., and Koole, M. (2020). Online university teaching during and after the COVID-19 crisis: Refocusing teacher presence and learning activity. *Postdigital Science Education, 2,* 923–945.

Shin, D. (2017). Conceptualizing and measuring quality of experience of the internet of things: Exploring how quality is perceived by users. *Information Management, 54*(8), 998–1011.

Six F. (2005). *The Trouble With Trust. The Dynamics of Interpersonal Trust Building.* Cornwall, GB: MPG Books Ltd, Bodmin.

Wang, C. R., and Jeong, M. (2018). What makes you choose Airbnb again? An examination of users' perceptions toward the website and their stay. *International Journal of Hospital Management, 74,* 162–170.

Wang, C. H., Shannon, D. M., and Ross, M. E. (2013). Students' characteristics, self-regulated learning, technology self-efficacy, and course outcomes in online learning. *Distance Education, 34*(3), 302–323.

Wang, Y. D. (2014). Building student trust in online learning environments. *Distance Education, 35*(3), 345–359.

Wilde, N., and Hsu, A. (2019). The influence of general self-efficacy on the interpretation of vicarious experience information within online learning. *International Journal of Educational Technology in Higher Education, 16*(1), 1–20.

Chapter 12

Face Detection with Applications in Education

Juan Carlos Bonilla-Robles,[1] José Alberto Hernández Aguilar,[1] and Guillermo Santamaría-Bonfil[2]

Abstract

E-learning has grown in importance, particularly nowadays under the COVID pandemic context. In this type of educational application, it is extremely useful to apply face-detection techniques to support online teachers—not only for the automation of roll call and for proctoring (supervision functions) in online assessments, but also to identify academic emotions, learning engagement, or boredom to carry out automatic adaptive tasks. In this research, we discuss the application of Haar filters and the AdaBoost classifier (Viola, 2001) for the detection of faces, in order to facilitate the counting and proctoring in online education activities. For this purpose, we analyzed 1,100 positive images (faces) and 1,100 negative images (no faces) to train a model; we obtained our own Myhaar.xml file and compared it with the default frontal .XML file of OpenCV; for this test we use

---

[1] Autonomous University of the State of Morelos (UAEMor), Av. Universidad 1001, Col. Chamilpa, Cuernavaca, Morelos, México

[2] National Council of Science and Technology—National Institute of Electricity and Clean Energy (CONACYT-INEEL), Reforma 113, Col. Palmira, Cuernavaca, Morelos, México

150 positive images and 150 negative images collected from different real-world video conferences. Results show the balance accuracy of our proposal is better (87% vs. 82%) than the default frontal classification of OpenCV. The main contribution of this paper is the application of a classic, low-cost technique for the detection of faces in online educational settings.

Keywords: Computer vision, Haar filters and AdaBoost, online teaching

Introduction

Face detection is emerging as an active area of research, covering various disciplines such as image processing, pattern recognition, computational vision, and neural networks (Chellappa et al., 1995).

Detection of faces using a computer system is the process of identifying faces in images or frames. This process has gained great importance in areas such as security, marketing, social media, and education, among many more (Wechsler, 2009).

Learning analytics (LA) is an emerging field that seeks to define the analytics of learning, its processes, and its potential to advance teaching and learning in online education (Elias, 2011).

In the area of learning analytics, facial recognition plays an important role, both in the human-in-the-loop and the automation, for customization of the learning and the systems that deliver it. In schools and educational settings, facial recognition is a preliminary step required for tasks that are more complex, such as the automatic attendance roll management to reduce the burden of carrying the roll call and preventing fake attendances. In other settings, facial recognition is used for e-assessment for identifying intruders during virtual examinations and in school security monitoring for identifying intruders and other threats, such as gun-shaped objects. Similarly, the analysis of facial actions, micro-expressions, eye tracking, and other facial landmarks are used for the detection of academic emotions (e.g., contentment, anxiety, hope, etc.) (Wentzel, 2009), cues of learning, and engagement, which can be exploited by adaptive systems (Andrejevic, 2019).

Although humans do not require much effort for detecting and recognizing faces, the problem is not the case when it is intended to be solved from a computational vision approach (Suarez, 2000). Since its inception, different techniques have emerged to perform face detection. The first algorithms based on heuristic and anthropometric techniques emerged in the 1980s. These techniques have different approaches. The holistic or image-based approach works with the full image, in which features representing the object to be detected are extracted. Focus based on facial features or local features looks for key elements that conform to the human face, such as the eyes, nose, and mouth. Finally, the hybrid approach is a method that combines the two previous approaches using both local and global characteristics (Guevara et al., 2008).

Facial features have been used to detect emotions such as boredom, confusion, delight, engagement, frustration, and surprise when students are involved in deep-level learning (McDaniel et al., 2007) and uses human judges and correlational analysis to classify emotional states. Bosch et al. (2015) use computer vision and machine learning techniques to detect emotions from data collected in a real-world environment of a school computer lab; up to 30 students at a time participated in the class, and results were cross-validated to ensure generalization to new students. The classification process was successful (AUC = .816).

Problem Statement

In the current context of the SARS-COV-2 pandemic, it is extremely useful to apply face-detection techniques to help teachers move through the list, monitor (supervisory functions), and analyze the acceptance of educational content to students—among other activities being carried out online—so it is necessary to improve effectiveness and give greater credibility to the education sector as well as distance education.

Because of the above, many institutions are incorporating biometric recognition for this purpose. With advances in technology, systems capable of solving the various problems have now been implemented. Some of the techniques used in systems have a high degree of effectiveness for face detection; however, the human face is a dynamic object with a high degree of variability in lighting, angle, and image size making its detection an active problem to address.

That is why in this research it is proposed to design and implement an algorithm, based on Haar filters for training and AdaBoost for the detection of faces derived from online evaluations, and compare the results obtained with the results of openCV and others reported in the literature.

Literature Review

As online education has soared, face detection is required to help count and monitor online education activities.

Singh et al. (2014) developed a system of control of assistance through detection and facial recognition to facilitate and improve the process of the passing list (mark attendance). This process, carried out by the teacher manually, is time consuming for the class, which could be used constructively in teaching or clarifying doubts.

To perform facial recognition, they used Principal Component Analysis (PCA); the system works by projecting the face image into a feature space that encompasses significant variations between images of known faces. PCA produces a set of *Eigenfaces*, which correspond to the larger eigenvectors of the covariance of the training data.

These are known as "Eigenfaces" to the significant characteristics because they are the oxygenators (main components) of the whole of faces. This does not necessarily correspond to characteristics such as eyes, ears, and nose.

On the other hand, Gutierrez et al. (2017) implemented techniques such as Eigenfaces and Fisherfaces for face detection. "Emotion Experience" is a system that, in its first stage, performs face detection and subsequently recognizes the emotional state to evaluate the experience of users (children) interacting in front of the computer while performing activities such as watching movie fragments or playing a video game. For this project, they propose to analyze Eigenfaces and Fisherfaces.

Fisherfaces uses linear discriminating analysis (LDA), which works by reducing the dimensionality of the image to find the best features, which allow recognition. It has a good recognition rate, but is lower than the effectiveness rate of Eigenfaces.

With 97% effectiveness rate and 2.5% error rate for Eigenfaces against 94% effectiveness rate and 50.5% error rate for Fisherfaces, it is concluded that the best Eigenfaces are better for face detection.

Krithika et al. (2017) developed a system for analysis in images, describing student behavior in learning environments through face detection and facial trait analysis.

Face Detection Techniques

Geometric Approach

Feature-based methods perform analysis of face properties and geometry, such as areas, distances, and angles between face elements. PCA (Principal Component Analysis), Eigenfaces, and Fisherfaces techniques, based on geometric characteristics, give importance to the structural shape of facial components such as the nose, mouth, and eyes (Mehta et al., 2018) (see Figure 12.1).

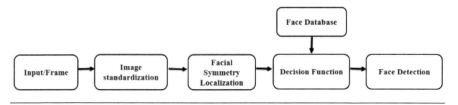

Figure 12.1   Methodology for the Geometric Focus Detection of Faces (Mehta et al., 2018)

Machine Learning Approach

This approach is based on appearance, where attributes such as intensities, pixel values, and histograms are considered. After extensive training with the help of pre-labeled datasets, machine learning techniques are applied to detect faces (Mehta et al., 2018). Figure 12.2 shows some of the techniques used for machine learning, such as Support Vector Machines, Deep Neural Networks, and Decision Trees.

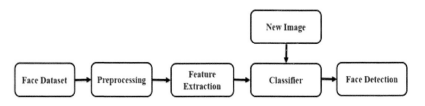

Figure 12.2 Methodology for Face Detection Approach Machine Learning (Mehta et al., 2018)

Methodology

The methodology implemented in this research work is based on the proposal of Viola and Jones (2001). This methodology is divided into six stages, as shown in Figure 12.3. In the first stage, the input image is received, and preprocessing is

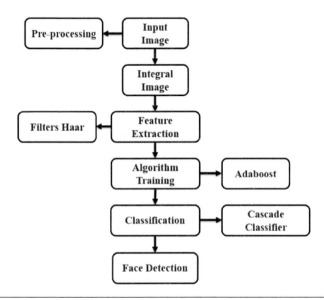

Figure 12.3 Face Detection Methodology (Based on Viola & Jones, 2001)

applied. In the second stage, a transformation of the previous image into a new image occurs, called the *integral image*. The third stage consists of the extraction of characteristics (features) using Haar filters, with the characteristics obtained from the previous stage. The process continues with the fourth stage, where the training of the AdaBoost algorithm is performed. In the fifth stage, a cascading classifier classifies the characteristics. Finally, face detection is performed, and its accuracy metrics are estimated.

Image

An image is a two-dimensional (two-dimensional) representation of an image through a numeric array in the binary system (ones and zeros); this can be defined as the following function:

$$f(x, y)$$

where (x, y) are the spatial coordinates (flat) and amplitude of the function f at some pair of coordinates (González & Woods, 1992).

Kumar and Verma (2010) classify images in three types:

- **Binary image.** An image that in its pixels contains only values 0 and 1, interpreted as black and white, respectively, or you can also use any other color scheme.
- **Grayscale image.** Such images are known as gray-level intensity images. These images contain values ranging from [0,1] to [0,65535] depending on the bit depth.
- **True-color image.** Also known as an RGB image; in this type of image, each pixel is specified by the intensity of its corresponding RGB components or channels (Red, Green, Blue). For single or double arrays, its range of values is [0,1]. The normal data type for an image is uint8; this indicates an integer presented in 8 bits. That is, $2 \wedge 8 = 256$ values that are distributed in the range of [0,255] for each pixel. For uint16 indicates an integer presented by 16 bits, $2 \wedge 16 = 65536$ values in a range of [0,65535] for each pixel.

Database Construction

The total database consists of 2,200 images, of which 1,100 are positive and 1,100 are negative. For positive images, we use several databases available on the Internet, and additionally, we collect other positive images of video sessions called from higher education institutions. For these images, the faces were trimmed individually, considering the total face, partial, front, or some other position, and were named consecutively.

With this procedure, 400 positive images are generated. To expand the number of samples, positive images are collected from other freely accessible and published databases. The databases used are: Eigenfaces and a Simple Face Detector with PCA/SVD in Python (2018); Rezaei, M. (2013); Computational Intelligence and Photography Lab, Yonsei University (2019); and Yale Face Database | vision.ucsd. edu (2021). These images are color scale and other grayscale images in .jpg and .png, and the size varies from 64 to 430 pixels.

Negative images are obtained from cocodataset.org (COCO, 2020), and images that do not contain human faces are selected. These images are in .jpg, color format, and the sizes vary from 250 to 640 pixels.

Preprocessing

Converting RGB Image to Grayscale Image

At this stage of preprocessing, if the input image is in RGB format, it is converted to grayscale to facilitate feature extraction, data storage, and reduction in computational complexity (Raveendran et al., 2018). The conversion is done by adding the RGB components of each pixel and is divided by the number of components—three components corresponding to Red, Green, and Blue. This process is represented by the following equation (Urueña et al., 2011).

$$Grey_{(x,y)} = \frac{R_{(x,y)} + G_{(x,y)} + B_{(x,y)}}{3}$$

Normalization

By normalization, we refer to having certain independence from the properties of the image, such as brightness and contrast.

The purpose of applying histogram normalization processing on the image is to correct images that are too dark or excessively light.

This process is represented by the following mathematical equation (Universidad de la República, 2003):

$$N(x,y) = \frac{\left(N^0\ Levels - 1\right)}{\left(\left(I\right) - \left(I\right)\right)} . I(x,y) - min(I)$$

Be $I(x,y)$ the input image
Where:

- $I(x, y)$, the gray level of the image at the coordinate (x, y).
- $min(I)$, $max(I)$: minimum and maximum gray level in the image, respectively.
- $N(x, y)$, the gray level of the normalized image at the coordinate (x, y).

All images are subjected to preprocessing color-to-grayscale conversion and histogram normalization. OpenCV libraries in Python language were used for this purpose. In this line of code with the method `cv2.imread` the image is loaded.

```
img = cv2.imread('/path/image.jpg')
```

In the second line of the code, we convert the RGB image to grayscale with the method `cv2.COLOR _ BGR2GRAY`.

```
img _ gray = cv2.cvtColor(img,cv2.COLOR _ BGR2GRAY)
```

The next line of code with the method `cv2.NORM _ MINMAX` we normalize histogram levels with parameters of [0,255]

```
img _ norm = cv2.normalize(img _ gray,None,0,255,cv2.
NORM _ MINMAX)
```

Integral Image

An integral image, also called a *summative area table*, is a tool used when you have a function from pixels to real numbers $f(x, y)$, and it is required to calculate the sum of a function over a rectangular region of the image (Bradley & Roth, 2007).

The sum is calculated in linear time per rectangle, initially calculating the value of the function pixel by pixel. However, the integral image allows you to calculate the sum over multiple overlapping rectangular windows.

This image allows to quickly extract features at different scales, containing the sum of the pixels at the top and left of the image (Guevara et al., 2008).

To perform the calculation of the integral image, it is stored in each location $I(x, y)$ the sum of all terms $f(x, y)$ left and top of the pixel (x, y).

For each pixel, the following mathematical equation is used and is performed linearly (Bradley & Roth, 2007).

$$I(x, y) = f(x, y) + I(x - 1, y) + I(x, y - 1) - (x - 1, y - 1)$$

Figure 12.4 shows the input of the values of a simple image, then as a second image we have the integral image calculated, and finally, using the integral image, the sum of $f(x,y)$ is calculated over the rectangle D. The latter is equivalent to the summation defined by the rectangles $(A + B + C + D) - (A + B) - (A + C) + A$, which are shown in the right hand of Figure 12.4.

4	1	2	2
0	4	1	3
3	1	0	4
2	1	3	2

4	5	7	9
4	9	12	17
7	13	16	25
9	16	22	33

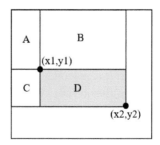

Figure 12.4   Integral Image Calculation

Once the integral image is obtained, we can calculate in linear time, the sum of the function for any rectangle with the upper left corner (x_1,y_1) and the top right corner (x_2,y_2), with the following equation.

$$\sum_{x=x_1}^{x_2} \sum_{y=y_1}^{y_2} f(x,y) = I(x_2,y_2) - I(x_2,y_1-1) - I(x_1-1,y_2) + I(x_1-1,y_1-1)$$

Removing Haar Features

Geraci et al. (1990) define feature extraction as an important step in pattern recognition, in which measurements or observations are processed to find attributes that are used to map objects to a particular class. Features in images are extracted when applying functions that allow the representation and description of interest of the image (patterns).

In this research work, the extraction of features is done by applying Haar filters to the image. These filters are calculated on the top image, traverse the entire image from top to bottom and from left to right at all possible scales, both horizontally and vertically, each possible position and scale corresponding to a Haar feature.

Experimentation

Creating the Haar Cascading Classifier

The Haar cascading classifier was created based on the article by Rezaei (2013), which provides a detailed step-by-step tutorial on what it takes to create the .xml. The process is divided into five steps:

A. Collection of positive and negative training images

We will take the images of the previously created database.

Positive images are those containing the object to be detected—in this particular case, images containing human faces, and negative images are those that do not contain the object to be detected.

B. Organization of negative images

Create a file .txt that contains the list name of the negative images. Example:

```
image001.jpg
image002.jpg
image003.jpg
...
```

C. Crop and mark positive images

This step creates a vector file that contains the names of the positive images and also the location of the objects to be detected. For this process, the authors share two tools: Objectmarket and ImageClipper.

D. Creating the vector of positive images

A batch file is created in this file; you must specify the following:

```
createsamples.exe -info positive/info.txt -vec
vector/facevector.vec -num 1100 -w 24 -h 24
```

`info positive/info.txt` Represents the file path of positive images

`-vec vector/facevector.vec` Represents the path of the output vector

`-num 1100` Number of positive files

`-w 24` Object width

`-h 24` Object height

After running the batch file, a file is generated, *facevector.vec,* in the folder `-training-vector`

E. Haar training

The Haartraining.exe collects a new set of negative samples for each stage. It uses the information from the previous stages to determine which of the *candidate samples* are poorly classified.

Training ends when the proportion of samples misclassified with respect to candidate samples is less than the unemployment condition.

Once the training process is complete, get the MyHaar.xml, which is used for face detection.

Tuning Parameters

The following experimentation aims to find the best scale factor (scaleFactor) and minimal neighbors (minNeighbors) parameters for OpenCV classifiers and the classifier previously created by us.

The experiment is performed with 300 images, of which 150 images are positive and 150 images are negative. These images are not found in the database with which the classifier was made. The parameters used are scaleFactor and minNeighbors. The first is a parameter that specifies how much the image size is reduced on each image scale. The scaleFactor values used range from [1.1, 1.9]. The second is a parameter that specifies how many neighbors each candidate rectangle must have to retain it. As the parameter gets larger, less detection is obtained, but with higher quality. It takes integer values from [1, 10].

Experimentation Results

By tuning parameters and selecting the best ones for each of the classifiers to compare, the following results are obtained.

Figure 12.5 shows that in a good part of the parameter tuning experiments the performance of the algorithm developed is better than that of OpenCV.

For the OpenCV classifier *'frontalface_default'* its best parameters for face detection are: scaleFactor: 1.2, minNeighbors: 4.

With these parameters we get:

	Positive	Negative
Faces	105	9
No Faces	45	141

The best parameters for our classifier *'MyHaar'* are scaleFactor: 1.3, minNeighbors: 8.

With these parameters we get:

	Positive	Negative
Faces	122	11
No Faces	28	139

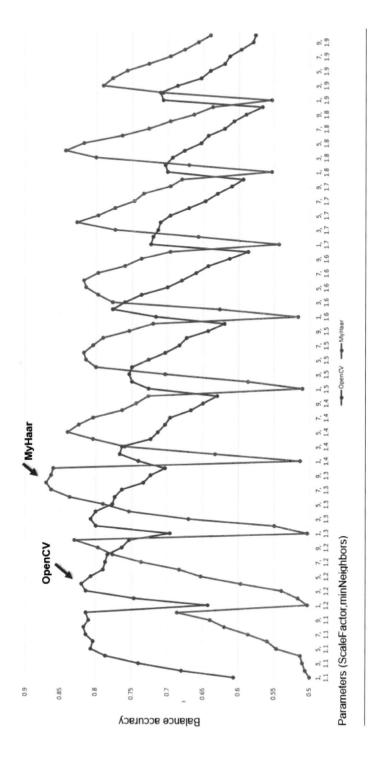

Figure 12.5 Comparison OpenCV with MyHaar

Results Metrics

True Positive Rate

The rate of true positives (TPR, also called *sensitivity*) is calculated as TP / (TP + FN). TPR is the probability that a real positive result will test positive.

True Negative Rate

The rate of true negatives (TNR, also called *specificity*), which is the probability that an actual negative result will give a negative result. It is calculated as TN / (TN + FP).

Recall

Recall is the relationship TP / (TP + FN). This metric intuitively captures the classifier's ability to find all positive samples.
    The best value is 1 and the worst value is 0.

Balanced Accuracy

Balanced accuracy in binary and multiclass classification problems is used to address unbalanced datasets. It is defined as the average of *Recall* obtained in each class.
    The best value is 1 and the worst value is 0 when set to False.
    It is calculated as (TPR + TNR) / 2

Results Comparison Table

Table 12.1 shows the results of the measurement metrics mentioned above, obtained from the experiments performed. A higher effectiveness rate is obtained with the 'MyHaar' classifier carried out in this research project with respect to the 'frontal face_default' classifier created by OpenCV.

Table 12.1 Comparison of OpenCV and MyHaar Classifiers

	TPR	TNR	Recall	Ba
OpenCV	0.70	0.94	[0.94, 0.70]	82%
MyHaar	0.81	0.92	[0.92, 0.81]	87%

Conclusions and Future Work

We can conclude that the performance of the classifier designed and developed in this investigation has a slightly (5%) higher effectiveness rate for detecting faces with respect to the OpenCV classifier.

During the early days of face detection, many of the developed methods were designed on an ensemble classifier approach such as the popular Haar-Cascades. These types of approaches employed handcrafted features obtained from a sliding window over an image, to detect face regions over it (Minaee, 2021). This type of model excels when the task involves the detection of objects that can be well represented with blob-like features such as those commonly found on frontal faces.

Nevertheless, Haar-Cascades or similar performing algorithms have several drawbacks for face recognition, such as managing images with objects with multiple scales several orders of magnitude different, variations in poses, face occlusion, emotional expressions, illumination, and other image variants (Minaee, 2021). Further, the Haar-cascades algorithm has an upper limit on the improvement it can achieve to the face detection problem, even when larger datasets are available.

In the last 10 years, deep learning algorithms have considerably improved the performance of face detection to human-like performance through the usage of Convolutional Neural Networks (CNN), Cascade-CNN, and more recently architectures such as Recurring CNN, single-shot detection models such as You Only Look Once (YOLO) algorithm (Redmon et al. 2016), and Feature Pyramid Networks such as RetinaFace, to mention a few (Minaee, 2021). These deep learning models have considerable advantages over the classical models, such as allowing one to obtain complex features, improve with larger datasets, good in representing edge features for shape outlines, have a shorter detection time (Murillo et al., 2017), with a human-like accuracy (Minaee, 2021). Therefore, future work involves the usage of these state-of-the-art algorithms for the detection of face recognition in online educational settings.

A final note needs to be made regarding concerns that arise from automatic facial recognition technologies. These relate to the development of authoritarian behaviors, compromised civil rights, the misuse of biometric information, and racist and intolerant behaviors given by racially skewed datasets biased by skin color and ethnicity (Andrejevic, 2019). Thus, the recollection of data in school settings needs to be carried out with full consent of parents, and through a very rigorous process that guarantees the de-identification of individuals to minimize possible misuses of the information and segregation.

Acknowledgments

We want to thank CONACYT-México for the granted scholarship that supported this research.

References

Andrejevic, M., and Selwyn, N. (2020). Facial recognition technology in schools: Critical questions and concerns. *Learning, Media and Technology, 45*(2), 115–128.

Bosch, N., D'Mello, S., Baker, R., Ocumpaugh, J., Shute, V., Ventura, M., Wang, L., and Zhao, W. (2015, March). Automatic detection of learning-centered affective states in the wild. *Proceedings of the 20th International Conference on Intelligent User Interfaces,* 379–388.

Bradley, D., and Roth, G. (2007). Adaptive thresholding using the integral image. *Journal of Graphics Tools, 12*(2), 13–21.

COCO—Common Objects in Context. (2020). Retrieved April 30, 2021, from Cocodata set.org website: https://cocodataset.org/

Computational Intelligence and Photography Lab, Yonsei University. (2019). Real and fake face detection. Retrieved April 30, 2021, from https://www.kaggle.com/ciplab/real-and-fake-face-detection

Chellappa, R., Wilson, C. L., and Sirohey, S. (1995). Human and machine recognition of faces: A survey. *Proceedings of the IEEE, 83*(5), 705–741.

EigenFaces and a Simple Face Detector with PCA/SVD in Python. (2018, January 6). Retrieved March 30, 2021, from https://sandipanweb.wordpress.com/2018/01/06/eigenfaces-and-a-simple-face-detector-with-pca-svd-in-python/

Elias, T. (2011). Learning analytics. *Learning,* 1–22.

Geraci, A. et al. (1990). IEEE Standard Glossary of Image Processing and Pattern Recognition Terminology. Institute of Electrical and Electronics Engineers (IEEE) Std., 610–614.

Gonzalez, R. C., and Woods, R. E. (1992). *Digital Image Processing.* Reading, MA: Addison-Wesley, 2.

Guevara, M. L., Echeverry, J. D., and Urueña, W. A. (2008). *Detección de rostros en imágenes digitales usando clasificadores en cascada. Scientia et technica, 1*(38).

Gutierrez, E. J., Duque, L. A., and Cano, S. (2017). *Midiendo la Experiencia de Usuario en Niños a Través del Reconocimiento de las Emociones.*

Krithika, L., Venkatesh, K., Rathore, S., and Kumar, M. H. (2017). Facial recognition in education system. In *IOP Conference Series: Materials Science and Engineering.* IOP Publishing.

Kumar, T., and Verma, K. (2010). A theory based on conversion of rgb image to gray image. *International Journal of Computer Applications, 7*(2), 7–10.

Mehta, D., Siddiqui, M. F. H., and Javaid, A. Y. (2018). Facial emotion recognition: A survey and real-world user experiences in mixed reality. *Sensors, 18*(2), 416.

McDaniel, B., D'Mello, S., King, B., Chipman, P., Tapp, K., and Graesser, A. (2007). Facial features for affective state detection in learning environments. *Proceedings of the Annual Meeting of the Cognitive Science Society, 29*(29).

Minaee, S. L. (2021). *Going deeper into face detection: A survey.* arXiv preprint, 1–17.

Murillo, P. C. U., Moreno, R. J., and Arenas, J. O. P. (2017). Comparison between cnn and Haar classifiers for surgical instrumentation classification. *Contemporary Engineering Sciences, 10*(28), 1351–1363.

Raveendran, S., Edavoor, P. J., YB, N. K., and Vasantha, M. (2018). Design and implementation of reversible logic-based rgb to grayscale color space converter. In *TENCON 2018–2018 IEEE Region 10 Conference.* IEEE.

Redmon, J., Divvala, S., Girshick, R., & Farhadi, A. (2016). You only look once: Unified, real-time object detection. In *Proceedings of the IEEE Conference on Computer Vision and Pattern Recognition, 779–788.*

Rezaei, M. (2013). Creating a cascade of haar-like classifiers: Step by step. *Aplikasi Pendeteksian Ras kucing dengan mendeteksi wajah kucing dengan metode viola jones.*

Singh, D., Hadke, R. S., Khonde, S. S., Patil, V. D., Kamnani, M., and Ingle, M. R. (2014). Attendance monitoring using face recognition. *International Journal of Computer Science and Mobile Computing, 3,* 633–636.

Suárez, O. D. (2000). *Introducción al reconocimiento de caras. Buran,* 39–42.

Universidad de la República, I. (2003). *Normalización de la imagen.* Retrieved January 16, 2021, from https://iie.fing.edu.uy/investigacion/grupos/gti/timag/trabajos/2003/huellas/html/node8.html

Urueña, W. A., Osorio, J. A. C., and Vargas, J. A. M. (2011). *Técnicas alternativas para la conversión de imágenes a color a escala de grises en el tratamiento digital de imágenes. Scientia et Technica, 1*(47), 207–212.

Viola, P., and Jones, M. (2001). Rapid object detection using a boosted cascade of simple features. *Proceedings of the 2001 IEEE Computer Society Conference on Computer Vision and Pattern Recognition. CVPR 2001.* IEEE.

Wechsler, H. (2009). *Reliable Face Recognition Methods: System Design, Implementation and Evaluation* (Vol. 7). Springer Science and Business Media.

Wentzel, K. R. (2009). Students' relationships with teachers as motivational contexts. In K. R. Wenzel and A. Wigfield (Eds.), *Handbook of Motivation at School,* 301–322. Routledge/Taylor & Francis Group.

Yale Face Database | vision.ucsd.edu. (2021). Retrieved March 30, 2021, from http://vision.ucsd.edu/content/yale-face-database

Index

For Product Safety Concerns and Information please contact our
EU representative GPSR@taylorandfrancis.com Taylor & Francis
Verlag GmbH, Kaufingerstraße 24, 80331 München, Germany